BOSTON'S
100
GREATEST
GAMES

BOSTON'S
100
GREATEST
GAMES

ROB SNEDDON

Candlepin Press

BOSTON'S 100 GREATEST GAMES

Rob Sneddon

Copyright © 2013 by Rob Sneddon
All rights reserved.

ISBN: 978-0615932712

Cover and book design
Tammy Francoeur Sneddon

Front cover photos
AP Photo/NFL Photos (Vince Lombardi Trophy)
AP Photo/Matt Slocum (inset)

Published by Candlepin Press
Somersworth, New Hampshire

First edition, December 2013
Printed in the United States of America

To my mom, who supported my efforts to write about sports, even if she couldn't resist adding (in her Glasgow accent), "I just wish it didn't seem so pointless." To my dad, a (nearly) lifelong baseball hater who became Red Sox Nation's least-likely pink hat in 2004, a year before he died. To my in-laws, as loyal a group of indigenous New England sports fans as you'll find. To Will, who watched his first Patriots game with me when he was two days old (it's No. 74 on the list). And to Tammy, for reasons that don't need to be explained to anyone who has ever met her.

Contents

Introduction

It's hard to overstate the accomplishments of Boston's sports teams in the 21st century. But that hasn't stopped people from trying. Each new milestone sends New England into fits of self-referential (and self-reverential) hyperbole. When the Bruins stunned the Maple Leafs during the opening round of the 2013 Stanley Cup Playoffs, becoming the first team in NHL history to overcome a three-goal deficit in the third period of a seventh game, the Twitterati groped for the appropriate comparison. Was it a better last-gasp comeback than the Red Sox' ninth-inning rally against the Angels in '86? The greatest overtime win since the Tuck Rule game? The most dramatic finish to a Game 7 since Havlicek stole the ball?

Already up to my bleary eyeballs in the research for this book, I immediately thought of a parallel that was both obvious and obscure. In the 2009 NCAA men's Division I hockey championship, Boston University trailed Miami of Ohio 3–1 in the final minute. With their goaltender off for an extra skater, BU scored twice in 40 seconds to tie the game, then won it in overtime. Terriers coach Jack Parker called it "the greatest championship game ever played." In college towns across America it would have become an instant legend.

In Boston it barely survived a news cycle.

There were a couple of reasons for that. First, Boston has set an absurdly high standard for sports drama. Second, not all "greatest games" are created equal. In one sense, it's hard to argue with Parker: Combine the implausibility of the BU comeback with the stakes—an NCAA title—and that probably *was* the greatest championship game ever played. Not just in Boston but anywhere, in any sport, at any level.

Still, it would be ridiculous to suggest that a college hockey game deserves to be ranked as the greatest game in Boston sports history. In terms of influence, NCAA hockey just doesn't compare to the NHL variety. (And *nothing* compares to the NFL's influence.) If you purport to rate the significance of a particular sporting event among a specific population, the percentage of that population that cares about the outcome ought to factor into the equation.

But it shouldn't be the only factor. If you appreciate sports at a fundamental level, instead of just as a series of mass-media conversation pieces, then you have to admit it would be hard to top that BU game for sheer drama. So is that reason enough to include it among the 100 greatest games in Boston sports history? To me, that's a legitimate question.

And it's the sort of question I asked myself as I refined the methodology for the rankings in this book. I used a loose formula, but it was a formula nonetheless, incorporating the following criteria:

Magnitude
On June 18, 1961, the Red Sox trailed the Washington Senators 12–5 in the last of the ninth with two outs and a runner on first. Despite one of the weakest lineups in club history—four starters that day were hitting less than .240, and no one was even close to .300—Boston scored eight two-out runs to win, 13–12. It was, in all likelihood, the greatest one-out-away rally in major league history. And yet, because it involved two bad teams bumbling through a Father's Day doubleheader, the game had little significance beyond providing an afternoon's entertainment at Fenway Park. So it didn't make the cut for this book. To crack the top 100, a game had to mean something. The tiniest ninth-inning rally in October trumped the largest ninth-inning rally in June.

That's not to say I restricted the list to playoff games—although I could have. Collectively, Boston's four major pro franchises have won almost 750 postseason games. The Celtics alone have won almost 350. Not all of them were spine-chillers, of course. Remember that 113–88 dismantling of the New York Knicks in Game 1 of the 1974 Eastern Conference Finals? Of course you don't (unless you're Bill Simmons). That's because it lacked the next ingredient:

Drama

Close games are more exciting. Pretty simple.

Level of Play

A game can be both significant and suspenseful—and still kinda suck. The Celtics' 66–64 win over the Pistons in Game 3 of the 2002 NBA Eastern Conference Semifinals is Exhibit A. (Actually, call it Exhibit D. It didn't deserve an A. "We were playing bad. They were playing badder," was Celtics point guard Kenny Anderson's summary.) When pressure brings out the best in an individual player, or an entire team, the results can be transcendent. Larry Bird's series-saving steal against Detroit in 1987. Tim Thomas's overtime save against Montreal in 2011. Doug Flutie's Hail Mary against Miami in 1984. The 2001 Patriots' collective performance against the Rams in Super Bowl XXXVI. David Ortiz's grand slam against the Tigers in October 2013. It's just more satisfying when somebody makes a great play to win the game than when the opponent makes a hideous gaffe to lose the game.

Historical Context

This was the trickiest element to factor into the equation. Fair or not, we end up rewarding some teams and penalizing others based on how their predecessors performed. The 2004 Red Sox are the best example of the former and the 2007 Red Sox are the best example of the latter—because of the former. Overcoming a three-games-to-one deficit in a League Championship Series en route to a World Series title is a rare feat—only four teams have done it. But when it happens just three years after the same team overcame a three-games-to-*none* deficit in a League Championship Series—against their hated rivals, no less—en route to a World Series title that ended an 86-year drought … it's just not going to have the same impact it otherwise would have. Through no fault of their own, the 2007 Red Sox suffer by comparison to the 2004 Red Sox. (The 2013 Red Sox, on the other hand, inspired comparisons to the 1967 Red Sox, not just because they were so much better than their immediate predecessors but also because they were *likable*—something that couldn't be said of the Sox from September 2011 through the Bobby Valentine fustercluck.)

The Russell Era Celtics were also victims of their own success. The more precious metal you accumulate, the less precious it becomes—and

Russell's Celtics stockpiled the most in pro sports history. Trying to grade each of the eleven titles Russell won in that thirteen-year span is like evaluating multiple MVP candidates on the same team. Each teammate's accomplishments diminish the others', and the award goes elsewhere—to the Patriots, in this analogy. That brings us to the apples-and-oranges problem. Because the NFL season consists of far fewer games than those of the other major sports, each game carries more weight. This disparity is magnified in the postseason. Every NFL playoff game is win–or–go–home. And that's why fourteen of the Pats' 24 playoff wins are on this list, by far the highest percentage of any franchise.

Another challenge was to overcome recency bias. I wanted the list to represent the greatest games of all time, not just our time. I tried, for example, to give due consideration to Harvard's reign as a national football powerhouse. This was trickier than it sounds. In the grand tradition of BCS chaos, the Crimson can claim anywhere from one to thirteen national championships, depending on which sources you use. How can you say a game was great when you can't even determine what the stakes were?

I ran into a different problem when evaluating games from the Braves franchise, which won nine titles while in Boston. Most came in an era when the champion was simply the team with the best winning percentage. Win the pennant by 8½ games, as the 1892 iteration of the Braves franchise did, and it's hard to say that any one win was more important than the others.

Same story with the 1872 Red Stockings, who finished with a record of 39–8 to take the National Association championship by 7½ games over the Baltimore Canaries. Their inclusion would have added a dash of sabermetric cachet to the list because that team can lay claim to Boston's first-ever pro sports title. But the Stockings' run to the championship lacked any suspense (at least any that I could detect more than 140 years later). Boston sprinted to a 22–1 start, including a 26–3 win over the Washington Nationals on Opening Day. They won by the same score over the Brooklyn Atlantics—not to be confused with the Brooklyn Eckfords, whom the Red Stockings beat 20–0.

National Association pennant fever! Catch it!

The 1904 Red Sox were another great team that never got to prove themselves in the postseason—much as they would have liked to. (And yes, I know the team wasn't actually called the Red Sox until 1908, but it's just too awkward to call them the Americans or the Pilgrims or the Puritans or the Plymouth Rocks or the Somersets or any of the other wacky-ass names that the newspapers hung on them at the time.) Those 1904 Sox were defending champions of the first modern World Series, having beaten the Pirates the previous October. (And I've chosen to spell the Pirates' hometown *Pittsburgh* in this book, even though it was officially spelled *Pittsburg*, minus the *h*, from 1890 to 1911 because of an arbitrary decree from the United States Board on Geographic Names.) The Red Sox repeated as American League champions in 1904, but the National League champion New York Giants refused to play them in a postseason series. Even so, the '04 Red Sox are in this book because they won the pennant in a tense October showdown with the Yankees (I *know*—Highlanders). Just like those *other* '04 Red Sox.

That's a roundabout way of saying that a regular-season game had to be pretty special to make the top 100. In general, a regular-season game had to be a steppingstone to a championship (a criterion that also figured in the ranking of postseason games); mark a significant milestone; involve an extraordinary comeback; or feature a record-setting individual performance.

In short: Games that scored high in each of those four categories— Magnitude, Suspense, Level of Play, Historical Context—dominate the top of the list. Games at the other end of the list scored high in two or three categories but not all four.

Oh—and 99 times out of 100, the Boston team won. (There was one tie.) This was not an objective exercise. An impartial observer in Yazoo City, Mississippi might argue that the Bill Buckner and Grady Little games were great, too. But you won't find them in this book, because....

Do I really need to explain that?

Finally, I drew a distinction between great games and great moments. It was a great moment when Mark Henderson used a snowplow to clear a spot for John Smith's field goal attempt with 4:45 left in the fourth quarter at Schaefer Stadium on December 12, 1982. But the Pats' 3–0 win over the Miami Dolphins was not a great game. Unlike BU's 4–3 win over Miami of Ohio on April 11, 2009.

And, yes, that one's in here.

Depending on how you look at it, assembling this book was an act of either incredible optimism or deep pessimism. The implication of publishing *Boston's 100 Greatest Games* is that the list isn't going to change. But I expect to revise this book frequently. (In fact, I had to revise this first edition just before publication to make room for those 2013 Red Sox.) Any additional Super Bowls or World Series or Stanley Cups or NBA championships (pro basketball needs a better name for its title round) will force me to bump games from the bottom of the list, reshuffle the order at the top, and publish a new edition. And when that next great game happens, if you want to weigh in on where you think it belongs in the top 100, feel free. Just go to **100greatestgames.com**.

And, of course, you're also welcome to take issue with the list presented here. If your argument is persuasive enough, I'll revise the next edition accordingly.

100

Patriots 28, Titans 24
September 17, 1960

The first win in Patriots history was also one of the most controversial

This game featured an improbable fourth-quarter comeback. It ended with the Patriots scoring on a play more peculiar than any not involving a snowplow. It involved a call at least as controversial as the Tuck Rule. And it was the first regular-season win in franchise history. All of which should have made it a bright strand in the fabric of New England sports history. Ask the average Pats fan about it, though, and you'll probably get a blank stare. Despite its deep reservoir of sports lore, New England remains strangely ignorant of the events of September 17, 1960.

After a stunning loss to Denver in their home opener—another landmark event: first game in American Football League history—the Patriots hit the road to take on the Titans in week two. (That would be the New York Titans, who are now known as the Jets—not the Tennessee Titans, who were then known as the Houston Oilers.)

The Titans seemed more a vestige of the NFL circa World War II than an entry in the newfangled AFL. Their home field was the Polo Grounds, of Bobby Thomson fame. Their head coach, Slingin' Sammy Baugh, had ended his Hall of Fame career as the Redskins quarterback eight years earlier. His previous coaching experience had come at Hardin–Simmons University, a small school near his Texas ranch. Nevertheless, his Titans salary, an estimated $100,000 over three years, was guaranteed, even if the AFL folded.

Baugh said the deal "made me happier than anything I ever got in pro football"—as opposed to the brand of football that the Titans played.

Actually, the Titans had looked impressive in their debut, beating the Buffalo Bills 27–3. And they were well on their way to a second win against the Patriots on a Saturday night at the Polo Grounds. New York built a 24–7 lead through three quarters behind three touchdown passes from Al Dorow, another former Redskins quarterback.

The Pats' quarterback corps had no such pedigree. With 36-year-old former BC QB Butch Songin unable to move the offense in the opener, Patriots coach Lou Saban went with rookie Tom Greene of Holy Cross against New York. By the time Greene threw his first career touchdown pass, a fifteen-yarder to receiver Oscar Lofton in the fourth quarter, the game appeared out of reach. Songin came on for the next drive and capped it with a six-yard touchdown pass to flanker Jim Colclough on fourth-and-goal that made it 24–21.

The Titans had only to kill the clock, but they couldn't do it. On fourth-and-four at the Patriots 48, Baugh faced a decision. He later said he "didn't know whether we had twenty or 30 seconds left to play." And although the clock was running, Baugh elected to kick the ball away. Just seven seconds remained when Titans long snapper Mike Hudock delivered the ball to punter Rick Sapienza. Sapienza, a Boston native who had previously played for the semipro North Attleboro Jewelers (and who would rejoin them shortly after this game), fumbled the low snap. He then compounded the problem by kicking the ball while it was on the ground. That should have drawn a flag but didn't. Another player, Patriots backup defensive end Tony Sardisco, also kicked the ball. That also should have drawn a flag but didn't.

From a massive scrum, Pats defensive back Chuck Shonta emerged with the ball at the Titans 25-yard line. "It was the wildest scramble I ever saw for a loose ball," Shonta later told the Associated Press. He sprinted into the end zone for the go-ahead score, although he was convinced it wouldn't count. "I was afraid to turn around for fear there would be flags all over the place," he said.

But the touchdown stood. Gino Cappelletti added the conversion, and the Pats escaped from New York with a wild 28–24 victory.

Firing the first volley in the long and contentious rivalry between these two franchises, New York owner Harry Wismer filed a protest, claiming he had video evidence confirming that Sardisco had illegally kicked the ball. Said Wismer, employing the overblown rhetoric that would come to characterize Pats–Jets relations, "The obvious mistake in the ruling by the officials prevented the Titans from protecting their undefeated mark in AFL play and first place in the Eastern Division." Keep in mind, the AFL was all of ten days old at that point. Commissioner Joe Foss acknowledged that officials had committed "an error in judgment," but he let the result stand. Said Foss, "Our games will always be decided on the field and not by viewing movies." (It wasn't the last time that the commissioner would get involved in a dispute involving these two teams and some video.) The Globe estimated that the amazing finish and resulting controversy translated to roughly 10,000 additional ticket sales for the Pats' next home game at BU's Nickerson Field. Considering that the attendance was only around 20,000, that was a significant boost for a franchise struggling to get a toehold in a town that had shown a disdain for pro football in the past.

99

Patriots 23, Ravens 20
January 22, 2012

It was an ugly win, but it was good enough to put the Pats
in the Super Bowl for the seventh time

OK, so Tom Brady played like Joe Flacco and Joe Flacco played like Tom Brady. (Brady: 22-of-36, 239 yards, no touchdowns, two interceptions; Flacco: 22-of-36, 306 yards, two touchdowns, one interception). So it took back-to-back, by-his-fingernails (and a fistful of jersey) plays from one of the most-maligned members of the Patriots' much-maligned secondary to keep the Pats from losing outright. (Undrafted rookie defensive back Sterling Moore, picked up from the discard pile in October, knocked a pass out of Ravens receiver Lee Evans' hands in the end zone on second-and-one with 27 seconds left. Then, assisted by an uncalled hold, he batted a pass away from tight end Dennis Pitta on third-and-one with 22 seconds left.) And it took a hideous hook from Baltimore kicker Billy Cundiff on a 32-yard field goal attempt with fifteen seconds left to keep the Pats from having to fend off the relentless Ravens in overtime. And OK, the 23–20 nail-biter over Baltimore was the 2011 Patriots' *only* victory against a team that finished with a winning record.

A simple fact remains: With a Super Bowl berth on the line, the Patriots won a tense, ugly game that wasn't decided until the final seconds. And it was a measure of how far the franchise had progressed that the fan base now had the luxury of fretting about style points.

OK, so maybe they weren't just style points. Maybe they were real points. And the Patriots left too many of them on the field two weeks later, in a

21–17 loss to the Giants in Super Bowl XLVI. Then they did it again in an AFC title game rematch with the Ravens a year later, in which Flacco (en route to a Super Bowl MVP award) again outperformed Brady in Baltimore's 28–13 victory.

98

Beaneaters 19, Orioles 10
September 27, 1897

The deciding game in Boston's first down-to-the-wire pennant race

Y ou can trace Boston's major league baseball history to Day One: April 22, 1876. On that spring Saturday, the Boston Red Caps beat the Philadelphia Athletics 6–5 in the first National League game ever played.

The Red Caps (renamed the Beaneaters in 1883) were an early baseball dynasty. (Incidentally, could somebody please come up with a less pretentious term for an extended run of sports success than *dynasty*?) Boston won six of the National League's first eighteen pennants, including three straight from 1891 to 1893. Then they were shoved aside by an unlikely upstart: the Baltimore Orioles. After going 106–171 in their first two National League seasons, this former American Association franchise suddenly morphed from a joke to a juggernaut under innovative manager Ned Hanlon.

Hanlon inherited a team built around one future Hall of Famer—third baseman John McGraw—and he imported three more: shortstop Hugh Jennings and outfielders Joe Kelley and Wee Willie Keeler. Hanlon also introduced a "small ball" style of offense that put constant pressure on the defense through running and contact plays. (This was the team that put the *Baltimore* in Baltimore chop.) Playing this new brand of ball, the Orioles won three straight NL pennants from 1894 to 1896.

After finishing fourth, seventeen games out, in 1896, the Beaneaters re-emerged as contenders in '97. This was due largely to a couple of newcomers: rookie outfielder Chick Stahl, who hit .354, and left-handed pitcher Fred Klobedanz, who won 26 games. The Beaneaters now had a potent one-two punch at the top of the rotation, as Klobedanz teamed with staff ace Kid Nichols, a 31-game winner.

Boston and Baltimore waged a seesaw battle all season and ended August in a first-place tie. During the stretch run they showed why they were the class of the National League. The Beaneaters went 15–3 to start September. The Orioles matched them almost stride for stride, at 15–4. Finally, the two teams met head to head at Baltimore's Union Park for three games in the penultimate series of 1897, with the Beaneaters holding a half-game lead. Boston won the first game, Baltimore the second. That made the rubber match, on Monday, September 27, a de facto playoff game. "The attendance broke all records in Baltimore," the New York *Times* reported.

Nichols squared off against 24-game winner Joe Corbett. But the expected pitchers' duel didn't happen. Corbett surrendered a single to Beaneaters outfielder Billy Hamilton to start the game, followed by a walk to first baseman Fred Tenney and a sacrifice by second baseman Bobby Lowe. Then came the decisive moment. Stahl lined a ball off of Corbett's pitching hand. The hit not only scored the first run, but it also knocked Corbett out of the box with a nasty cut. Baltimore would have to go the rest of the way with a patchwork of relievers, against a lineup in which everybody but the battery hit better than .300.

But Baltimore had a combustible lineup of its own, with Keeler providing the kindling. He once described his approach as "Hit 'em where they ain't," and he never did it better than in 1897, when he hit .424.

Keeler's one-out single in the bottom of the first started a rally that put the O's ahead 2–1. After just two innings it was 5–4, Baltimore.

At that point Nichols settled down, holding the Orioles scoreless for four innings. The Beaneaters tied the game with a run in the third and took the lead with three in the fourth. Baltimore was still within striking distance in the seventh when the Beaneaters blew the game open with nine runs on eleven hits. With the pennant all but assured— Boston officially clinched with a win in Brooklyn three days later—the Beaneaters began the celebration. "The visiting 'Rooters' own the town tonight," the *New York Times* reported. "Their brass band is parading through the principal streets, and their cry 'Hit her up! Hit her up! Hit her up again! B-O-S-T-O-N!' is heard everywhere."

The Beaneaters bested the Orioles again in 1898, this time by six games. But the rivalry was short-lived. The National League contracted to eight teams after the 1899 season, and the Orioles were one of the victims. Still, the DNA of that rivalry survives today. After the contraction, former Oriole John McGraw helped bring baseball back to Baltimore, as the player/manager of a revamped Orioles team in the newly launched American League in 1901. That team later moved to New York and eventually became the Yankees.

97

Celtics 106, Bulls 104, OT
April 28, 2009

The pivotal game in the tightest NBA playoff series ever

This was supposed to be a best-of-seven series. It ended up being a best-of-seven-and-three-quarters. The second-seeded Celtics, defending NBA champions, met the seventh-seeded Bulls in a first-round playoff series that was the tightest in NBA history.

The Bulls, an ascendant team led by rookie guard Derrick Rose, had immediately proved that they were tougher than their 41–41 regular-season record showed. They took Game 1 on the road, in overtime, 105–103. Boston evened the series with a throwback to the 1980s, a 118–115 shootout (in regulation) that featured eight lead changes and two ties in the fourth quarter. Game 3 was the outlier, an easy 107–86 Celtics win at Chicago. The Bulls answered with a 121–118 win in double overtime.

Which set the table for Game 5 at Boston.

Already down one member of the Big Three—Kevin Garnett, who was out with a knee injury—the Celtics played half of Game 5 without foul-plagued Ray Allen. Allen, who contributed just ten points on 3-of-8 shooting, left the game for good with 5:27 left in regulation. This on a night when the bench contributed just five points.

Paul Pierce, playing the role of the Big One, delivered in appropriate style, drilling a series of clutch shots in isolation. He scored Boston's last four points in regulation to force overtime, including a fifteen-footer with ten seconds left. And he scored Boston's last six points in overtime, all on contested jumpers from beyond fifteen feet, including the game winner with 3.4 seconds left.

But Pierce was far from a one-man show. Glen Davis added 21 points on 7-of-11 shooting. Kendrick Perkins had perhaps his best game as a Celtic, scoring sixteen points on 7-of-13 shooting, grabbing nineteen rebounds, and blocking seven shots. Just as important, Perkins had zero personal fouls. That allowed him to stay on the floor for more than 48 minutes.

And then there was Rajon Rondo. Boston's third-year guard had come with unique wiring and no schematic. His freakishly large hands gave him remarkable ball-handling skills but no consistent shooting touch. And he submitted long stretches of intense, driven play broken by lapses in which his focus seemed to evaporate.

Fortunately for the Celtics, Rondo was locked in for this one. He scored a team-high 28 points on 12-of-22 shooting, including 2-of-2 from three-point range. He hit a pair of high-pressure free throws in overtime. He did his usual superb job of multitasking (eleven assists, eight rebounds, two steals). But his signature play, the vintage Rondo moment—Celtic green, clouded with shades of gray—came just after Chicago inbounded the ball in the Celtics frontcourt after Pierce's go-ahead fall-away. Chicago's Brad Miller, all seven feet and 250 pounds, took the pass just beyond the foul line and steamed into the lane. Perkins moved in to make the block. But before that happened, the 6'1", 170-pound Rondo flew in from the wing and clamped his right hand across Miller's face as if administering chloroform. Was it a flagrant foul, which would have given Chicago two shots plus the ball? Or just a hard foul on which Rondo simply missed the ball (as he later claimed)? Chicago coach Vinny Del Negro offered a third alternative, calling it "a playoff foul."

The refs apparently agreed. In the regular season Rondo's foul might have been deemed flagrant, but in this game, at this critical moment, it was not.

Miller, an 82% free-throw shooter that season, seemed rattled, mentally if not physically. He front-rimmed the first shot. He missed the second deliberately, hoping for an offensive rebound. But he fired the ball off the backboard so hard that it never touched the rim—a violation. Celtics ball, game over.

On a night marked by plenty of offensive heroics, the decisive play turned out to be a foul. "You always talk about playoff basketball—no layups," Celtics coach Doc Rivers said. "Rondo did it on the very last play, and it won the game for us."

Game 6 of this epic seven-game series was most epic of all, as the Bulls survived with a 128–127 win in triple overtime. Although Boston took the series with a ten-point win in Game 7, the 35 minutes of overtime they had logged against Chicago took its toll. The Celtics couldn't hold a 3–2 edge over Orlando in the Eastern Conference semis, scoring just 75 points in a Game 6 loss at Orlando and getting blown out, 101–82, on their own floor in Game 7.

96

Bruins 6, Whalers 5
April 11, 1990

Until 2013, this was the Bruins' greatest come-from-behind
Stanley Cup victory

B oston has an awkward relationship with Hartford. Unlike
Providence, which is a legitimate part of the New England fam-
ily—a cousin whose means of support are a mystery but who is
always pleasant company—Hartford is like a relative by marriage. Any
attempt to include them in the proceedings feels perfunctory. Remember when the Celtics used to play three "home" games a year at the
Hartford Civic Center because … why did they do that again?

And so it is astounding, in hindsight, that at the height of their popularity, the Big Bad Bruins were driven to fits of irrational insecurity by
the *Whalers*.

It was 1972. The Bobby Orr/Phil Esposito/Derek Sanderson/Wayne
Cashman/Gerry Cheevers Bruins had just won the Stanley Cup for the
second time in three years. The World Hockey Association, challenging
the supremacy of the NHL, began play with such franchises as the
Alberta Oilers and the Houston Aeros (or was it the Houston Oilers and
the Alberta Aeros?)—and the Boston-based New England Whalers.

The Bruins gave their newborn brother an icy reception. They rel-
egated the Whalers to the worst Garden dates—Saturday afternoons and
Monday nights. Even at that the newcomers had to play half their home
games at the old Boston Arena. By 1974 the Whalers were so tired of
the second-class treatment that they sought a new home. They explored
a move to Foxboro, which made a kind of sense. Like fellow Boston
ex-pats the Pats, the Whalers had chosen the identifier *New England* not

only as a marketing ploy (to broaden their prospective fan base), but also because it gave them multiple options to relocate. But after exploring the idea of moving in with the Patriots, the Whalers ultimately spurned Foxboro for Hartford. (Twenty-five years later, Pats owner Robert Kraft more than evened the score by agreeing to move the Patriots to a proposed $380 million stadium in Hartford, only to change his mind and double down in Foxboro.)

At any rate, the Bruins were happy to see those annoying interlopers go. The Whalers could languish in America's insurance capital until the WHA met its inevitable demise. This occurred at last in 1979—but with a twist. The NHL, seizing an opportunity for rapid expansion, formed a plan to absorb four former WHA franchises, including the Whalers. The plan, which required approval from 75% of NHL owners, passed by a vote of 14–3. One of the no votes came from the Bruins.

Once the Whalers—rechristened the *Hartford* Whalers—joined the NHL it was hard to understand what the Bruins were so concerned about. Even though they were now in the same league as the Bruins, the Whalers still weren't in the Bruins' league. With sixteen of the NHL's 21 teams making the playoffs each year, Hartford somehow failed to qualify five times in their first six seasons. The Bruins, meanwhile, methodically added to a run of postseason appearances that would eventually reach a record 29 consecutive years.

When at last the teams' divergent paths crossed in the Stanley Cup Playoffs, in 1990, the Whalers seemed like little more than a first-round bye for the Bruins. Boston had the NHL's best record; Hartford had qualified for the playoffs only because of the epic ineptitude of the last-place Quebec Nordiques. But it took the Whalers just eight shots—four of which whizzed past Bruins goalie Reggie Lemelin—to make it plain that they had come to the playoffs to *play*. Hartford hung on to win Game 1 at the Garden, 4–3. And although the Bruins recovered to win Game 2, the price was steep: Raymond Bourque injured his hip on a check by the Whalers' Grant Jennings and would be out indefinitely.

It didn't take the Whalers long to capitalize; they won Game 3 at the Hartford Civic Center to take a 2–1 series lead. In Game 4, the Whalers were on the verge of not just beating the Bruins but also embarrassing them. After two periods Hartford led 5–2. But the Bruins' superiority resurfaced rapidly. Andy Moog replaced the unreliable Lemelin in the third period. Then the Boston offense relentlessly chipped away at the three-goal deficit. Center Dave Poulin got the comeback started by scoring just 1:28 into the final period to make it a two-goal game. By the seven-minute mark it was a one-goal game, after defenseman Bob Beers, a recent call-up from the Maine Mariners, scored his first NHL goal. Barely a minute later, right winger Dave Christian, who had scored the first Bruins goal in the second period, got his second of the night by one-timing a feed from Poulin to make it 5–5.

As the last ten minutes of the third period ticked down, sudden-death overtime seemed inevitable. Then Poulin—who had scored just six goals all season—struck again. With Whalers defenseman Ulf Samuelsson riding him hard, Poulin took a pass from left winger Randy Burridge and crashed the net. Somehow—Poulin later confessed that he had "no idea how it went in"—the puck got past Whalers goalie Peter Sidorkiewicz with just 1:44 left. It was like one of those old table-hockey goals, when you just shove the handle on your center as hard as you can and hope to jam the puck home.

Regardless of how it occurred, the outcome was undeniable. Bruins GM Harry Sinden called it "maybe the greatest comeback ever by the Bruins in a playoff game." (At least until 2013; see Game No. 35.)

Whalers coach Rick Ley offered a different perspective. Said Ley, "Our old team reared its ugly head."

To their credit, the Whalers hung tough and eventually forced a seventh game at the Garden. That's when Raymond Bourque, who again wasn't expected to play, pulled a Willis Reed. Bourque entered the game 52 seconds into the first period, to a thunderous ovation. Thirty-eight seconds later he assisted on the Bruins' first goal. The Whalers had no chance. The charged-up Bruins won the game handily and advanced to the Stanley Cup Final before losing to the Edmonton Oilers in five games.

95

Harvard 12, Yale 6
November 22, 1890

Harvard snapped The Game's longest winless streak to complete an undefeated season and give the Crimson their only undisputed national championship

The Game really wasn't a game at first. With the soccer/rugby-style rules of the day, a better description would have been The Match. When Harvard beat Yale in the first-ever "football" game between the two schools, on November 13, 1875, the score was 4–0, a result of "four goals and two touchdowns." (Imagine trying to play fantasy football with *that* scoring system.)

Nor, in those days, was The Game much of a game in the competitive sense. After losing the first one, Yale dominated to a degree not seen since. From 1876 through 1889, Yale went 10–0–1 against Harvard (the teams didn't play in 1877, '85, or '88). In fact, Yale's principal rival in that period was Princeton. Between them, those two schools either won or shared every national championship for fourteen consecutive years (even if the "national championship" is essentially a 20th century invention, applied retroactively to 19th century results).

Yale's attitude toward Harvard was downright dismissive. In 1888, the Harvard–Yale game was tentatively scheduled for Thanksgiving Day at the Polo Grounds in New York, where it had been played twice before. When Harvard's faculty asked for a change of venue, Yale flatly refused. The Bulldogs were focused on their meeting with undefeated Princeton, the Saturday before Thanksgiving. According to a Boston *Daily Globe* account of the dispute, "Yale cares very little whether they play Harvard or not."

It's not as if Harvard sucked. They were much better than most of the other dozen or so major-college programs of the time. But they were still several levels below Princeton and Yale.

Take the 1886 season, when Harvard went 12–2. The Crimson averaged 63 points a game in their twelve victories and allowed zero. Their two losses, of course, were to Princeton (by a 12–0 score) and Yale (29–4).

So when the 1890 Harvard team got off to a 10–0 start, it didn't mean much. Sure, the Crimson had beaten up on the likes of Amherst (74–6), but they didn't schedule Princeton that year. And they still had to deal with 12–0 Yale, and legendary coach Walter Camp.

The game was played at Springfield's Hampden Park before a crowd of about 20,000. (That sounds modest until you consider that the seating capacity was only 8,500.) Another 1,000 or so Harvard supporters gathered outside the *Daily Globe's* office in Boston to await updates.

Per 1890 rules, there were two 45-minute halves. Scoring had evolved to where a field goal was worth five points, a touchdown was worth four, and the conversion kick was worth two. (Another Gay Nineties touch: The two schools openly bet on the outcome, with Yale sending Harvard $1,000 and requesting two-to-one odds.)

Oddly, a Harvard injury turned the tide in the Crimson's favor. Harvard had trouble playing against the wind in the first half and was lucky that Yale's Bum McClung (future U.S. Treasurer) missed two field goal attempts. The game was still scoreless in the second half when Harvard's promising young back, Everett Lake, was carried off the field with what the *Daily Globe* called "a bad sprain." In his place Harvard subbed J.P. Lee, a track star who had set a world record in the low hurdles six months earlier. But for all his speed, Lee was a confounding player—"a riddle to his captain, his fellow players, and the interested public," the *Daily Globe* had declared in a scathing assessment a month earlier. "He seems to be absolutely without courage … stopping when he expects to be tackled."

The *Daily Globe's* correspondent, a former player identified only as "Rusher," concluded that Lee would be a serious liability against Yale, "unless he can convince himself that he is blessed with exceptional natural football advantages, and make up his mind to use them."

Whether motivated by this criticism or some other force, Lee finally lived up to his potential shortly after entering the game. He lined up deep in the backfield, took a handoff from quarterback Dudley Dean, swept around the right end, and sprinted 55 yards for a touchdown. The conversion kick made it 6–0, Harvard. "The play was astounding to Yale men," the *New York Times* reported. "To think that 'Jimmy' Lee should score a touchdown seemed preposterous."

Fired up by this unlikely turn, Yale was marching toward the potential tying touchdown when freshman quarterback Frank Barbour fumbled. Dean (who would later distinguish himself with Teddy Roosevelt's Rough Riders in the Battle of San Juan Hill) picked up the ball and returned it 70 yards for a touchdown.

McClung scored late to add some drama, but the Crimson held on in the gathering dusk for a landmark victory. In 19th century fashion, the players returned to Cambridge on a special railroad car while some of their supporters stayed behind to paint the town crimson—at Springfield's opera house. "The lingering ones are having no end of fun," the *New York Times* reported, "and some of it pretty severe, too."

Harvard remained a college football powerhouse for the next 30 years, claiming a share of nine additional national championships.

94

Bruins 3, Sabres 2
May 1, 1992

A spectacular save by Andy Moog helped the Bruins survive
Game 7 of a scrappy first-round series

Not much had separated Boston and Buffalo in the NHL's 1991–
92 Adams Division race. Although the Bruins had finished second, ten points ahead of the third-place Sabres, the teams had
split eight games, each winning three and losing three, with two ties.
Little surprise, then, that their opening-round series in the Stanley Cup
Playoffs went the distance. Or that Game 7 turned into a tense bout of
call-and-response. Glen Murray gave the Bruins a 1–0 lead in the first
period. The Sabres' Pat LaFontaine tied it at 2:07 of the second with a
shorthanded goal. Boston regained the lead at 2:55 of the third when
Stephen Leach swept one through the five hole on Buffalo goalie Tom
Draper. Buffalo tied it less than two minutes later when Dale Hawerchuk
tucked in a short rebound. Dave Reid put Boston back up, 3–2, on a slap
shot with just 8:20 left in regulation.

And now another tie, and sudden-death overtime, appeared inevitable. With a little over four minutes remaining in the third period,
Sabres defenseman Keith Carney wound up from the right point. The
Bruins' Raymond Bourque committed early, hitting the ice before
Carney pulled the trigger. Carney re-aimed and wristed a left-handed
shot on net. Boston goalie Andy Moog made the save but failed to corral
the puck. It caromed to the weak side, where LaFontaine loomed.

Moog had a solid playoff pedigree; he had been a part of three
Stanley Cup-winning teams with the Edmonton Oilers, and he had led
all goalies with a 2.21 goals-against average for the Bruins in the 1990

postseason. But his two most recent playoff starts had ended badly. In Game 5, a 2–0 Buffalo victory at Boston Garden, he had received a game misconduct in the second period for spearing in retaliation for having been speared earlier. (Buffalo's intent, Moog conceded later, was "to try to get me off my game, and it worked tonight.") In Game 6 at Buffalo, he had been pulled during a 9–3 pasting. And now, at the decisive moment of the deciding game, he was off his feet, half the goalmouth was unguarded, the puck was loose, and the series' most potent offensive force was teeing up from within ten feet. LaFontaine, a gifted center, already had scored at least one goal in each of the seven games. But Moog had a couple of intangibles going for him. One, he had a short memory. "I don't think I can get anything out of [Game 6] by thinking about what happened," he'd said before Game 7. Two, he relished the moment. "It's why you play the game," he said. "All of this added anxiety is great."

Whether that added anxiety got to LaFontaine, or whether he was victimized by the vagaries of a six-ounce vulcanized rubber disk skittering on a sheet of ice, he didn't get good wood on the shot. Moog, who looked like a first baseman stretching for the throw as he dived across the crease, made the glove save. He held onto the puck—and the Bruins held on for the last four minutes and change. Afterward Bourque made it clear why Boston had lived to play another day: "I've said it before and I'll say it again. We've gotten where we've been the past few years because of Andy Moog."

After backstopping the Bruins to four one-goal victories over Buffalo, Moog led Boston to a shocking sweep of the top-seeded Canadians in the Adams Division Final. The Bruins then fell to eventual champion Pittsburgh, 4–0, in the Prince of Wales Conference Final.

93

Boston College 19, Tennessee 13
January 1, 1941

BC's first bowl win completed an undefeated season and should have put the Eagles into the conversation regarding the national championship—if there had *been* a conversation regarding the national championship

Sports-talk radio would have been a hard sell in Boston in 1940. There just wasn't much to talk about. The Red Sox finished eight games out that season—and that was the closest they'd come to a pennant since 1918. The Braves—or "Bees," as they were called then—were even worse. They finished 34½ games out, and it had been 24 years since they had finished higher than fourth. The Celtics wouldn't exist for another six years, the Patriots for twenty. (An earlier NFL team, the Boston Redskins, had already come and gone, arousing little interest.) In the pro ranks, the Bruins were the lone bright spot. They were the NHL's best team—but at that point the NHL consisted only of the Original Six plus the moribund New York Americans.

In college football—still the second-most-popular team sport nationally, behind baseball—Boston had lost its place of prominence. Since Harvard's last claim to a national championship in 1920, the Crimson had receded into mediocrity. (Harvard's records in the three most recent seasons: 4–4, 4–4, 3–2–3.)

All of which made BC's sudden emergence on the national stage one of Boston's biggest sports stories in those lean prewar years.

Although the Eagles had had some good teams in the past—they'd had three unbeaten seasons in the '20s—the perception was that they benefitted from a soft "Eastern" schedule. The 1939 team's 6–3 loss to Clemson in the Cotton Bowl, BC's first bowl invitation, did nothing to burnish the school's national reputation. Nor did the Eagles' 1940 schedule: nine of ten games at home, including a platter of cupcakes. In one four-week stretch, the Eagles dispatched Idaho (0–3), St. Anselm (0–1), Manhattan (2–3), and Boston University (1–2) by a combined 161–0.

Then Georgetown came to town.

Hard as it is to imagine now, the Hoyas were once a football powerhouse. Georgetown brought a 23-game unbeaten streak to Fenway Park on November 16, 1940, having last lost three years ago that week. The current team was 7–0 and had just blown out Syracuse and Maryland in consecutive road games. And they jumped out to a 10–0 lead against the Eagles just five minutes into the game. But behind "Chuckin' Charley" O'Rourke, a 158-pound senior quarterback, BC came back for a thrilling 19–18 victory in what the iconic (if awful) sportswriter Grantland Rice called "probably the greatest football game ever played." Wrote Rice, "I doubt that any other team in the country could have beaten either [team]."

Two more home wins, against Auburn and Holy Cross, completed a 10–0 regular season, after which Boston College accepted a Sugar Bowl invitation. Their opponent: SEC champion Tennessee, also 10–0. In keeping with the prevailing bias, Tennessee was an 8–5 favorite.

The game, on a muggy afternoon in New Orleans, began as expected. A short punt by O'Rourke in the first quarter set Tennessee up at the BC 46-yard line. Aided by a questionable pass-interference call, the Vols cashed in to make it 7–0. But that was the only score of the first half. And after a blocked punt, BC scored on a two-play, seventeen-yard drive to tie it in the third quarter.

This was a much more evenly matched game than most "experts" had predicted. Tennessee ended up with twelve first downs to BC's eleven. BC had 248 total yards to 245 for Tennessee. The teams even traded missed conversions. After Tennessee had taken a 13–7 lead, Boston College tied it on a fourth-and-one plunge from sophomore running back (and future Pats coach) Mike Holovak. Needing only a PAT to take a 14–13 lead, BC inexplicably opted to try for two after a half-the-distance penalty. Tennessee stoned the attempt.

The game was still tied at thirteen halfway through the fourth quarter when BC's Don Currivan blocked a 23-yard field goal attempt. The Eagles took over at their own twenty. Having kept the ball on the ground for most of the day, the Eagles now took to the air. O'Rourke threw on four straight downs, completing three, as Boston College moved to the Tennessee 24. O'Rourke then executed the perfect play for the circumstances: a quarterback draw. His pump fake froze the Tennessee defense, and he scrambled untouched for what he called the "last and best and most important touchdown" of his BC career. Then, playing defensive back, the "Malden Meal Ticket," as O'Rourke was also known, had an interception to put the game away.

Notwithstanding this outcome, Tennessee finished fourth in the final 1940 AP college football poll and BC finished fifth. Why? Because in those days the final rankings were released before the bowl games. On the basis of this essentially meaningless poll, the NCAA recognizes 8–0 Minnesota— whose season ended on Thanksgiving weekend, and who declined to participate in a bowl game—as the 1940 national champion.

92

Red Sox 13, Yankees 1
October 16, 1999

In the Yankees' first-ever postseason visit to Fenway Park,
the Red Sox offense (and Boston fans) ripped Roger Clemens
while Pedro Martinez silenced the potent New York lineup

This wasn't the greatest win in the history of the Red Sox franchise, but it was the greatest in the history of Red Sox *fans*. Never has the Nation played a more conspicuous role in the outcome.

Sox fans didn't need extra incentive for Boston's first official postseason home game against the Yankees. (The '78 tiebreaker was the 163rd game of the regular season.) But they got it anyway when the pitching match-up was announced for Game 3 of the 1999 American League Championship Series: Pedro Martinez, 27, the Red Sox current ace, vs. Roger Clemens, 37, the Red Sox former ace. Or, in the talk-radio shorthand: Cy Young vs. Cy Old. Sox GM Dan Duquette had allowed Clemens to leave as a free agent after the '96 season and had replaced him with Martinez. In the three years since, Martinez had secured his place in Sox history. His '99 season (23–4, 2.07 ERA, 313 strikeouts) was one of the best ever. He had been the stopper all year, and he would have to come through again; the Sox were in an 0–2 hole after dropping a pair of one-run games at Yankee Stadium.

Clemens, meanwhile, had secured his reputation as a faded carpetbagger by signing with New York, the defending World Series champions. The expectation that the Rocket would crash and burn was palpable. Sox chief executive officer John Harrington said ticket demand was the highest in Fenway history. Sox fans knew all too well that Clemens, despite a 3–0 win over Texas in the division series, had a history of postseason meltdowns. What chance would he have pitching in the most hostile environment imaginable, against a Sox offense that had set postseason records for hits (24) and runs (23) against the Indians in its last Fenway appearance?

None, it turned out.

The crowd started in on Clemens immediately. A haunting, taunting chant of *Ro-ger Ro-ger* resounded through Fenway throughout Clemens's stint on the mound—which wasn't long. Second baseman Jose Offerman led off the bottom of the first with a triple and third baseman John Valentin followed with a homer. Seven pitches, seven total bases.

Staked to a 2–0 lead, Martinez kept Fenway at full boil in the second by striking out the side, all swinging. Clemens surrendered a single, a walk, two doubles, and two more runs in the bottom half. His day ended with an appropriate indignity in the third. Yankees manager Joe Torre yanked him during an at-bat following a leadoff single by Mike Stanley and a first-pitch strike to Brian Daubach. But the Red Sox didn't let up— Daubach promptly homered off of Hideki Irabu—and neither did the fans. They continued to serenade Clemens long after he had left: *Where is Roger? In the shower!*

"I don't know who comes up with that stuff," Sox pitcher Bret Saberhagen said afterward. "I always thought New York fans were pretty good, but what these fans have come up with, they have it, hands down."

The flip side of Fenway's emotional crowd was on display the next night. With the Sox down 9–2 in the ninth, manager Jimy Williams was ejected for arguing another in a series of calls that went against Boston. Fans pelted the field with debris, forcing both the Yankees and the umpires to take refuge. The Yankees eliminated the Red Sox in five games, and Clemens ended up with his first World Series ring when the Yankees swept the Braves. Even worse for Sox fans, Clemens was the winning pitcher in the final game.

91

Boston University 4, Miami (Ohio) 3, OT
April 11, 2009

"The greatest championship game ever played"

This might have been Jack Parker's best team. It certainly gave him his best moment. Parker's Boston University Terriers had won their eighth regular season title in Hockey East with a record of 27–5–4, and just one loss after Thanksgiving. (They had also won the Bean Pot for the 29th time.) They won the Hockey East tournament for the seventh time, putting them into the NCAA tournament for the 31st time. They won with impressive offense in the first round (8–3 over Ohio State). They won with tough defense in the Northeast Regional final (2–1 over New Hampshire, as senior forward Jason Lawrence got the game winner with just 14.4 seconds remaining). They won by using a little bit of everything in round one of the Frozen Four (5–4 over Vermont). Now all that separated BU from a fifth national championship was Miami University of Oxford, Ohio. The RedHawks, from the Central Collegiate Hockey Association, were in the Frozen Four for the first time. When Parker took over behind the Terriers bench in 1973, Miami's hockey program didn't even exist.

But once the puck dropped to start the 2009 Division I Men's Ice Hockey championship game at the Verizon Center in Washington, D.C., BU's pedigree meant nothing. Not at first, anyway.

The score was 1–1 after two periods. The longer the game wore on, and the more the pressure mounted, the more the odds would have seemed to favor BU and their experience. But it was the RedHawks who scored in the thirteenth minute of the third period to break the tie.

25

Parker didn't panic. He knew that all BU needed was one goal to stay alive. They had seven minutes to get it.

Six minutes.

Five minutes.

When a late goal finally came, with 4:08 remaining, it wasn't a BU veteran who got it. It was Miami freshman Trent Vogelhuber, netting just the second goal of his college career.

Still Parker didn't panic. He knew BU could be explosive. They had scored three goals in 44 seconds to overcome a 1–0 deficit against Boston College in the semifinals of the Hockey East tournament. But how could he give them their best chance?

Parker deliberated through a TV timeout with 3:32 remaining, and when he still hadn't settled his mind, he extended the break with a timeout of his own. Really, his strategic options came down to a simple matter of risk versus reward. If Parker pulled goalie Kieran Millan for an extra attacker, that would leave the BU net empty for up to 3½ minutes—considerably longer than most coaches would be comfortable with. On the other hand, if BU continued to play straight up, there was a chance that Millan might not get off the ice until it was too late. So should Parker be aggressive or conservative?

His decision, as he later summarized it: "The hell with it." He ordered Millan to the bench.

Facing BU's extra attacker, Miami finally began to feel the pressure. With just over two minutes left, the RedHawks had a chance for a rush on the empty net, but in their haste they were offside.

Miami simply couldn't control the puck. BU attacked with urgency while the RedHawks skated in tight circles near their own net. When junior forward Zach Cohen bounced the puck off Miami goaltender Cody Reichard's leg pads and into the net with 59.5 seconds left, Miami's margin for error was gone.

BU's superiority truly showed on the tying goal. With just twenty seconds remaining, the consensus pick as America's best college player—Hobey Baker Award winner Matt Gilroy, a senior defenseman—suddenly had the puck about 25 feet in front of the Miami net. He darted left, causing RedHawks forward Justin Mercier to hit the ice in anticipation of a shot that didn't come. As Gilroy moved in on net, the rest of the Miami defense moved with him, like a listing ship.

Put yourself in Gilroy's skates. You're the best player on the ice. This could be your team's last hope. You're closing on the net. What do you do? As ESPN analyst Barry Melrose noted a moment later, "Most guys would have just blasted it."

Instead, Gilroy slipped a crisp backhand pass to junior forward Nick Bonino, who one-timed it over Reichard's left shoulder before the defense could recover.

The game ended with another abrupt change of direction. In the twelfth minute of overtime, Miami defenseman Kevin Roeder threw himself in front of a shot from BU junior defenseman Colby Cohen. Rather than stop the puck, however, Roeder simply altered its attitude, from a straight slap shot to a fluttering knuckleball. The puck floated over Reichard and into the net to complete BU's stunning turnaround. Later, Parker stated the obvious: "It's the greatest comeback I've been involved in."

The level of self-regard required to excel in sports doesn't always translate well in real life. In 2012, after two BU players were charged with sexual assault (charges were later dropped against one and reduced against the other), the school conducted an internal investigation, which concluded "that there are a number of important structures and processes that are failing to achieve the full level and quality of oversight of the men's ice hockey program that is expected and appropriate at a major university." Among the findings was that some members of the 2009 national championship team celebrated with a bacchanalia at Agganis Arena. As part of the fallout, Jack Parker was removed as athletic director. He continued as BU's hockey coach for one more season and then retired.

90

Patriots 26, Vikings 20, OT
November 13, 1994

Drew Bledsoe's record-setting performance started the
slow turnaround that made the Patriots respectable

A fter a 1992 season in which they had twice as many starting
quarterbacks (four) as wins (two), the Patriots hit "select all"
and "delete." First, they enticed Bill Parcells out of retirement
to replace Dick MacPherson. ("Coaching the Patriots will be my last
job," Parcells declared.) Then they unveiled a new logo and new uniforms. Finally, they used the number-one draft pick on Washington
State quarterback Drew Bledsoe.

Even as the new-look Pats sold season tickets at an unprecedented
rate, Parcells tried to manage expectations. "I really detest the term 'franchise quarterback,' " he said on draft day. "For now, [Bledsoe's] role will
be to learn our system."

With a couple of exceptions—including a stirring 33–27 overtime
win over the Dolphins to conclude a 5–11 season in '93—Parcells took
a conservative approach with Bledsoe. It ended in the second half of
the tenth game of the 1994 season, after the 3–6 Patriots had fallen into
a twenty-point hole against the 7–2 Vikings.

The two-minute offense had produced a field goal on the final play
of the first half, cutting the deficit to 20–3. So Parcells decided to treat
the entire second half as a two-minute drill. "I thought maybe if we
could surprise them with that," Parcells said later, "we might get something out of it quickly before they adjusted."

The Pats did indeed score quickly on the opening drive. Barely a
minute and a half had elapsed when Bledsoe hit Ray Crittenden with a

31-yard strike that made it a game at 20–10. And while the Pats didn't score again until late in the fourth quarter, the Vikings never really did adjust to Bledsoe's rapid-fire assault. His numbers: 37-of-53 for 354 yards and three touchdowns.

In the second half.

For the game, Bledsoe completed 45 passes in 70 attempts, both of which still stand as NFL records. Just as important—and perhaps even harder to believe—he had no interceptions and no sacks.

And still the Patriots needed overtime to win. The second touchdown drive, an 87-yard masterpiece that culminated in a five-yard toss to running back Leroy Thompson, didn't begin until just 5:05 remained in the game. After the Pats' defense—which deserved its share of credit for pitching a shutout in the second half—forced a three-and-out, Bledsoe got the ball back with 1:51 left.

The drive started on the New England 39. After three straight incompletions, it almost ended there. But Bledsoe hit Vincent Brisby for 25 yards on fourth and ten, and the Pats were on their way to a 23-yard field goal that tied the game at twenty with fourteen seconds left. The Patriots got the ball to start overtime and never gave it back. Bledsoe's fourteen-yard pass to fullback Kevin Turner capped a 67-yard touchdown drive. "We needed this more than any team has ever needed a win," Turner said. "Morale was low around here."

Just as it had been for the better part of 34 years.

The comeback against the Vikings sparked a seven-game winning streak that propelled the Patriots to a 10–6 record and a wild-card berth. (Their season ended with a first-round loss to the Cleveland Browns—and coach Bill Belichick.) It also quieted many of the skeptics who had begun to question whether Bledsoe was really the Pats' quarterback of the future. Not that Bledsoe himself had any doubts. "I want everybody to realize I'm here for the long haul," he said after the Vikings game. "I'm going to be the Patriots' quarterback for a while, barring injury."

89

Boston College 41, Notre Dame 39
November 20, 1993

The so-called Holy War had a "Holy s---!" ending, thanks to
BC's walk-on kicker, David Gordon

I n the big picture of Boston sports, BC football is usually out of the
frame. After a landmark win over Tennessee in the 1941 Sugar Bowl
(see Game No. 93), Boston College didn't win another bowl game
until Doug Flutie's swan song on the first day of 1985. Interest waned
again until 1991, when BC hired Tom Coughlin to coach the team in
the Big East's new football conference. Season ticket sales doubled in
Coughlin's first two years. An 8–3–1 mark in 1992 and a trip to the Hall
of Fame Bowl stoked expectations for 1993.

The Eagles promptly lost their first two games, including a 22–21
heartbreaker at Northwestern. Walk-on kicker David Gordon missed a
40-yard field goal attempt with just over a minute left.

BC football receded to the fringes.

The Eagles then reeled off seven straight wins en route to the biggest
game of the season, at Notre Dame in late November. The so-called
Holy War would have been significant under any circumstances. But
these weren't just any circumstances. Unbeaten Notre Dame, ranked
number two the week before, had just knocked off number-one Florida
State in the "Game of the Century." As the new number one, Notre
Dame now had a clear path to the national championship game. All the
Irish had to do was beat BC—something Notre Dame had done in all
four of their previous meetings, including a 54–7 pounding at South
Bend the year before.

This was perfect timing for the Eagles. Eager to avenge that whipping, BC came in on an emotional high, while Notre Dame suffered an understandable letdown. Boston College quarterback Glenn Foley shredded the Notre Dame defense (30-of-48 for 315 yards and four touchdowns). Coughlin engineered an aggressive game plan that featured a fake punt and a surprise onside kick, among other wrinkles. It all added up to a 38–17 BC lead early in the fourth quarter.

At which point each team seemed to suddenly remember its place in the college football hierarchy. Assisted by two Foley fumbles, Notre Dame piled up 22 points in ten minutes to take a 39–38 lead. Just 1:01 remained when the reeling Eagles got the ball back at their own 25.

Foley drove BC to the Notre Dame 24 in seven plays. Boston College had a chance—if not a very good one.

Five seconds remained for Gordon, the left-footed walk-on, to try the winning kick from 41 yards. It was longer than any field goal he had ever made. (He had missed from 40 yards earlier that day.) He was kicking on a natural grass field for the first time all season. This was the same kid who had missed the potential winning kick from almost the same distance against Northwestern. And this was unbeaten, number-one Notre Dame.

The kick was not an esthetic success. The snap was high and Foley, the holder, did a good job just to get it down in time. Then Gordon caught the ball with more toe than he'd intended. The kick started low and tracked to the right. But then it drifted left. Gordon described it as "kind of a knuckleball," but it was more like a slider that starts outside the strike zone and then breaks over the plate. Still, when it cleared the crossbar with the clock at 00:00, that homely kick was breathtaking for BC.

For Notre Dame, it was something else. Said coach Lou Holtz, whose team saw a shot at its twelfth national championship evaporate, "It's heartbreaking."

A week later BC was back to its "Others Receiving Votes" status of Boston sports relevance. The Eagles lost to West Virginia, costing them a share of the Big East title and a shot at a major bowl bid. Tom Coughlin left to become an NFL head coach after the season. His accomplishments in the National Football League include knocking off another previously unbeaten powerhouse, in Super Bowl XLII. But that upset didn't play as well in Boston as BC–Notre Dame had.

88

Patriots 26, Jets 14
December 28, 1985

For the first time in 22 years, the Patriots won a playoff game

Expectations were high and the bar was low. The Patriots had won just one playoff game in their 25-year history, exactly 22 years earlier: December 28, 1963. And that wasn't a playoff game per se; it was a tiebreaker. Neither the 7–6–1 Patriots nor their AFL East co-champs, the Buffalo Bills, had sufficiently transcended mediocrity to claim the division outright. The Patriots beat the Bills for the right to get demolished by the Chargers in the AFL championship game, 51–10.

The Pats' most recent trip to the playoffs, in the strike-shortened 1982 season, had also been a fraud. The Patriots had sneaked in with a 5–4 record and the Dolphins quickly escorted them out, 28–13. In between, there were just two other postseason games: the infamous 24–21 loss at Oakland in 1976 (featuring a controversial roughing-the-passer call by referee Ben Dreith that extended the Raiders' winning drive) and an embarrassing 31–14 home loss to Houston on New Year's Eve 1978, with head coach Chuck Fairbanks having already bid New England *Auld Lang Syne.*

That was it. That was the playoff pedigree of the Patriots team that took the field at the Meadowlands on wild-card weekend in 1985.

Still, there was reason for optimism. The Pats had split the season series with the Jets, winning by a touchdown at home and losing by an overtime field goal in New Jersey. When two even teams meet in the playoffs, the difference often comes down to better coaching and preparation.

Good sign for New England. During his playing days as a receiver with the Baltimore Colts, Patriots head coach Raymond Berry had pioneered the art of obsessive preparation. He'd brought that same approach to the Patriots, and it was working. They had won nine of their last eleven and flipped their turnover differential from –4 in the first half of the season to +9 in the second half. This was not a glamorous team—but neither was it a team with glaring weaknesses. They had a solid defense and a conservative, run-based offense featuring the fullback, Craig James.

Against the Jets, that added up to a performance that was not particularly pretty anywhere but the scoreboard, which read New England 26, New York 14 at the end. With James struggling (22 carries for just 49 yards) the Patriots mustered only one offensive touchdown. But they added another on special teams, and kicker Tony Franklin booted four field goals. On defense, New England recorded five sacks (and knocked Jets starting quarterback Ken O'Brien out of the game) and won the turnover battle, 4–0.

So the outcome was legitimate if unspectacular. The Patriots had simply won a football game. It just happened to be in the postseason.

And that made it a landmark occasion for the current generation of Patriots players and their fans. "I kind of lost it at the end," admitted Pats linebacker Steve Nelson, a veteran of three prior postseason deflations. "I've lost it on the football field before—but never in joy."

If they wanted to prove that they were genuine contenders, the Patriots couldn't wait 22 years for their next playoff win. In eight days they would face the Raiders in Los Angeles (see Game No. 64).

87

Red Sox 11, Yankees 10
July 24, 2004

The midsummer promo for the greatest October story ever told

I t was a rebirth with a nine-month gestation. No need to go back to 1918 or 1978 or even 1999. All relevant developments in the Red Sox–Yankees rivalry, as of late July 2004, had occurred since October 16, 2003, when Grady Little hanged himself on the Yankee Stadium mound.

The '04 Red Sox had a new manager, Terry Francona. They had a new ace, Curt Schilling. They had a new closer, Keith Foulke. The one off-season move that hadn't panned out was an attempt to acquire Alex Rodriguez from Texas. A-Rod wound up with the Yankees instead.

How had it all worked out so far? Less than 24 hours earlier, on a Friday night at Fenway, Schilling had been unable to hold a 4–1 lead. The Yankees won, 8–7. A-Rod drove in the go-ahead run in the top of the ninth. Off of Foulke. Yankees closer Mariano Rivera then set the Sox down in order as New York pushed its AL East lead to 9½ games.

In other words, not much had changed, despite all the off-season maneuvering. The Sox were still wild-card contenders, but their prospects of unseating the Yankees as AL champions seemed as dismal as Saturday's rainy weather, which delayed the start.

The game was slow to begin but the Yankees weren't. Boston starter Bronson Arroyo was already trailing 3–0 in the top of the third. Rodriguez was batting with two outs and no one on when Arroyo hit him with a curveball. A-Rod yelled something at Arroyo. Home plate umpire Bruce Froemming stepped between them. So did Sox catcher Jason Varitek.

They had a lively exchange. "I told [Rodriguez] in choice words to go to first base," Varitek later said. "Then things got out of hand."

A moment later, Varitek stuffed his mitt in A-Rod's race. It became a snapshot of the 2004 season.

The fight lit a fuse, albeit a slow-burning one. The Sox trailed 9–4 after 5½ innings. That's when the resurrection started. The Sox scored four runs on four hits and three walks in the bottom of the sixth to cut the deficit to 9-8. But it appeared that the Yankees would once again have just enough to keep Boston at bay when Nomar Garciaparra struck out with the bases loaded to end the inning.

It was 10–8 Yanks in the bottom of the ninth and Rivera was once again protecting the lead. A Garciaparra double and a Kevin Millar single, sandwiched around a Trot Nixon flyout to deep right, made it 10–9. With the wind blowing in and Boston at the bottom of the order, small ball was the obvious play. Dave McCarty went in to run for Millar, and Red Sox third baseman Bill Mueller went to bat with a simple objective: "See some pitches, get on base."

Meuller saw five pitches. And he did more than get on base—he created a dog pile at home plate when he drilled a 93-mph cutter into the Yankees bullpen for an improbable walk-off win.

New York still had an 8½-game lead, but the Red Sox felt re-energized. Sox slugger David Ortiz, who called the brawl "the best thing that ever happened to us," offered a prediction: "It's the start of something good."

Even A-Rod, who could have avoided putting a spark to the tinder just by keeping his mouth shut, admitted that the tide was rising. "I think it's going to take this rivalry to a new level," he said.

It reached a new level, all right. And in October, Sox fans got a second classic photo to go with the mitt-in-the-mug shot: A-Rod desperately slapping the ball out of Arroyo's glove, a pointed symbol of the Yankees' futile attempt to stave off the Red Sox in the greatest postseason comeback in baseball history (see games 2–5).

86

Red Sox 3, Yankees 2
October 10, 1904

In 1904, as in 2004, the American League pennant came down
to four games between the Red Sox and Yankees—two in Boston
followed by two in New York. Different century, same result:
The Sox came from behind to win

There was no American League Championship Series in 1904.
Not officially, anyway. But thanks to some scheduling quirks and
what the *Globe* called "the greatest race since baseball was invented," the Red Sox and Yankees settled the American League pennant
with a five-game showdown that prefigured the modern postseason.

In some ways the baseball schedule was more manageable in 1904.
There were just eight teams in the American League—none west of
St. Louis. Teams played only 154 games. The schedule was perfectly
equitable; each team played the others 22 times—eleven at home, eleven
on the road.

But in other ways the schedule was a nightmare. There were no night
games. Just two AL cities (St. Louis and Chicago) permitted Sunday baseball. Teams traveled by train. Any game that ended in a tie because of
darkness or weather was replayed from scratch. Finally, there was no All-
Star break. As a result, teams were dragging by September—and because
of all the postponements that had accrued by then, September was the
most grueling month of all. In September 1904, for instance, the Red Sox
played eleven doubleheaders, including four in as many days against the
same team (the Washington Senators). Which makes it even more
remarkable that the Red Sox and Yankees (who played ten September
doubleheaders) stayed even down the stretch. From August 22 until the
final weekend, no more than a game and a half separated Boston and
New York atop the American League standings.

A mid-September series before SRO crowds at Boston's Huntington Avenue Grounds illustrated how extraordinarily taut (and fraught) the race was. The Sox led by half a game when the Yankees came to town for what was originally to have been a four-game series in three days, including a doubleheader. But because of a May rainout, the Sox added a second doubleheader. Then game two of the opening doubleheader was called after five innings because of fog, with the score 1–1. So Boston was compelled to add a third straight doubleheader. But the second game of the second doubleheader also ended in a useless 1–1 tie, called after nine innings due to September's early dusk.

As for the four games that counted: They split 'em. So after playing six games in three days, the Red Sox and Yankees ended up right where they'd started: Boston up a half-game, with a critical rained-out game still to be made up somehow.

New York unwittingly provided a solution.

The season was supposed to end with the Sox playing four games in New York the second weekend in October. But the Yankees had rented out their home field, Manhattan's Hilltop Park, to the Columbia University football team that Saturday, leaving them with a game of their own to reschedule. There was already a season-ending doubleheader scheduled for Monday (remember—no games on Sunday). And each team needed all day Thursday, and then some, to reach New York by train from the Midwest (the Sox from Chicago, the Yanks from St. Louis). So New York agreed to move their orphaned Saturday home game to Boston and combine it with the remaining makeup game in a doubleheader.

When the climactic weekend finally arrived, the Sox still had a half-game lead. (New York had played three fewer games, which would not be made up.) The upshot: New York and Boston ended up with what amounted to a best-of-five playoff series with a 1–2–2 format. Game 1 was in New York on Friday, games 2 and 3 were in Boston on Saturday, and games 4 and 5 were back in New York on Monday.

Although they were the home team for the opening game, the Yankees were just as wrung-out as the Red Sox. In fact, having reached New York just three hours before the first pitch, the Yankees stuck with their dark blue road uniforms. Still, New York had one major advantage: 40-game winner Jack Chesbro was on the mound. When it was over, Chesbro was a 41-game winner. Playing on a day cold enough for overcoats, the sluggish Red Sox made three costly errors and New York cashed in for a 3–2 win. The Yankees leapfrogged into first, and jubilant New York fans carried Chesbro off the field.

The rivals reconvened in Boston at one o'clock Saturday afternoon. With a doubleheader sweep, New York could've clinched the pennant. And maybe that's what enticed Yankees manager Clark Griffith into a tactical blunder. Chesbro started the first game, less than 24 hours (and a late-night train ride) after he had just won the tensest game of his life.

Bad move. Boston chased Chesbro with a six-run fourth en route to a 13–2 rout. And the Sox refused to let up; there wasn't even a break between games. As soon as Bill Dinneen (22–14) fanned Yankees leadoff man Patsy Dougherty to end the first game, Dougherty had to step right back into the box against Cy Young (25–16) to start the second game. Young wriggled out of several jams in a gripping 1–0 victory.

So it all came down to the season-ending doubleheader back in New York on Monday. Griffith started Chesbro again for the opener. Boston's fourth starter, Norwood Gibson, was due up next in Sox rotation. But manager Jimmy Collins decided to bring back Dinneen on short rest.

The Yankees struck first, with two runs in the fifth. The rally included a key hit by Dougherty, the left fielder. He had been a vital member of the Sox team that had beaten the Pirates the year before in the first World Series (see Game No. 28). But with his average down almost 60 points, the Sox had dealt him to New York in June. Since then Dougherty had haunted his old mates, hitting .381 with nine extra-base hits in sixteen games against Boston.

It was still 2–0 in the seventh when New York became unnerved against the bottom of the Boston order. First baseman Candy LaChance led off with a single. Then Yankees second baseman Jimmy Williams couldn't handle a hot grounder by his Sox counterpart, Hobe Ferris. It was scored a hit, putting runners at first and second. Catcher Lou Criger sacrificed the runners over. Collins left Dinneen (a .208 hitter) in the game, and he rolled a grounder to Williams. Instead of taking the force-out at first, Williams fired the ball to the plate. It eluded catcher Red Kleinow and rolled to the backstop, allowing the tying runs to score.

It was still 2–2 starting the ninth. Criger led off with an infield single and advanced to third on a sacrifice and a groundout. Sox shortstop Freddy Parent needed a hit to drive him in. Unless the Yankees decided to help the Sox cause again.

They did. Chesbro had achieved his 41 wins through deft use of the spitball, a legal pitch at the time. But the wet one worked against him at the worst possible time. He sailed a pitch over Kleinow's head, and the Red Sox scored their third run, all on balls to the backstop.

But the drama of the 1904 pennant race wasn't over yet. In the home half, a pair of walks put runners on first and second with two out. In stepped Dougherty, Boston's friend-turned-nemesis. With the count 2–2, Dinneen fired a waist-high fastball over the inside corner. Dougherty swung and missed—"the last man out in the most important game of ball ever played," declared the *Globe*'s T.H. Murnane.

Outlasting the Yankees for the pennant was its own reward. There was no formal World Series in those days—nor was there an informal one that season, thanks to the shortsightedness of the New York Giants. The National League champions haughtily declared that they saw no purpose in playing the champion of "a minor league."

85

Celtics 138, Bucks 137, 2OT
May 10, 1987

With the aging Big Three defending what turned out to be their last title, the Celtics pulled off one of their grittiest playoff wins on the road

The 1986–87 Boston Celtics seemed older than they were. When the season began, on Halloween night, Robert Parish was the only member of the Big Three who was approaching the limits of the NBA actuarial table. He was 33. Larry Bird was 29. Kevin McHale was just 28. But they had already played together for six years. (For perspective, Paul Pierce was 30, Kevin Garnett was 31, and Ray Allen was 32 when they played their first game together.) They had been to the NBA Finals four times, winning three, and had logged more than a full season's worth of playoff basketball: 98 games.

All those hard minutes on hard wood had accelerated the aging process. The Celtics had become crotchety homebodies. Life on the road was a dreary grind. The Big Three preferred to putter around Boston and tend their Garden, barking at trespassers to get off their leprechaun-green lawn. They lost just once at Boston Garden all season—same as the year before. But whereas the 1985–86 team played tough everywhere, the 1986–87 team had a losing road record (20–21), including 0–3 in overtime games.

In short, this was not a team that you would have expected to win a double-overtime playoff thriller at a breakneck pace in a hostile arena. But they did it, in Game 4 of the Eastern Conference Semifinals at Milwaukee.

The Celtics, as expected, had beaten the Bucks in the first two games, at Boston Garden. Milwaukee, as expected, won Game 3 at the

MECCA Arena. (The Bucks, who had won 50 games in the regular season, were 3–0 at home versus the Celtics.) That game, on a Friday night, required overtime. With Game 4 less than 48 hours later, on Sunday afternoon, there was little time for the Celtics to recuperate from that enervating defeat.

All of which made the Game 4 outcome so unexpected.

And it's not as if the second unit saved the day. Boston's starting five (which also included 32-year-old Dennis Johnson and 28-year-old Danny Ainge) accounted for 130 of Boston's 138 points. Other than Parish, who fouled out, every starter logged at least 51 minutes. There was no time for a breather; neither team ever led by more than six. The game had a competitive flow that stoked the Celtics' veterans—McHale and Bird in particular. Each played all but two minutes while seemingly impervious to fatigue. Bird had 42 points on 13-of-23 shooting, including 3-of-5 from three-point range and 13-of-15 from the free-throw line. He added eight assists, seven rebounds, and two blocks. McHale had 34 points on 15-of-25 shooting, along with eleven rebounds—six at the offensive end—four blocks, two assists, and a steal.

And the Celtics still nearly lost, thanks to an equally dogged effort by Milwaukee. Six Bucks scored in double figures, led by Terry Cummings with 31. Five of those six shot better than 50% from the floor. The game started as an offensive clinic at both ends—the Celtics led just 32–31 after one quarter, despite shooting 67%—and stayed that way.

But for all the offensive pyrotechnics, it was some last-minute defense that decided the game. And again, Bird and McHale stepped up. With exactly 60 seconds left in the second overtime, Celtics backup forward Darren Daye, of all people, scored the game's final points, hitting a pair of free throws. Fifty seconds later, after running the shot clock all the way down, Dennis Johnson missed a jumper that would have extended Boston's lead to three. Milwaukee's Ricky Pierce grabbed the rebound and got the ball to John Lucas, a veteran point guard. Rather than call timeout, Milwaukee pressed the attack. Lucas, who had averaged a career-high 17.5 points per game that season, pushed the ball up the floor. Only Bird, back at the foul line, stood in his way. Said Bird later, "I didn't like my chances."

No wonder. Lucas, who thrived in the transition game, had already scored eighteen points that afternoon on 7-of-9 shooting. He'd also dished out six assists—and he had Cummings on the wing.

Bird simultaneously stepped in front of Lucas and reached out to deflect the anticipated pass to Cummings. He caught just enough of the ball to knock it away. Lucas recovered the loose ball, but by then McHale had arrived to help. McHale's long arms disrupted the desperate final shot and caused Lucas to miss badly. The Celtics had survived what McHale called "the kind of game I'll look back on and smile about."

McHale, who was already hobbled by a hairline fracture in his right foot and a sprained right ankle, reinjured the ankle on the final play. Attrition finally caught up with the Celtics in Game 5. Milwaukee became just the second team to win at Boston Garden in the last 81 games. The Bucks then squared the series with a ten-point win in Milwaukee, sending the series to a seventh game back at the Garden (see Game No. 84).

84

Celtics 119, Bucks 113
May 17, 1987

The Celtics overcame an eight-point deficit in the last six minutes
to win Game 7 of the 1987 Eastern Conference Semifinals

Basketball is such an easy game when the shots are dropping. All you have to do is create enough space to squeeze off another and another and another … like the Celtics had done in outlasting Milwaukee in Game 4 of the 1987 Eastern Conference Semifinals (see Game No. 85). What sets a truly great team apart is how they react when the shots are *not* dropping. Then it becomes a matter of manufacturing offense with defense, second-chance points, or both. And there was never a better demonstration of this than the Celtics' victory over the Bucks in Game 7, exactly one week after that Game 4 classic.

Led by small forward Paul Pressey (28 points on 12-of-17 shooting for the day), Milwaukee came out firing. The Bucks put up 36 points in the first quarter to grab a nine-point lead. Milwaukee, coached by former Celtic Don Nelson, was frighteningly efficient on offense. The Bucks hit sixteen shots from the perimeter in the first half. For the game they converted 28 of 30 free throws, including five from center Jack Sikma, who didn't miss once from the line during the series in 35 attempts. They had 46 fast-break points in Game 7 while committing just six turnovers. All of this on a day when A) Larry Bird, Dennis Johnson, and Robert Parish shot a combined 25-of-57; B) Danny Ainge joined the growing list of wounded Celts with a knee sprain that sidelined him in the third quarter; and C) Boston was victimized by a dreadful call on their home floor.

At the end of the third quarter, officials allowed Sidney Moncrief's three-pointer, which clearly came after the buzzer, to stand (no replay in those days). The psychological swing was huge. Rather than trailing by two to start the fourth, Milwaukee led by one, 89–88. The Bucks built the lead to eight, 108–100, over the next six minutes.

And yet the Celtics found a way. They maintained their poise at the line despite being cold from the floor. Bird was 13-of-13. Johnson and Parish were each 5-of-6. The seldom-used bench came through in Ainge's absence. Guard Jerry Sichting had just six points—but he was perfect from the field (2-of-2) and the line (ditto). The Celtics clamped down at crunch time, outscoring Milwaukee 19–5 over the final 5:52. They made the hustle plays, as when Parish blocked Sikma's shot and Johnson then hurled the ball off of Sikma while falling out of bounds to give Boston possession with a four-point lead and 1:31 to play.

But more than anything, on a day when they weren't able to simply drain shot after shot, the Celtics gave themselves second chance after second chance, with a remarkable 25 offensive rebounds. Both Parish (eleven) and McHale (ten) hit season highs when the season was on the line.

When veterans talk about the importance of experience in winning playoff games, they don't just mean experience at putting the ball in the basket. "A lot of guys, the day of a seventh game, will come out early to shoot," Bird said. "Never did it all year, but now they are. That doesn't get it. I believe that you work hard all year and games like this is when it pays off. That's what my high school coach said and I still believe it."

The Celtics had to work even harder against the Detroit Pistons in the Eastern Conference Finals (see games 58 and 59).

83

Harvard 29, Yale 29
November 23, 1968

Unbeaten Yale was fit to be tied—and Harvard obliged with one of the greatest last-minute comebacks in college football history

America hates muddy outcomes. The goal in any 21st century conflict is, to use Charlie Sheen's crude channeling of Vince Lombardi: "Duh. Winning." No time for losers. It's an outlook that leaves no room for compromise in politics—and no place for ties in sports.

It wasn't always that way, and America is probably poorer for it. For most of the twentieth century, a tie was considered a legitimate outcome in just about any contest, including a baseball game. (The Red Sox have had 83 ties in their history, but none since 1985.) College football, in particular, embraced the tie. And there was never a better illustration of the beauty of a tie game than the battle for the 1968 Ivy League title.

Harvard and Yale were tied for first, each at 8–0, going into The Game at Harvard Stadium. And they were still tied for first, at 8–0–1, coming out of it. And yet no one on either side could dispute the sentiment of the Harvard *Crimson*'s brilliant headline: HARVARD BEATS YALE 29–29. Yale coach Carmen Cozza didn't even try to put a good face on it. "We feel like we lost the game," he said.

Yale was the better team. In theory. The defending Ivy League champions had the nation's longest winning streak, at sixteen. They had breezed through the 1968 Ivy League schedule, winning every game by at least twelve points. They were ranked eighteenth in the UPI poll. They had a Heisman Trophy candidate, Brian Dowling, at quarterback.

(Dowling was the inspiration for the *Doonsebury* character B.D.) They had another genuine NFL prospect, Calvin Hill, at running back.

The only player on Harvard's roster who would become a household name was all-Ivy offensive tackle Tommy Lee Jones.

The Game went as expected for most of the afternoon. Yale jumped to a 22–0 lead. Late in the first half Harvard head coach John Yovicsin pulled starting quarterback George Lalich and replaced him with Frank Champi, a junior English major from Everett, Massachusetts. Champi had played fewer than three quarters in two years.

Champi rallied Harvard to a couple of touchdowns, but Yale led, 29–13, with 42 seconds to go. Harvard had a first down at the Yale fifteen. It was still just a "two-possession game," to use the modern term. But describing a sixteen-point deficit with less than a minute remaining as a two-possession game conveys only a remote theoretical possibility, like the odds of being struck by lightning. Harvard not only needed two possessions, but they also needed to turn those possessions into the maximum number of points possible—two touchdowns and a pair of two-point conversions. This on a day when they had managed just two touchdowns in the first 59 minutes and had botched a *one*-point conversion.

Champi took the first step of that improbable journey on the next play, hitting wideout Bruce Freeman for a touchdown. Champi then tried to hit tight end Pete Varney for the conversion. The pass fell incomplete. Game over.

No—wait. Flag. Pass interference.

With the ball now on the one, Champi handed off to fullback Gus Crim, who plunged in to make it 29–21.

On the expected onside kick, Yale guard Brad Lee had a clear shot at the ball but muffed it. Harvard safety Bill Kelly fell on the ball at the Yale 49.

On first down, Champi scrambled to the 35. Officials tacked on fifteen yards for a facemask penalty. A pair of incompletions made it third-and-ten. Champi crossed up Yale with a draw to Crim, who rumbled to the six-yard line. On first-and-goal, Champi was sacked for a two-yard loss. Harvard called time. Just three seconds remained.

The next pass was supposed to go to Crim, but he was covered. The clock read all zeroes as Champi scrambled to keep the play, and Harvard's last hope, alive. Just before he was leveled, Champi threw across his body and somehow got the ball past the Yale defense to half-back Vic Gatto, the Harvard captain, in the end zone.

Touchdown.

The comeback that had seemed implausible a mere 42 seconds earlier was now just one play away from becoming a reality. As on the first conversion attempt, Champi looked for Varney, the 6'3" 235-pound tight end—and this time he hit him. Harvard fans swarmed the field. A guy whose name almost spelled *champion* had come off the bench to beat Yale with a tie.

Under today's rules this game would have gone into overtime and Harvard might well have won it outright, given their obvious momentum. But could that possibly have felt any better than forcing Yale to share the Ivy League title with them?

82

Red Sox 8, Rays 7
October 16, 2008

The Red Sox staged the biggest comeback in a postseason game
since 1929 to stay alive in the American League Championship Series

Imagine that the Red Sox' 2004 and 2007 World Series wins didn't
happen. Now try to imagine the seismic response that this comeback against the Tampa Bay Rays would have generated. It likely
would rank right alongside Game 6 of the '75 Series (Fisk's pole dance;
see Game No. 30) in Sox history.

But those two World Series wins *did* happen. And their long shadow
dimmed the luster of the biggest comeback in a postseason game since
1929. Instead of a rally for the ages, it felt more like a nice little bonus,
a check in the mail that Sox fans didn't expect.

Part of the reason is that the comeback happened so late, both in
the series and in the game. When you trail the ALCS three games to one
and you bring in your closer in the seventh inning of Game 5 on the
wrong end of a 5-0 score, with two on and no outs, you know you're in
desperate straits. But that was the situation Sox manager Terry Francona
faced when he summoned Jonathan Papelbon. The Rays promptly
pulled a double steal, and B.J. Upton drilled a two-run double to make
it 7-0.

Papelbon escaped further damage. But in the mood of the moment,
that was like saying that the Titanic escaped further damage after it hit
bottom.

The Sox scratched out a run against Grant Balfour, a fiery Aus-
tralian right-hander, in the bottom of the seventh. Then, with two outs
and two on and David Ortiz, the greatest clutch hitter in team history,

due up, everyone at Fenway expected Rays manager Joe Maddon to bring in a lefty.

Instead, Maddon kept Balfour in the game. And Balfour kept Boston in the game when he tried to get a 1–0 fastball in on Ortiz's hands. Ortiz drove the pitch deep into the right-field grandstand, which was jubilant long before the ball landed. "This place came unglued," Francona said afterward. "I've seen it before. Because of the situation we were in, it was pretty magical."

Never had a team trailing 7–4 in a game and 3–1 in a series seemed so in control. Boston tied it in the eighth on J.D. Drew's two-run homer and Coco Crisp's clutch two-out single, which came on the tenth pitch of the at-bat.

The game's reversal-of-fortune theme continued in the ninth. The Rays appeared to have Sox rookie Justin Masterson on the ropes with runners on first and second, one out, and Rays slugger Carlos Pena (three homers in the series) at the plate. But the rally came to a swift end when Pena grounded into a double play. In the bottom half, Dustin Pedroia grounded to third and Ortiz, now facing the lefty reliever (J.P. Howell) that Maddon had neglected to bring in earlier, went down swinging. The two outs came on just six pitches.

Then came another epic at-bat, this time from Kevin Youkilis. "I kept trying to challenge him with curveballs and heaters and he kept fouling them off," Howell said. "He showed a lot of will."

And he found a way. Youkilis sent the tenth pitch down the third base line for an infield hit, advancing to second on third baseman Evan Longoria's wild throw to first.

This time Maddon elected to play the percentages. He had Howell intentionally walk Jason Bay, a righty to get to Drew, a lefty. Didn't matter. Over the last three innings, all the percentages went Boston's way. They had to. According to Baseball Prospectus, the Red Sox had a 0.6% chance of winning the game when trailing 7–0 in the seventh. Drew lined a Howell change-up to right for a run-scoring single, and the Sox had beaten lottery-ticket odds. Their prize: A trip to Tampa, Florida. Said Francona, "I've never seen a group so happy to get on a plane at 1:30 in the morning."

Another unlikely win followed in Game 6, when ailing Josh Beckett pitched five gritty innings and the bullpen shut the Rays out. When Pedroia's first-inning homer gave the Sox a 1–0 lead in Game 7, another miraculous ALCS comeback seemed destined. But the offense evaporated, and Tampa Bay nicked lefty Jon Lester for three runs, including their ALCS-record sixteenth homer, in a 3–1 win.

81

Bruins 3, Sabres 2
April 24, 1983

The Bruins overcame a 2–0 deficit (and a dogged underdog)
to win Game 7 of the 1983 Adams Division Final

W ho knew what to expect? The 1983 Stanley Cup Playoffs had followed no pattern. The Bruins, who had the NHL's best record, struggled to get past the mediocre Quebec Nordiques in the best-of-five first round. It was a low-scoring series that featured three one-goal games. Meanwhile, with goalie Bob Sauve pitching back-to-back shutouts at the Montreal Forum, the third-seeded Buffalo Sabres had swept the Canadiens in a shocker. But when the Bruins and Sabres met in the best-of-seven Adams Division Final, lockdown defense and miserly goaltending gave way to intermittent outbursts of offense. Buffalo erupted for seven goals in the opening game to stun the Bruins at the Garden. Trailing 2–1 in the series, the Bruins smacked the Sabres 6–2 in Buffalo to draw even. Then, in Game 5 at the Garden, the Bruins blasted their first two shots past Sauve—the same guy who had allowed just two goals in the entire Montreal series—in a 9–0 blowout. The Bruins put two more quick ones past Sauve in Game 6 at Buffalo ... before the Sabres rallied to win 5–3 and force Game 7. That also set up a unique Sunday in Boston sports. The Bruins–Sabres finale would be the second half of an elimination-game twin bill at the Garden, following Celtics–Hawks in Game 3 of their best-of-three opening-round series.

The Celtics allowed the home folks to ease into the day with a 98–79 rout. The only high-blood-pressure moment occurred during a fight in which Atlanta's 7'1" center, Tree Rollins, bit Danny Ainge's finger.

The nightcap had Bruins fans chewing their own fingers from the outset. Buffalo grabbed the lead halfway through the first period when forward Ric Seiling put one through the five hole of Boston goalie Pete Peeters on a shot from the left faceoff circle. Seiling added a second goal 3:50 into the second period on a deflection to make it 2–0. But less than three minutes later—before the Garden crowd's anxiety even had time to metastasize into a full-on panic—Bruins center Barry Pederson turned a Buffalo turnover into a point-blank goal to halve the deficit. And less than three minutes after that, Boston's 34-year-old defenseman, Brad Park, drove home his left-handed slap shot from the right point on a power play to tie it.

And that's the way it stayed for the remaining 30 minutes and 39 seconds of regulation. Despite outshooting the Sabres 8–5 in the third period, the Bruins couldn't get that third goal past Sauve.

One of the it's-a-cliché-because-it's-true chestnuts of sudden-death hockey is that if you just put the puck on net good things can happen. It was proven again less than two minutes into overtime. The Bruins had just won a faceoff in the Sabres' end when Park wound up again from near the same spot he had scored from in the second period. But he didn't get good wood on his slapper this time. "[The Sabres] were expecting a real hard shot and it just kind of rolled," Park said later.

Still, the puck was on net. Like a batter who's been badly fooled by a changeup, Sauve toppled onto his back as he went for the save. Two Sabres defenders also hit the ice, as if executing an air-raid drill. The puck squirted out of the scrum in the crease and tricked out in front of the net to Park, 30 feet away. It was almost stationary and perfectly placed, like a golf ball on a tee. And the Sabres, having lost track of the rebound, offered no resistance. "I said, 'Just get it up, just get it up—make sure it's on net,' " Park said afterward.

Park succeeded on both counts. His top-shelf goal gave the Bruins their first overtime victory in a Game 7 since 1939 (see Game No. 10).

After that unpredictable start, the 1983 Stanley Cup Playoffs had a predictable finish. The New York Islanders bounced the Bruins in six games to win the conference final, en route to their fourth straight championship.

80

Red Sox 5, Reds 4
October 15, 1975

Luis Tiant's incredible effort led to Carlton Fisk's indelible moment

Without Luis Tiant and Game 4, there would have been no Carlton Fisk and Game 6 (see Game No. 30). The Red Sox, trailing the Reds two games to one in the 1975 World Series, were clinging to a 5–4 lead in the bottom of the ninth at Cincinnati's Riverfront Stadium. Tiant, Boston's starter, was still in the game. So far in the postseason he'd already done more than Sox manager Darrell Johnson could reasonably have asked. He'd thrown a three-hitter at the A's as the Red Sox swept the American League Championship Series. He'd shut out the Reds in Game 1 of the World Series. He'd even been a vital part of the Sox offense against Cincinnati, despite having made just one plate appearance in the previous three years (since the introduction of the DH). In Game 1 he'd scored the run that broke a 0–0 tie after a leadoff single in the seventh. Tonight, in Game 4, he'd singled and scored during a five-run fourth.

But it turned out that Johnson had one more thing to ask of Tiant—as unreasonable as it might have been. With the tying run at second, one out, and Tiant's pitch count already at 150, Johnson asked Tiant to serve as his own closer. And he had to do it against the top of the Big Red Machine's imposing order.

The first challenge was Pete Rose, who had collected his customary 200 hits from the leadoff spot that season. Tiant pitched him carefully. Rose took a walk.

Finally, Johnson emerged from the dugout. But when he returned, Tiant was still in the game.

The tension mounted. By walking Rose, Tiant had set up the possibility of a game-ending double play for the Red Sox—but also of a game-winning double for the Reds. To add still more tension, Tiant then ran the count full on the next batter, Ken Griffey Sr. A left-handed hitter, Griffey drove the payoff pitch to the wall in deep center, 404 feet away. Fred Lynn, Boston's rookie centerfielder, needed almost every one of those 404 feet to run the ball down and make an over-the-shoulder catch.

But Tiant still had to get one more out. And it was probably the toughest out in the Cincinnati lineup, at least for a right-handed pitcher: Joe Morgan. Morgan, a left-handed-hitting second baseman, had hit .327 during the season, with seventeen home runs and 94 RBI. A patient hitter, he had also led the National League in walks, with 132, and on-base percentage, with a career-high .466. So far in the two games against Tiant, his OBP was an even .500.

For the third straight batter, Tiant fell behind 1–0. How long could he get away with pitching to good hitters in hitter's counts? The next pitch, Tiant's 163rd of the night, provided the answer. Morgan took a rip—and popped up to Carl Yastrzemski at first. And that meant, among many other things, that Darrell Johnson wouldn't have to deal with the second-guessers. Said Tiant, "I told him, 'I started this thing—I want to finish it.'"

How important was Luis Tiant to the 1975 Red Sox? Boston won the three World Series games that Tiant started and lost the four that he didn't.

79

Bruins 2, Canadiens 1
April 29, 1991

For the first time ever, the Bruins beat the Canadians in a Game 7

For Bruins fans, the years were etched in the memory, each as vivid as a date on a tombstone: 1952. 1971. 1979. Three times the Bruins had skated against the hated Canadiens in the seventh game of a playoff series. Three times they had lost. First it was Rocket Richard, breaking a 1-1 tie with less than four minutes remaining to help Montreal complete a comeback from a 3–2 series deficit in the '52 semifinal. Then it was Ken Dryden, the 24-year-old law student/goalie who rebutted the Bruins attempt at a title defense in '71. And then there were Guy Lafleur and Yvon Lambert and too many men on the ice and sudden death in '79.

It's not as if the Bruins couldn't beat the Canadiens in the playoffs. They had done it as far back as 1929, when Boston had swept Montreal en route to their first Stanley Cup championship. They had done it as recently as 1990, coasting past the Canadiens in five games in the Adams Division Final. But a seventh game brought special pressure. So when the Bruins failed to close the deal in Game 6 at the Montreal Forum in the '91 Adams Division Final, dropping a 3–2 decision 17:47 into overtime, it was hard not to expect the worst. Because that's what every previous Game 7 with Montreal had delivered.

If Bruins fans were scared the Bruins themselves were not. They had won the division. They had beaten Montreal in the season series. They were playing at the Garden. And they came out determined to show that they were not intimidated. Said Chris Nilan, the pugnacious Boston native who had spent the bulk of his career as an enforcer in Montreal before joining the Bruins that season, "I wanted to start the game physical." He did, tussling with Canadiens tough guy Mario Roberge within the first ten seconds.

The physical play may have set the tone, but it was the netminders who determined the outcome. And on this night the Bruins' Andy Moog outplayed future Hall of Famer Patrick Roy. Moog stopped 35 shots, several from point-blank range, and didn't allow a goal until the final minute. (And *that* goal should have been disallowed because Shayne Corson had just leveled Raymond Bourque with a vicious cross-check to the back of the head, which left Bourque motionless in front of the crease. Moog, hoping for a stoppage, dislodged the net from its magnets just before Montreal scored, but the goal stood.)

Roy made 31 saves but failed to provide the kind of lockdown playoff goaltending he delivered in other years. (He ended up with 23 career playoff shutouts.) The two goals he allowed—to Dave Christian in the second period and Cam Neely on a power play two minutes into the third—weren't exactly soft. In fact, Bruins coach Mike Milbury called Neely's blast, a blistering slapper from just outside the blue line, "as hard a shot as I've seen." But a Hall of Fame goalie isn't supposed to miss an unscreened slap shot from 65 feet in a Game 7.

Montreal's controversial last-minute goal added an element of suspense that Bruins fans could have done without. Boston fanned on several chances at an open net in the frantic final moments, and Montreal almost made them pay, which would have been the greatest Game 7 disaster yet. But again, the Bruins themselves weren't dwelling on past catastrophes. "I never read about us," center Craig Janney said. "It's all crap most of the time. I just like to read about the Celtics and the Red Sox."

Soon Bruins fans were back to reading about the Celtics and the Red Sox, too. After jumping to a 2–0 lead over Mario Lemieux and the Pittsburgh Penguins in the Prince of Wales Conference Final, Boston dropped four straight.

78

Red Sox 3, A's 1, 11 innings
October 4, 2003

Thanks to some boneheaded A's baserunning, and Boston's first walk-off home run in the postseason since Carlton Fisk's famous blast in 1975, the Red Sox avoided elimination in the 2003 ALDS

C all it an unkempt dress rehearsal for 2004. The scruffy Red Sox, down two games to none to the Oakland A's in the best-of-five 2003 American League Division Series, not only found a way to stay alive in Game 3, but they also did so in a way that instilled self-doubt in their opponent. Not that the latter was terribly difficult. Oakland had blown leads of 2–0 and 2–1 in the 2001 and 2002 ALDS, respectively. And you could almost see the words *Here we go again* in thought balloons above the young Athletics' heads as another winnable game slipped away in ghastly fashion.

In the second inning the A's looked more like the E's. Boston was able to parlay Kevin Millar's leadoff single into a run thanks to three Oakland errors—all on potential double-play grounders. Two were by third baseman Eric Chavez. On the second one, Chavez passed up a probable 5–4–3 double play to try to get Sox catcher Jason Varitek at home. Chavez was charged with obstruction during the subsequent rundown, allowing Varitek to score the game's first run.

Oakland made several mental errors on offense as well. Sox starter Derek Lowe was working on just two days' rest, having thrown 42 pitches out of the bullpen in Game 1. (Lowe was the losing pitcher as Oakland won in twelve innings on catcher Ramon Hernandez's squeeze bunt with the bases loaded and two outs.) But the overanxious A's barely made Lowe sweat through the first five innings of Game 3. He gave up just two hits and threw only 57 pitches. And when the A's finally applied some pressure in the sixth, they ran themselves out of a potential big inning by having two runners gunned down at the plate.

Well, not *gunned down*, exactly. The first victim, centerfielder Eric Byrnes, looked more like he had been anesthetized with a tranquilizer dart. With runners at the corners and one out, Byrnes tried to score from third on a tapper to Lowe from A's shortstop Miguel Tejada. Varitek blocked the plate with his shin guard. After jamming his left knee on an attempted slide, Byrnes gave Varitek a shove before hobbling away.

But the play wasn't over. Lowe's throw had rolled past Varitek toward the backstop. Byrnes had never touched the plate, however. Nor did he attempt to dot that i as Varitek retrieved the ball. Varitek tagged the staggering Byrnes out, while the remaining runners each moved up.

Tejada made the next mental mistake. An intentional walk to Chavez loaded the bases. Hernandez then hit a lazy bouncer to short. The ball skipped under Nomar Garciaparra's glove and into short left field for an error, allowing Erubiel Durazo to score.

Tejada also attempted to score, but he collided with Red Sox third baseman Bill Mueller while rounding the bag. Third base umpire Tim Welke signaled obstruction—but as he (sort of) explained later, his call meant only that Tejada was awarded *third*. With the ball still in play, Tejada had continued toward home "at his own peril," in the language of the rulebook. Had he kept running hard, it's likely that he would have scored even without the benefit of an obstruction call. Left fielder Manny Ramirez's throw was high and up the third-base line. Instead, Tejada stopped about 25 feet short of home, looking for someone to argue with. Varitek tagged him out.

After all that—a single, two walks, an error, and two runners tagged out at home who weren't even trying to *reach* home—Oakland managed just one run. And that's all the A's got, thanks to some stellar work by the Boston bullpen (four perfect frames), which sent the game—and the Sox season—into extra innings.

With one on and one out in the last of the eleventh, Boston manager Grady Little called on Trot Nixon to pinch-hit. Nixon, who was nursing a calf injury, had been absent from Boston's starting lineup against A's lefty Ted Lilly. But Little preferred the left-handed-hitting Nixon over Gabe Kapler against hard-throwing righty Rich Harden, Oakland's fifth pitcher. When Nixon drove a 1–1 pitch into the centerfield bleachers, the Red Sox had their first walk-off home run in a postseason game since Carlton Fisk in 1975 (see Game No. 30).

Like the Fisk homer, which had also come in extra innings, Nixon's shot allowed the Sox to live for another day (see Game No. 77).

77

Red Sox 5, A's 4
October 5, 2003

The Red Sox rallied against Oakland's All-Star closer, Keith Foulke, to even the 2003 ALDS at two games each

If mojo, like momentum, lasted only as long as tomorrow's starting pitcher, then the Oakland A's needed their starter to be a stopper. After losing what third baseman Eric Chavez called "probably the ugliest game I've ever been involved in" (see Game No. 78), the A's returned to Fenway Park the next afternoon still holding a 2–1 lead over the Red Sox in the best-of-five 2003 American League Division Series. And they had their ace, Tim Hudson (16–7, 2.40 ERA), on the mound in Game 4, versus Boston's fourth starter, John Burkett (12–9, 5.15 ERA).

Hudson breezed through the first. He retired Boston's first three hitters, Johnny Damon, Nomar Garciaparra, and Todd Walker, on nine pitches, seven for strikes.

And then he was done for the day. The diagnosis: strained oblique.

Strained and *oblique* were also fitting descriptions of Oakland's approach as they desperately tried to avoid a third straight postseason collapse. What had seemed a direct path to the American League Championship Series a mere 24 hours earlier now resembled an Escher sketch. Knuckleballer Steve Sparks, picked off the late-summer scrap heap from the historically horrid Detroit Tigers (43–119), was pressed into service in the second inning. Sparks and the high-octane Sox offense seemed like an explosive combination. But Boston managed only Johnny Damon's two-run homer through Sparks's four innings of work. Burkett, meanwhile, looked every bit the back-of-the rotation starter: four runs on nine hits, plus two walks, through 5⅓ innings.

And so the twin mo's—mojo and momentum—appeared to have switched sides again. Oakland led 4–2 heading into the home half of the sixth. The bullpens would decide the game, and the A's appeared to have a decided advantage. With Boston's erstwhile closer, Byung–Hyun Kim, reassigned from the bullpen to the doghouse—he had looked shaky in Game 1 and flipped off the Fenway faithful before Game 3— the Red Sox had had to stretch their setup men. Mike Timlin, who had thrown three innings the night before, was unavailable. So the Red Sox resorted to *their* stopgap knuckleballer, Tim Wakefield.

Oakland countered with Ricardo Rincon, one of Billy Beane's more celebrated *Moneyball* finds. All-Star closer Keith Foulke lurked behind him.

Red Sox second baseman Todd Walker greeted Rincon with a homer. It was Walker's third home run of the series, and just the second that Rincon had allowed to a left-handed batter all year. Rincon allowed no further damage—but Wakefield allowed no damage at all. He held the A's scoreless over an inning and two-thirds, one his many unsung post-season performances. With Oakland holding a one-run lead after seven, each manager turned to his closer in the eighth. Scott Williamson, given a battlefield promotion over the unreliable Kim, set the A's down in order. Then Foulke entered in the bottom half.

Besides fighting Foulke, Sox hitters were also battling creeping shadows from the low, late-afternoon October sun. Watching a white baseball travel from sun to shadow within 60 feet, six inches, in less than half a second, was like tracking a miniature eclipse. And yet, with one out, Garciaparra connected with the dark side of the cowhide for a wall-ball double. With two outs, Manny Ramirez stroked a hard single to left, sending Garciaparra to third.

And now, with the Red Sox season on the line, designated hitter David Ortiz stepped in. Far from being a postseason hero at that point, Ortiz was in line to become a goat. He was 0-for-16 in the series, with six strikeouts. If he failed again here, his lack of production would be cited as one of the primary reasons that the Sox had fallen short of their considerable "Cowboy up" promise.

Ortiz worked the count full. And then the man who had been a shadow of his September self (eight homers, including his first walk-off with Boston, along with 23 runs batted in), suddenly launched the ball out of the October shadows and into the brilliant sunshine. The ball sailed over right fielder Jermaine Dye's head. More bad A's mojo: The ball caromed off the wall instead of bouncing over it. That allowed not only the tying run to score from third, but also the go-ahead run from first.

After Williams blew away the A's in the ninth to seal the win, the ever-confident Ortiz expressed surprise that anyone had ever doubted him. "Don't give up on me, people," he said. "Come on."

No one in Boston was giving up on the Red Sox now—not with Pedro Martinez scheduled to start Game 5 in Oakland the next day (see Game No 76).

76

Red Sox 4, A's 3
October 6, 2003

The "Cowboy-up" Red Sox won their third straight elimination game, escaping a bases-loaded jam in the bottom of the ninth, to overtake the A's in the 2003 ALDS

T his was a chance to get back the one that got away. In Game 1 of the 2003 American League Division Series, Boston had Pedro Martinez on the mound at Oakland's Network Associates Coliseum. While not as sharp as usual—he needed 130 pitches to get through seven innings—Martinez nonetheless delivered a performance that was good enough to win; Boston led 4–3 when he left. But the bullpen blew the lead in the ninth and lost the game in the twelfth.

Now, five days, 29 dizzying innings, and some 5,400 air miles later, Martinez was back on the Oakland mound in Game 5. The winner would take all.

One again Martinez had less than lights-out stuff. But once again he yielded just three runs through seven innings (seven innings plus two batters, to be precise). Once again he left the game with Boston holding a 4–3 lead, thanks to a pair of homers in the sixth off of Oakland's Barry Zito: a solo shot from Jason Varitek and a three-run bomb from Manny Ramirez.

Once again it was up to the bullpen to hold a one-run lead. And this time they did—by the frayed tips of their overworked fingers.

Left-hander Allan Embree, charged with the blown save in Game 1, redeemed himself by retiring lefty sluggers Erubiel Durazo and Eric Chavez (50 homers between them that season) with one on and no outs in the eighth. Mike Timlin (who had thrown three full innings in

Saturday's extra-inning win) then got free-swinging shortstop Miguel Tejada to end the threat.

Scott Williamson, the de facto closer since Byung–Hyun Kim had fallen out of favor, came on for the ninth. But Williamson, winner of both games in Boston, was fatigued from his two-inning stint the day before, followed by a cross-country flight. He walked Scott Hatteberg and Jose Guillen to put both the potential tying and winning runs on base with no outs.

Enter Derek Lowe.

Lowe had been the hard-luck loser in Game 1 (Oakland won on a bases-loaded squeeze bunt with two outs). He had been Boston's starter in Game 3, a mere 48 hours earlier, when he had thrown 100 pitches in seven innings. And yet Boston manager Grady Little had decided that Lowe was the best option to quell a two-on-and-no-out rally with a one-run lead in the bottom of the ninth of an elimination game.

Little was right.

Oakland catcher Ramon Hernandez, who had delivered the walk-off squeeze in Game 1, dropped down another successful bunt to put both runners in scoring position. Oakland then went into full-on work-the-count mode. Pinch hitter Adam Melhuse looked at strike three. Center fielder Chris Singleton took ball four. That loaded the bases with two outs—and no doubt sent another couple of hundred thousand New Englanders into I-can't-watch mode.

Lowe's slack was gone. Another walk would force in the tying run, and Boston couldn't afford to go into extra innings. In addition to a depleted bullpen, the Red Sox had lost starting center fielder Johnny Damon to a concussion in a frightening collision with second baseman Damian Jackson in the seventh.

Oakland manager Ken Macha sent up Terrence Long, one of Oakland's least disciplined hitters, to bat for second baseman Frank Menechino. Lowe immediately took command with a first-pitch strike. He missed with his second pitch to even the count at 1–1. Long fouled off the next pitch to fall behind 1–2.

Baseball analysts have long insisted that sinkerball pitchers tend to do better when they're tired. Maybe that explains what happened next. Lowe, who had to be nearing the point of exhaustion, snapped off one of the nastiest sinkers he had thrown all year. Long watched helplessly as it dipped over the plate. Against the team that had popularized *Moneyball*, Derek Lowe had delivered the ultimate money strike.

Next up for the Red Sox: an ALCS showdown with the Yankees—now invariably referred to as the Hated Yankees across New England. Said Red Sox CEO Larry Lucchino, "I hope we have a chance to write a memorable chapter in what has been a rivalry for the ages." It was a memorable chapter all right, but for all the wrong reasons. But it also resulted in a historic "To be continued...."

75

Celtics 118, Hawks 116
May 22, 1988

Larry Bird got the better of Dominique Wilkins in a fourth-quarter shootout to win Game 7 of the 1988 Eastern Conference Semifinals

The Celtics were two years removed from what would be their final NBA championship in the Larry Bird Era. But Bird himself was still going strong. In fact, his 29.9-points-per game average during the 1987–88 season was the highest of his career. He was the third-leading scorer in the NBA, behind the Bulls' Michael Jordan (35 PPG)—and the Atlanta Hawks' Dominique Wilkins (30.7). So when Wilkins tried to singlehandedly outgun the Celtics in Game 7 of the 1988 Eastern Conference Semifinals, it's not surprising that Bird rose to the challenge. Or that he saved his best for the fourth quarter.

It was a fitting conclusion to a series that got tighter as it went along. Each team went 2–0 at home over the first four games, with the margin of victory at least nine points in each. Then the Hawks stunned the Celtics 112–104 in Game 5 at the Garden. Boston responded by jumping out to an early nine-point lead at Atlanta in Game 6 and holding off a late surge from Wilkins (35 points) to win 102–100 and force a seventh game back in Boston. And what a seventh game it was.

Years later players from each team would claim that they were reduced to little more than spectators in this game, watching Bird and Wilkins play one on one. That's an exaggeration, of course. Both Boston and Atlanta got critical contributions from up and down the roster. Future Celtics coach Doc Rivers dished out eighteen assists for the Hawks, to go with his sixteen points. (He also committed a critical goaltending violation against his future boss, Danny Ainge, late in the fourth quarter.) The Hawks' Randy Wittman added 22 points on 11-of-13 shooting. Seven Celtics shot at least 50% from the floor. Kevin McHale was particularly effective. He was 10-of-14 from the field and perfect on thirteen free-throw attempts. For most of the game *he* was the one matching Wilkins blow for blow; each had 31 points through three quarters. The Celtics led 84–82.

Another player, having the kind of day McHale was having, might have demanded the ball in the fourth quarter and pouted if he didn't get it. Not McHale. As he said afterward, "Larry got that look in his eye—the one that says, 'Get the hell out of my way, boys, I'm going to go to work.' "

Bird, who'd scored just fourteen points to that point, logged a terrific afternoon's work in one quarter. Over the final twelve minutes he scored twenty points on 9-of-10 shooting, including an acrobatic continuation-and-one off the glass with his left hand to put the Celtics up 93–90 with nine minutes left. Wilkins answered with his only three-pointer of the day to tie it. Three minutes later, Wilkins nailed a perimeter jumper to tie it at 99, beginning a stretch of five straight possessions on which he and Bird traded baskets. Bird untied it with another left-hander in the lane. Wilkins tied it with a seventeen-footer. Bird untied it with virtually the same shot at the other end. Wilkins tied it again, at 103, by using the glass from the baseline.

Finally the Celtics went on a 9–2 run, the exclamation point coming on a Bird three-pointer from the left wing that made it 112–105, Boston, with just 1:43 to go. The raucous Garden crowd was still cheering this apparent dagger when Wilkins hit a jump hook to make it a five-point game. Shortly after that he brought Atlanta to within three with a pair of free throws. Bird again appeared to seal the game, with a nifty spin move around Wilkins for a left-handed layup. And *again* Wilkins answered, putting back his own miss to make it 114–111.

It was 118–115, Boston, when Wilkins had the ball near midcourt with just one second left. Rather than let him attempt a tying three, even from that distance, Ainge deliberately fouled him.

Wilkins hit the first free throw, making him 8-of-8 from the line to go along with his 19-of-33 performance from the floor.

It was now a two-point game. For the Hawks to tie it, Wilkins would have to do something that was exceedingly difficult for him on this day: miss. He succeeded—but the attempt was so awkward that the Hawks had no chance for the rebound. Wilkins had outdueled Bird for the game, 47–34, but Bird had won the fourth quarter, 20–16. And the Celtics had won yet another Game 7 at the Garden.

Unfortunately for Boston, the momentum didn't carry over to the next round. For the first time since 1983 the Celtics failed to win the Eastern Conference Finals, falling to the Pistons in six games. And six games was all Bird managed to play the entire next season due to bone spurs in both heels. When he shut it down in November for surgery, Boston's title window abruptly slammed shut.

74

Patriots 24, Chargers 21
January 14, 2007

Playing the unaccustomed role of underdogs, the Patriots
upset the cocky Chargers on the road in the divisional round
of the 2006 AFC playoffs

This wasn't just a dose of reality—it was an overdose. Injuries and all the other tiny undercurrents that can undermine a successful NFL franchise—a tough schedule, lousy draft picks, salary cap sudoku—had finally caught up with the Patriots. During back-to-back Super Bowl runs in 2003 and 2004 the Pats had lost a total of four games. The 2005 Pats had already lost six—and, with a minute left in the third quarter of a divisional-round playoff game at Denver, it had suddenly become clear that they were about to lose a seventh. One moment the Patriots were on the Broncos' five-yard line, trailing 10–6 but poised to take the lead. The next moment Denver's Champ Bailey was streaking 100 yards down the sideline, having picked off Tom Brady's pass intended for Troy Brown in the end zone.

Then, just before Bailey crossed the goal line, Patriots tight end Benjamin Watson wiped him out. Watson had covered not only the length of the field but also the width; he had lined up on the opposite side of the play. His full-tilt hit jarred the ball loose, but it sailed out of bounds and the Broncos retained possession at the one-yard line.

Short term, Watson's extraordinary hustle accomplished nothing. Denver scored on the next play and went on to win 27–13, Bailey's pick and its fourteen-point swing being the difference. Still, it was the kind of effort that winning teams make even when they're losing. The attitude becomes contagious, and eventually it pays off.

Take what happened on the same date—January 14—one year later, under similar circumstances. Once again the Patriots were on the road, playing an AFC West opponent in the divisional round. But this team, the 2006 San Diego Chargers, was arguably tougher than the 2005 Broncos. San Diego had finished 14–2. They had won ten straight. They were undefeated at home. They had the AFC's top scoring offense and seventh-best defense. They had nine Pro Bowl selections, led by running back LaDainian Tomlinson. Other than the quarterback position—where Philip Rivers had replaced Drew Brees—this was essentially the same team that had whipped the Patriots 41–17 a year earlier. That loss hadn't merely snapped the Pats' 21-game winning streak at Gillette Stadium, it had splintered it into kindling and torched it.

That humiliating defeat stayed with the Patriots. And while they had given the talented Chargers a tougher fight than many people had anticipated, they still trailed 21–13 with less than seven minutes remaining. It was fourth-and-five from the San Diego 41. This was, in all likelihood, the Patriots' last chance. And Brady didn't have the same weapons he'd had in the past; both Deion Branch and David Givens had departed after the 2005 season. The 2006 Patriots' leading receiver was Reche Caldwell, who was nobody's idea of a game-breaker.

Just as he had on that decisive play in Denver a year earlier, Brady forced a pass into coverage and it was intercepted. That should have clinched the victory for San Diego, just as Bailey's pick had for Denver. But for all their ability, the Chargers under coach Marty Schottenheimer were an undisciplined team that made bad mistakes. This was one of the worst. San Diego free safety Marlon McCree, who made the interception, should have simply knocked the pass down. That would have given the Chargers the ball on downs. Instead McCree tried to turn it into a much bigger play than the Chargers needed by making a return.

Troy Brown, like Watson a year earlier, refused to give up on the play. Having spent some time shoring up the Pats' depleted secondary, he had honed his defensive chops—and he put them to good use against McCree. Brown stripped the ball and Caldwell recovered it at the San Diego 32.

It was, Tom Brady said later, "the best play I've ever seen." It had allowed a team that failed to convert on fourth down *and* committed a turnover on the same play to keep the ball, with a fresh set of downs and a nine-yard gain.

Less than two minutes later, Brady hit Caldwell for a four-yard touchdown pass. Kevin Faulk rushed for the two-point conversion on a direct snap, and the game was tied. New England's fired-up defense then forced a three-and-out, and suddenly the Patriots were in control.

On a critical third-and-ten with 2:42 left, Brady hit Caldwell—the former Charger who wasn't supposed to be a big-play receiver—for 49 yards. Three plays later, Stephen Gostkowski drilled the winning field goal from 31 yards. Afterward the Chargers devoted more energy to complaining about the Patriots' celebration than to explaining how they had allowed a less talented team to beat them on their own field. Their words, like their play, focused on the wrong things.

In the AFC Championship Game the following week, the Patriots were on the cusp of a second straight road upset, building a 21–3 lead at Indianapolis before Peyton Manning rallied the Colts to a 38–34 victory.

73

Celtics 94, Nets 90
May 25, 2002

The biggest postseason comeback in Celtics history was the highlight
of a surprising run to the 2002 Eastern Conference Finals

T he Celtics have had just one .500 season. This is not a franchise
prone to mediocrity. Mostly the C's have been very good
(seventeen NBA championships). Occasionally they have been
very bad—never more so than during the Sahara at the end of the
millennium, when they finished at least ten games under .500 for eight
straight years.

And that's what made the 2001–02 team such a pleasant surprise.
Without a substantial makeover—the team was still basically just Paul
Pierce, Antoine Walker, and a supporting cast—the Celtics graduated
from suckitude to success. In their first full year under coach Jim
O'Brien, who had taken over in midstream the season before when the
Rick Pitino Ice Age mercifully ended, the Celts finished third in the
Eastern Conference at 49–33. Still, no one considered them a legitimate
contender, even after Boston's late-season acquisition of veterans Tony
Delk and Rodney Rogers from Phoenix. That impression didn't change
when they needed the full five games to get by the sixth-seeded 76ers
in the first round. But then they ousted the Central Division champion
Pistons with relative ease in the second round. And they wrested home-
court advantage from the top-seeded Nets by stealing Game 2 of the
Eastern Conference Finals in New Jersey. Suddenly this team seemed
for real.

Then the Celtics fell into a 26-point third-quarter crater at home in
Game 3.

Unlike Pitino, whose micro-coaching never translated from the college ranks, O'Brien understood that there were times when the less a coach said to his team, the better. One of those moments occurred before the fourth quarter, when Walker cut O'Brien off as he spoke. And O'Brien had the good sense to defer. Besides, what X's and O's could he have come up with to address a 74–53 deficit after three quarters?

Walker's point was simple. "I saw New Jersey over there smiling and laughing," he said, "and the game wasn't even over."

Walker delivered a profane appeal to his teammates' pride. Among other things he told Pierce, who was just 2-for-14 from the floor, to stop settling for jump shots and take the ball to the rim. On the first possession of the final quarter, Pierce did. Those were the first decisive steps of Pierce's nineteen-point fourth-quarter eruption.

New Jersey's first fourth-quarter possession ended with a Delk steal that led to a Walker layup. After another stop, Pierce converted a drive plus one. Another stop, another Pierce drive. Another stop, another drive ... and this time New Jersey collapsed into the paint, leaving guard Kenny Anderson with an open jumper, which he nailed. An 11–0 run in less than three minutes had cut the lead to ten. The Nets were neither smiling nor laughing anymore.

As the Celtics continued to apply suffocating pressure, and the surround-sound crowd pumped up the volume, the Nets continued to tighten. New Jersey didn't make a field goal in the final four minutes. Meanwhile, five straight points from Pierce brought the Celtics within one, at 90–89, with just over a minute remaining.

Any doubt about the outcome evaporated on the Nets' next possession when Kerry Kittles air-balled a terrible three-point attempt. With 45 seconds left, Pierce hit two more free throws to give the Celtics their first lead since the opening minute. A steal and an Anderson layup pushed the lead to three. In the last twenty seconds the Nets bracketed a final Pierce free throw with five more bricks from beyond the arc.

The most impressive thing about the Celtics' 41–16 fourth-quarter blitz was that there was nothing freakish about it. On a team often criticized for relying on threes, the Celtics had just one in the fourth quarter. The comeback was simply a matter of penetrating the paint at one end and protecting it at the other, over and over.

Deciding on that strategy is one thing. Executing it is another. Pierce, who had lit up the Nets for 46 second-half points six months earlier after a 1-for-17 start, offered a simple explication of the inexplicable: "In the fourth quarter I'm a whole different player."

The 2001–02 Celtics delivered one last surprise, and it was an unpleasant one: After their stirring comeback, they didn't win again. The Nets took the series in six games before being swept by the Lakers in the Finals.

72

Patriots 20, Jaguars 6
January 12, 1997

The Patriots hosted the AFC Championship Game for the first time
and held off feisty Jacksonville (and former BC coach Tom Coughlin)
in a thriller

T he 1996 Patriots got a belated Christmas gift from the Jacksonville
Jaguars. Jacksonville's upset of top-seeded Denver in the divi-
sional round allowed second-seeded New England to host the
AFC Championship Game for the first time.

But like a "free" dinner that includes a timeshare pitch, the gift
came with strings attached. The Patriots had to play those same feisty
Jaguars in the title game. And New England didn't need to study film
of the Denver game to know that Jacksonville was for real. The Patriots
had received a live demonstration in week four, when the Jags had rallied from a 22–0 deficit to force overtime at Foxboro. (The Patriots
pulled that one out 28–25.) And that was back when Jacksonville
still looked like a second-year expansion team. The Jaguars started the
season 3–6 before rallying to a 6–1 finish under former BC coach Tom
Coughlin.

But the 1996 Patriots had finished strong too. They won eight of
their last ten, and overcame a 22–0 deficit of their own to beat the Giants
in the regular-season finale. Then they blew away the Steelers, 28-3, in
the divisional round.

So the AFC Championship Game matched two streaking teams
with potent offenses. New England had scored the most points in the
conference; Jacksonville had gained the most yards. Naturally, the
matchup produced an ugly defensive slugfest. The zero-degree wind
chill probably had something to do with that. So did the playoff pressure.

Both of those factors helped set up the game's only offensive touchdown, which came on the Patriots' first drive. It covered all of four yards, following a bad snap on a punt attempt. From there, New England's offense produced only two field goals from rookie kicker Adam Vinatieri.

But Jacksonville's offense could muster just two field goals, too. Still, as the game wore on and the New England offense continued to miss opportunities, an uneasy feeling pervaded Foxboro that the Patriots could contain Jacksonville's elusive quarterback, Mark Brunell, for only so long. (It was a reasonable fear; Pats fans had watched Brunell throw for a career high 432 yards in his earlier Foxboro visit.) When Vinatieri's third field-goal attempt, a 46-yarder into the wind, drifted left with 8:42 remaining, Brunell returned to the field still within a touchdown.

The uneasiness in Foxboro grew to alarm as the Jaguars marched to a first-and-goal just inside the New England seven. But on second-and-goal, Pats safety "Big Play" Willie Clay made the biggest big play of his career, stepping in front of a Brunell pass in the end zone to turn a potential touchdown into a touchback.

Still the Pats' sluggish offense couldn't put the game away. After an ugly New England three-and-out, the Jaguars got the ball back with 2:36 remaining. On the first play of the drive, the Patriots accepted another Jacksonville gift. Linebacker Chris Slade poked the ball out of running back James Stewart's hands on a draw play. Cornerback Otis Smith snatched it out of the air and ran it back 47 yards for a touchdown that made the final margin appear far more comfortable than it actually was.

The Patriots were the ones in a giving mood in Super Bowl XXXI. Drew Bledsoe threw four interceptions as the Packers beat the Pats 35–21.

71

Red Sox 5, Cardinals 0
October 5, 1967

Jim Lonborg followed up a career year with the best postseason pitching performance in Red Sox history

A quick backward glance makes it easy to see why the dream seemed impossible. Just compare the opposing pitching staffs in the 1967 World Series. The St. Louis Cardinals had two future Hall of Famers, Bob Gibson and rookie Steve Carlton. Between them they ended up winning 580 games and six Cy Young Awards.

The Boston Red Sox had Jim Lonborg. He went 22–9 that year. It was the only time any pitcher on that staff ever won twenty games in a season.

But what a season. Lonborg pitched like a Hall of Famer in 1967. He won the Cy Young Award. He had fifteen complete games. Besides leading the American League in wins, he also led in starts (39) and strikeouts (246).

And he led the majors in hit batsmen, with nineteen.

That last stat was the most telling. In his first two seasons, Lonborg had hit a total of ten batters—and was eight games under .500. But in 1967 Boston's pitching coach, Sal "The Barber" Maglie, gave Lonborg shaving lessons. Maglie, whom columnist Red Smith called "that swarthy and gimlet-eyed old headhunter," had earned a record of 119–62 in ten years on the mound—along with a reputation for brushing hitters back.

Lonborg learned his lessons well.

Because St. Louis won the National League pennant by 10½ games, at 101–60, the Cardinals were able to set up their rotation just the way they wanted for the World Series. Gibson pitched the opener at Fenway. And because the Red Sox had had to fight until the end, with Lonborg beating the Twins in the season finale (see Game No. 62), the Boston rotation was off its axis. Sox manager Dick Williams opened with Jose Santiago, who had spent most of the year pitching out of the bullpen. Santiago allowed just two runs in seven innings. He also, improbably, homered off Gibson. But that was the only run the Red Sox got, and the Cardinals took a 1–0 Series lead. So Lonborg started Game 2 facing what already felt like a must-win situation. The Red Sox couldn't afford to fall behind 0–2, knowing that the next three games were in St. Louis and that Gibson was available for two more starts.

Left fielder Lou Brock led off for St. Louis. Brock had tortured the Red Sox in Game 1, going 4-for-4 with a walk and three stolen bases and scoring both St. Louis runs. With the first of his 93 pitches on the afternoon, Lonborg sent Brock sprawling into the Fenway dirt. When told later that a couple of Cardinals had complained about the knock-down, Lonborg said, "What do they think I'm going to do—give them home plate?"

Through six innings Lonborg not only refused to give the Cardinals home plate—but he also refused to give them first base. By the top of the seventh, with the Sox up 2–0, Fenway began buzzing about the prospect that Lonborg might match Don Larsen's perfect game in the '56 Series. (Coincidentally, Maglie was the losing Brooklyn pitcher that day.) Lonborg had developed a blister on his right thumb, however. He tried to limit his breaking pitches. But he threw one down and away to Cardinals center fielder Curt Flood on a 3–2 count with one out. Flood checked his swing and took a walk.

Still, a no-hitter remained within reach. And when Triple Crown winner Carl Yastrzemski drilled his second homer of the day, a three-run shot over the Boston bullpen in the bottom of the seventh that made it 5–0, Lonborg's no-hit bid provided the only remaining suspense. He got broadcasters-to-be Tim McCarver and Mike Shannon on back-to-back groundouts in the eighth. Then he left a first-pitch slider upstairs to second baseman Julian Javier. Javier lined it into the left-field corner for a double.

Flood's walk and Javier's double were the only flaws in Lonborg's gem. He had lost his bid for history—but more important, the Red Sox had won the game and made it a series.

With the Red Sox trailing three games to one, Lonborg again faced a do-or-die start in Game 5 at St. Louis. And again he did. The Sox beat the Cards 3–1, with only Roger Maris's two-out homer in the ninth preventing Lonborg's second straight shutout. The Red Sox then stitched together enough innings from an unlikely trio of pitchers (rookie Gary Waslewski, John Wyatt, and Gary Bell) to outlast the Cardinals in Game 6 and even the series. In Game 7 the Cardinals started Gibson on three days' rest and the Red Sox started Lonborg on just two days' rest. The difference showed. Gibson pitched a complete game, with ten strikeouts, while Lonborg made it through just six innings, surrendering seven runs on ten hits—including a homer by Gibson—in the Cardinals' 7–2 victory.

70

Bruins 3, Rangers 0
May 11, 1972

The Bruins subdued the stubborn Rangers in Game 6 of the final
to claim their second Stanley Cup in three years

The 1971–72 Boston Bruins were one of hockey's greatest teams. In dominating every offensive category, they combined charismatic flash with deadly effectiveness. Center Phil Esposito led the league in goals (66) and points (133). Bobby Orr, the incomparable defenseman, led the league in assists (80) and only-he-could-pull-that-off moves (too numerous to count). The outré Derek Sanderson led the league in shorthanded goals (seven) and offensive fashion statements. Add a couple of veteran goaltenders—Eddie Johnston and future Hall of Famer Gerry Cheevers, each of whom won 27 games—and Boston was a solid defensive team, too. Put all that together, and it's easy to understand why the Bruins had such devoted fans not just in Boston, but also on rosters around the NHL. As his rookie-laden St. Louis Blues were being swept in the semifinal by the composite score of 28–8, coach Al Arbour made a stunning confession. "I think our young team is awed by the Bruins," Arbour said after Boston had rung up ten goals in Game 2. "We're playing in a trance. We're mesmerized."

The veteran New York Rangers had a different response. The Bruins' greatness inspired them. In Esposito and Orr Boston had the NHL's two leading scorers. But in Jean Ratelle, Vic Hadfield, and Rod Gilbert, New York had the next three. The Rangers fell ten points short of their Eastern Division rivals during the regular season, but they got another chance at them when the NHL's two best teams met, inevitably, in the Stanley Cup Final.

This Original Six rivalry could get heated at times. The Rangers–Bruins six-game quarterfinal matchup in 1970 had set an NHL record for penalty minutes. But according to Hadfield, the Rangers captain and an Oakville, Ontario native, the rivalry was rooted not in hatred but respect. Hadfield said his motivation was simple: "To go home to Canada and be able to say you beat the Bruins."

The only way to do that was to neutralize Orr. (In this feud, even the Hadfields acknowledged that Orr was the real McCoy; Hadfield's nine-year-old daughter had written to Orr requesting an autographed photo.) Five games into the final, with Boston holding a 3–2 edge, the correlation between Orr's success and his team's was obvious. In the three Boston wins, Orr had a total of five points. In the two Boston losses, he had just one. So, heading into Game 6 at Madison Square Garden, the Rangers knew what they had to do. They just couldn't do it.

Halfway through the first period, with the game still 0–0, the Bruins were massing inside New York's defensive zone, trying to muster a scoring chance. From in front of the net, Esposito flipped the puck to Orr at the right point. Orr was skating toward his own goal as he gathered the puck near the blue line. Rangers right winger Bruce MacGregor bore down on him from behind. The conservative play would have been to shield the puck and try to prevent MacGregor from clearing the zone. Instead, Orr whirled to his left, right back into attack mode as MacGregor whiffed on the check. It was the type of risky maneuver that few defensemen would even attempt—certainly not in Game 6 of the Stanley Cup Final. "MacGregor almost checked me," Orr said later, "and if he had checked me he would have had a breakaway."

But it was those *almost* plays that set Orr apart. After MacGregor missed the check, Orr got an uncontested shot off—even though, as he later said, "I wasn't shooting, really. I was trying to pass in front to anyone who might be trying to deflect it." But there was no need to deflect this pass. It wound up in the net, past the Rangers stunned goalie, Gilles Villemure.

Orr's game-winning goal in the 1970 Stanley Cup Final was a better photo op (see Game No. 22). But this goal—which also turned out to be the game-winner in the Bruins' 3–0 victory—might have been a better play.

Afterward, Hadfield summed up the series: "We played them pretty even—except they had Bobby Orr."

In leading the Bruins to their second Stanley Cup championship in three seasons, Orr became the first player to win the Conn Smythe Trophy for a second time. And he was still just 23. Said veteran goalie Eddie Johnston, "Right now we have the best players ever assembled." But they disassembled with depressing suddenness. Less than a month after the Stanley Cup Final, Orr had knee surgery. He missed fifteen games the next season. Cheever and Sanderson, along with right winger John McKenzie, jumped to the rival World Hockey Association. As a final blow, Esposito was lost to injury during Game 2 of the Stanley Cup Quarterfinal, a rematch with the hungry Rangers. New York eliminated the Bruins in five games.

69

Celtics 131, Lakers 92
June 17, 2008

The Celtics ended their longest championship drought
with a glorious deluge against Kobe Bryant and the Lakers

G ame 6 of the 2008 NBA Finals stretched the definition of a great
game. It wasn't dramatic. It wasn't close. It was, in fact, the most
lopsided title-clinching game in Celtics history.

But it also ended the longest dry spell in Celtics history. And it happened at home, before a delirious crowd of 18,624, against Kobe Bryant
and the Lakers.

All of which made it great.

But this game stood out for another reason. The 2007–08 Celtics
had put conventional NBA wisdom on trial: *You can't build a contender
overnight. Not in the salary-cap era.* Boston 131, LA 92 was a resounding
closing argument.

It was Rick Pitino who had expressed the harsh realities of modern
NBA economics most memorably. Toward the end of his dreary tenure
as Celtics coach and general manager, in a misguided lecture meant to
sell Boston on the idea of living with the likes of Vitaly Potapenko, Pitino
had declared: "Larry Bird's not walking through that door, fans. Kevin
McHale's not walking through that door, and Robert Parish is not walking through that door."

Pitino didn't mention another member of the 1980s glory years:
Danny Ainge.

Not long after Pitino left the Celtics in shambles, Ainge did indeed
walk through that door, as the new executive director of basketball operations. Then in the summer of 2007, just after the Celtics had con-

cluded a disastrous 24–58 season, Ainge channeled Red Auerbach, circa 1979. Kevin Garnett walked through that door. Ray Allen walked through that door. Paul Pierce didn't walk *out* that door.

Less than a year later, with their 39-point demolition of the Lakers, the Celtics' new Big Three had proven that, in Garnett's euphoric declaration, *"Anything's possi-bullllll!"*

Too bad the new Big Three couldn't have banked some of that 39-point margin. They could have used it in their only other trip to the Finals, in 2010. Boston mustered just 79 points in Game 7 at the Staples Center, blowing a thirteen-point third-quarter lead to Kobe and the Lakers.

68

Red Sox 3, Mariners 1
April 29, 1986

With one record-setting outing from Roger Clemens,
the Red Sox were suddenly relevant again

I t was early. Early in the evening. Early in the season. Early in the
bloated melodrama that was the career of Roger Clemens. But the
potential for something special was already evident.

Clemens had just struck out Jim Presley, the Seattle Mariners number-five hitter, on three pitches. Now he had two quick swinging strikes
on Ivan Calderon, the Seattle right fielder. It was only the top of the second
inning, in a matchup of the 9–8 Red Sox and 7–12 Mariners, on a Tuesday
night in April. Just 13,414 people were at Fenway Park. (This was roughly
1,400 fewer than were jammed into Boston Garden that night for Game
2 of the NBA Eastern Conference Semifinals between the Celtics and
Hawks.) But when the count reached 0–2 on Calderon, the noise level
spiked among the small but savvy Fenway crowd. As play-by-play man
Ned Martin noted on the NESN broadcast, "Fans are starting to get
excited early."

Calderon took the next pitch. Home plate umpire Vic Voltaggio rang
him up. The crowd erupted. Clemens had five strikeouts in two innings.
This was an irresistible force versus an eminently moveable object.

Clemens had missed the last two months of the '85 season with a
torn labrum. Following surgery, he had gradually regained the velocity
and the confidence he had shown as a 22-year-old call-up in 1984, when
he had fanned fifteen Kansas City Royals on an August night at Fenway.
He was 3–0 in three starts so far in the 1986 season. His strikeout totals
had climbed steadily, from two to seven to ten. Moreover, he was work-

ing on a full week's rest, thanks to a Sunday rainout and an off day on Monday.

The swing-and-miss Seattle Mariners, in the throes of a 2–9 slump, were the perfect foil. During their eleven-game funk they had hit a sickly .137 and scored just 21 runs while striking out 101 times. As the *Globe's* Larry Whiteside noted in his series preview, the '86 Mariners were on pace to shatter the single-season strikeout record set by the '68 Mets. Now, after a cross-country flight from Oakland, they had to face an amped-up young fireballer on a cool New England night with a brisk wind in their faces.

Clemens had had trouble with his control in the top of the first—a result, no doubt, of the extra rest. Eye-level fastballs had dropped Mariners leadoff hitter Spike Owen into the dirt on successive pitches. But the high heat also delivered a not-so-subtle message: With Clemens on the Fenway mound, no visiting hitter should get too comfortable at the plate—not even an old friend like Owen, Clemens's former University of Texas teammate.

From the second inning on Clemens had almost flawless command, to go with high velocity and wicked movement. The Fenway crowd was more energized when the visitors were up than when the Red Sox were. Any time a Seattle hitter put a ball in play, even for an easy out, fans reacted with palpable disappointment.

Another oddity: A Red Sox error turned into a cause for celebration. Don Baylor, normally a DH, was playing first base for just the second time in three years. (Bill Buckner, the starting first baseman, had taken Baylor's spot at DH with a sore elbow.) Baylor dropped an easy foul popup on a 3–2 pitch to Mariners DH Gorman Thomas with two outs in the fourth. Clemens got Thomas looking on the next pitch. That was the third of eight straight whiffs—a Red Sox record.

To add to the drama, Clemens got no run support through the first six innings. After two more strikeouts to start the seventh, Clemens got ahead of Thomas, 1–2. But his next pitch caught too much of the plate. Thomas, an all-or-nothing swinger, got *all* this time, for a home run to center. Suddenly Clemens was in danger of losing the best game he had ever pitched. After getting Presley on a groundout to end the inning, he hurled his glove into the dugout in disgust. But the downer didn't last long. Dwight Evans answered with a three-run shot in the home half, and after that the focus shifted from the scoreboard to the record book.

In the eighth, Clemens got Calderon and Dave Henderson (who was destined to become a Sox hitting hero within six months; see Game No. 50) to pass Bill Monbouquette (seventeen strikeouts) for the Red Sox single-game record. Owen became victim number nineteen leading off the ninth, as Clemens equaled the major league mark. Then came the record-breaker—the most telling K of the night.

Left fielder Phil Bradley had struck out three times already, all swinging. In the first he was late on a fastball up and away. In the fourth he was late on a fastball down and in. In the seventh he was late on a letter-high fastball right over the heart of the plate.

In the ninth Bradley didn't swing at all. He got ahead in the count, 2–0, then watched three straight strikes sail past. He looked like an over-matched Little Leaguer just praying to draw a walk. But Clemens hadn't walked a batter all night, and he didn't start now. Instead he rang up his twentieth strikeout. In 110 years of major league baseball, no pitcher had ever done that before in a nine-inning game.

Afterward Cooperstown came calling, soliciting mementoes for an instant shrine. Clemens, still just an impressionable 23-year-old kid, was thrilled to comply. "I'm in the Hall of Fame," he said. "That's something nobody can take away from me now."

The 1986 Red Sox season took on a different character after that night. Clemens's gem was the second game of a 12–2 streak that propelled Boston from an 8–8 team in third place to a 20–10 team in first. The Red Sox went on to make the postseason for the first time since 1975. Clemens ended up at 24–4, with a 2.48 ERA and 238 strikeouts, to win the first of his seven Cy Young Awards. As for the Hall of Fame, well….

67

Patriots 17, Titans 14
January 10, 2004

The Patriots overcame a tough Tennessee team and a minus-ten windchill to advance to the AFC Championship Game

S ome reward. A twelve-game winning streak had earned New England a league-best 14-2 record, a first-round bye, home field throughout the AFC playoffs—and the dubious honor of performing in the coldest conditions the franchise had ever played in. When the Patriots kicked off to the Titans on this frigid Saturday night, the temperature at Gillette Stadium was four degrees, with a windchill factor of minus-ten. Offense figured to be at a premium. But the Patriots needed just six plays to score, ending the 69-yard drive with a 41-yard strike from Tom Brady to Bethel Johnson. Then Titans quarterback Steve McNair immediately countered with a relatively easy six-play, 61-yard drive for the tying touchdown. After that brief flurry, the game settled into the kind of stone-cold trench warfare that everyone had anticipated. It came down, as playoff football often does, to three things:

1) Turnovers. Each team coughed up the ball once. The Patriots turned a Rodney Harrison interception into their second touchdown and a 14–7 lead. In the third quarter, with the game tied at fourteen, the Pats' ham-handed tight end, Daniel Graham, fumbled near midfield and Tennessee recovered. But Willie McGinest dropped Frank Wycheck for a ten-yard loss on a first-down screen pass, leading to a three-and-out. No damage.

2) Penalties. The Patriots had just two for fourteen yards. The Titans had nine for 55 yards, including intentional grounding on McNair and holding on guard Benji Olson (which wiped out a first down) during their final drive.

3) Special teams. The Titans had the AFC's best punter, Craig Hentrich. The Patriots had Ken Walter, whose season had been so shaky that the Pats actually waived him in December before bringing him back a week later. But it was a good punt from Walter (which pinned the Titans on their seven-yard line) in the fourth quarter followed by a poor one from Hentrich (which Troy Brown returned to the Tennessee 40) that resulted in a critical exchange of field position. That, in turn, set up Pats kicker Adam Vinatieri for a 46-yard field goal attempt in a 14–14 game with just over four minutes remaining....

Vinatieri was just a .500 kicker in attempts of 40 or more yards in 2003. He had already missed one that night from 44 yards, in the first quarter. (Titans kicker Gary Anderson had had his lone attempt, from 31 yards, blocked at the end of the first half.) And now he would have to attempt a slightly longer kick on a night when the football felt like a cinder block. (Said Walter, whose kicking foot was black and blue afterward, "It was brutal out there.")

Just as he had in the Snow Bowl two years earlier (see Game No. 9), Vinatieri delivered—if just barely. "I don't think that ball had more than a couple of extra yards on it," he said later.

But for all that the Patriots did right and the Titans did wrong, Tennessee still had a chance in the final two minutes. The game came down to a jump ball on fourth-and-twelve from the Patriots 42. McNair, under pressure from a Harrison blitz, put the ball up high for Titans wide receiver Drew Bennett, who had a seven-inch height advantage on Pats defensive back Asante Samuel. Bennett had enough yardage for the first down, and he had the ball in his hands. But he bobbled it, and that was all Samuel needed to jar it loose. "I had the chance," Bennett said afterward. "I just didn't catch it. That was a tough way to end it."

For the Titans. But for the Patriots, it was another close game with a happy ending. Good to the last drop.

The Patriots followed the same M.O. throughout the playoffs, doing just enough of whatever was necessary to win. The defense harassed Peyton Manning into four interceptions in a 24–14 win over the Colts in the AFC Championship Game (see Game No. 40), and the offense answered every Carolina Panthers punch in a 32–29 Super Bowl shootout (see Game No. 13), giving the Patriots their second title in three years.

66

Red Sox 10, Rockies 5
October 27, 2007

The Red Sox took command of the 2007 World Series
by strangling a Rockies rally in the thin air of Coors Field

I f it wasn't time to panic, it was certainly time to perspire. The Red
Sox had made things look a little too easy for most of the 2007
postseason. Sure, they had fallen behind the Indians three games
to one in the ALCS. But they won the next three games by a combined
score of 30–5. Then they opened the World Series by blowing out the
Rockies 13–1 at Fenway Park. Then, up two games to none, they sent
eleven men to the plate in the third inning of Game 3 at Coors Field and
seized a 6–0 lead. The most devastating blow was Daisuke Matsuzaka's
two-out, two-run single—the first hit of the Japanese pitcher's major
league career.

But, true to his exasperating form, Dice-K eventually undid his good
deed. Holding a six-run lead in the sixth, he issued back-to-back walks.
Both runners ended up scoring off of Javier Lopez to make it 6–2. The
game then got much tighter an inning later, when Boston's ace setup
man, Hideki Okajima, had his "Welcome to Coors Field" moment.
Okajima hadn't allowed a run so far in 9⅔ postseason innings. But Matt
Holliday blasted Okajima's first pitch 437 feet through the chilly moun-
tain air for a three-run homer that made it 6–5. Todd Helton followed
with a single to put the tying run on, still with no outs.

This was the pivotal juncture of the 2007 postseason. If the Red Sox
held on, they would have a 3–0 lead and a submission hold on the series.
But if they let this game get away—look out. The Rockies were as resilient a team as any in recent baseball history. They had won thirteen

of their last fourteen regular-season games just to force a one game play-off with the San Diego Padres for the National League wild-card spot. And they won that game 9–8 by scoring three runs off Trevor Hoffman in the bottom of the thirteenth after San Diego had scored twice in the top half. Then they swept the Phillies and Diamondbacks, respectively, in the NL playoffs. That's 21 wins in 22 games, all for high stakes, before the World Series.

In other words: It was critical that the Red Sox not give this team any reason to believe.

They didn't. Helton remained anchored at first as Okajima struck out Garrett Atkins and Brad Hawpe, then got Yorvit Torrealba on a comebacker to end the threat. Boston's explosive offense, dormant for four innings, then tacked on three runs in the eighth to extinguish any hope Rockies fans had of another miraculous Colorado rally. One night later, when indomitable closer Jonathan Papelbon (no runs allowed in 10⅔ postseason innings) struck out pinch hitter Seth Smith to nail down a 4–3 victory, the Red Sox made the inevitable official. The team that had waited 86 years to win one World Series had now swept a second World Series in three years.

In the euphoria that follows a championship it's tempting to attribute much of a team's success to a special chemistry. But even in the immediate aftermath of the 2007 World Series, Sox manager Terry Francona brushed aside such talk. "When you win, everything's fine," Francona said regarding his team's character. "When you lose, it's not good."

65

Red Sox 3, Athletics 0
May 5, 1904

Cy Young (who else?) threw the first perfect game in American League history—and the only perfect game in Red Sox history

There were no words to describe the accomplishment. At least not concisely. The modern designation—*perfect game*—hadn't been coined yet. So when Red Sox pitcher Cy Young retired all 27 Philadelphia Athletics that he faced on a bright Thursday afternoon at Huntington Avenue Grounds, newspapermen struggled to find perspective. The Boston *Globe*'s T.H. Murnane called it simply "the greatest game ever pitched by mortal man."

The feat was not unprecedented. Two National League pitchers, J. Lee Richmond and John M. Ward, had thrown perfect games five days apart in June 1880. But those games, which had been pitched under different rules, appeared to have been largely forgotten after 24 years. People didn't reflexively project the possibility of a perfect game after five unmarred innings, the way they do now. Partly because of that, Young's achievement had the power of a revelation.

In addition, Young was locked in a scoreless duel with Rube Waddell through six innings. Like Young, Waddell was a future Hall of Famer. These were the aces of what had been the American League's two best teams since its founding three years earlier. First-place Boston entered the game with a 12–3 record—but two of the three losses had been shutouts thrown by Waddell, including a one-hitter in the series opener just three days earlier. The marquee pitching matchup drew 10,267, a great crowd for a weekday. As each scoreless inning zipped past—the game took just an hour and 23 minutes—the suspense centered on which team would scratch out a run first.

Boston broke through on back-to-back triples by second baseman Hobe Ferris and catcher Lou Criger in the bottom of the sixth, and then tacked on two more in the seventh. "With the game practically won," Murnane wrote, "finally the vague idea of a no-hit game dawned … until in the last inning came a deathlike silence as each man stood at the plate." Said Young, "I never worked harder in my life than I did for those last three outs."

Young got shortstop Monte Cross looking, for his eighth strikeout. Catcher Ossee Schrecongost grounded to short. Then Athletics manager Connie Mack made the curious decision to let Waddell, Philadelphia's last hope, bat for himself. Waddell, who had hit just .122 the previous season and would duplicate that average in 1904, obliged with an easy fly to straightaway center. Said center fielder Chick Stahl, "I thought that ball would never come down."

When it did, Cy Young had achieved the greatest of his 511 career wins.

The first perfect game in American League history remains the only perfect game that a Boston pitcher has thrown.

64

Patriots 27, Raiders 20
January 5, 1986

The Pats and Raiders, two charter members of the AFL,
switched roles in a playoff upset

Acontinent separated them. Seemed about right. These charter
members of the American Football League had traveled different paths from the league's inception in 1959 through the
NFL merger in 1970 to this divisional-round playoff game at the Los
Angeles Coliseum in 1986. The Raiders had Al Davis and Commitment
to Excellence. The Patriots had Billy Sullivan and Consignment to
Irrelevance.

The one characteristic that the franchises shared was a vagabond
history. The Raiders had knocked around the Bay Area in their early
years, playing in San Francisco (at Kezar Stadium and Candlestick Park),
and then taking up temporary residence at Frank Youell Field (Youell
was an undertaker, in case you're wondering) while awaiting completion
of Oakland–Alameda County Coliseum. Finally, after protracted legal
wrangling, Davis headed south, to L.A., in 1982. Thus the Oakland
Raiders became the Los Angeles Raiders.

During their first decade the Pats were like a slacker who's always
imposing on his friends. They bummed around Boston, crashing on one
couch after another, from Nickerson Field to Fenway to BC to Harvard
Stadium. Finally, Sullivan headed south, to Foxboro, in 1971. Thus the
Boston Patriots became the New England Patriots.

But in neither case had the name change affected the product. It
took the Los Angeles Raiders just two years to win a Super Bowl. It took
the New England Patriots fifteen years to win a playoff game—and that

had happened just eight days earlier, when the Pats upset the Jets on wild-card weekend (see Game No. 88).

Little wonder, then, that not many outside of New England gave the Patriots much chance at LA, where the Raiders were 5½-point favorites. These expectations were based as much as on recent history as on long-term trends. In September, the Raiders had come to Sullivan Stadium and battered the Pats, 35–20, behind third-string quarterback Rusty Hilger. Now, after a bye week, playing at home, with a presumed upgrade at quarterback (second-stringer Marc Wilson; starter Jim Plunkett had been lost for the season), the Raiders remained confident.

But after stumbling early, the '85 Patriots had jelled under Raymond Berry, who was in his first full year as an NFL head coach. New England won nine of its last eleven games, behind a tag team of quarterbacks (Tony Eason and Steve Grogan), a career year from fullback Craig James (1,227 yards rushing), a defense that was solid if not elite, and special teams with a knack for special plays. Scoring on kickoffs, for example. Not kick returns—kick*offs*. Twice in the last three weeks, Pats special-teamers had turned fumbled kick returns into touchdowns, including Johnny Rembert's fifteen-yard runback against the Jets.

And then, incredibly, it happened *again*. After tying the game at twenty in the third quarter with a 32-yard field goal, Tony Franklin kicked off to Raiders return man Sam Seale, who muffed the catch at the five-yard line. Seale gathered the ball up but evidently didn't secure it. Patriots running back/special-teamer Mosi Tatupu drilled Seale at the ten and jarred the ball loose. It ended up in the end zone and the Patriots' Jim Bowman ended up on top of it. The Patriots' secret weapon, the kick-coverage team, had grabbed the lead.

The Pats never gave it back. While the offense played keep-away (New England's time of possession in the fourth quarter: 10:35) the defense made Marc Wilson look like every bit the backup that he was (11-of-27 for 135 yards, one touchdown, and three interceptions). When it was over, the role reversal was complete: The Raiders were forlorn, the Patriots were for real. "Destiny is on our side," James said afterward. "Or if he isn't, he's standing awfully close."

Even in the franchise's finest hour to that point, the Sullivans managed to sully the moment. General manager Pat Sullivan, who had been mouthing off at the Raiders from the sideline all day, got into a postgame tussle with Raiders defensive end Howie Long and linebacker Matt Millen. The incident left Sullivan with a cut on his face and his team with a public-relations black eye as they prepared to take on the Dolphins for the AFC championship (see Game No. 46).

63

Celtics 111, Nationals 105, 4 OT
March 21, 1953

In winning a postseason series for the first time, the Celtics
(and Bob Cousy) set two playoff records that still stand

T he Celtics' first-ever playoff clincher was also their most excruciating. It wasn't just the four overtimes—an NBA playoff record
that has stood for more than 60 years. It was also the 107 fouls.
(At least the officials called 'em both ways; Boston committed 52 fouls,
Syracuse 55.)

Those improbable numbers were a byproduct of early NBA rules.
There was no shot clock, so teams often stalled. (With the score tied at
77, Syracuse held the ball for the final 2:10 of regulation before missing
a shot at the buzzer.) On the other hand, the penalty for a personal foul
was a single free throw (or two attempts to make one, when a team was
in the bonus), which led to an obvious counter-strategy. In the second
half, the trailing team resorted to fouling in an attempt to trade two
points for one on every exchange of possession. In fact, Game 1 of the
best-of-three Eastern Division semifinals had produced an even more
egregious example of this tactic.

The Celtics were heavy underdogs. They had never won a playoff
series, while the Nationals had advanced to the Eastern Division finals
in each of the three previous seasons. Further, Syracuse had home-court
advantage, which was considerable. Boston had lost fourteen of their
last fifteen games at the 6,000-seat Onondaga War Memorial Coliseum
("that Syracuse barn," Bob Cousy called it). But simply by building a
53–49 lead after three quarters in the opening game, Boston effectively
seized control of the series. In the fourth quarter the Celtics had just

three field goals—but they converted 28 free throws, including 22 in a row, to hold off the Nats 87–81.

Hoping to avoid a repeat in Game 2, Syracuse jumped out to a quick start at the Garden, grabbing an 8–0 lead. The Nats' advantage was 29–27 halfway through the second quarter when Syracuse's Dolph Schayes and Boston's Bob Brannum got into a fight. Both were ejected. And because Schayes, a future Hall of Famer, was Syracuse's leading scorer and Brannum was the equivalent of an NHL enforcer, Boston clearly got the better end of the deal. So much so that it took Boston police five minutes to quell the enraged Nats' protests. (The *Globe*'s John Ahern wrote that Syracuse guard Billy Gabor "took on a whole platoon of cops and was holding his own with them.")

Despite losing their best player—or perhaps inspired by it—Syracuse managed to hang with Boston in a game that dragged on for more than three hours of real time (and this was long before games became marbled with media stoppages). But attrition—and Bob Cousy—finally caught up with them. By the third overtime, so many players had fouled out that each team had exhausted its bench and had to allow a player with six fouls to remain on the floor. The penalty for additional fouls on each of those players was a technical along with the personal. This happened to each side; Celtics forward Chuck Cooper and Syracuse player/coach Al Cervi each were charged with seven personals.

If a coach wanted to sub a fouled-out player back into the game due to an injury, the penalty was also a technical. Cervi faced this decision when Paul Seymour, Syracuse's second-leading scorer, suffered a badly sprained ankle two minutes into the third OT. Incredibly, rather than bite the bullet and take the T, Cervi left Seymour in the game, even though he couldn't do much more than limp around the backcourt. Just as incredibly, the Nats overcame this handicap to score the first five points of the fourth overtime.

Cousy to the rescue.

Boston's fleet guard had started slowly, with just one field goal in the first half. But with his ball-handling skills, quick hands, and free-throw accuracy (82% that season), he took over the game as it wore on. By the time it ended, he had set an NBA playoff record with 50 points—half of them in overtime.

Cousy scored Boston's last three points in regulation. He scored six points in the first overtime. He scored eight of Boston's nine points in the third overtime, including the tying 25-footer with three seconds left. And he scored nine of Boston's twelve points in the fourth overtime, flipping a five-point deficit into a six-point lead over the final 3½ minutes.

Each team wound up with 65 free-throw attempts. The Nats hit 51. The Celtics hit 57. And that's why they advanced to the second round for the first time ever. (It was a brief stay; the Knicks bounced them from the best-of-five Eastern Division Finals in four games.)

Cousy made 30 of 32 free throws in that four-overtime marathon. It stands as one of the great clutch performances in NBA history.

Those 32 free-throw attempts remained a playoff record until 2000, when Hack-a-Shaq supplanted Abuse-the-Cooz. The Indiana Pacers sent Shaquille O'Neal to the line 39 times in a 111–104 loss to the Lakers. O'Neal converted just eighteen, however, leaving Cousy's playoff record of 30 made free throws intact.

62

Red Sox 5, Twins 3
October 1, 1967

This game completed the founding of the modern Red Sox Nation

Today it would be a huge gamble to hire a 37-year-old manager with no major league experience. But it wasn't a gamble for the Red Sox in the dreary fall of 1966. To gamble you needed a stake. Boston didn't have one. The Red Sox hadn't been to the World Series in twenty years. They'd just finished their tenth straight losing season. Only the free-falling Yankees had kept them from finishing last in the American League. So, really, what did they risk by promoting Dick Williams, manager of the Triple-A Toronto Maple Leafs, to the big leagues for the modest salary of $25,000 a year?

If nothing else, Williams brought grit. "I'm a low-ball hitter and a highball drinker," he once said. (Actually that sounds like something he would have said more than once.) A .260 lifetime hitter, he clung to his career as an itinerant utility man for thirteen major league seasons. Dick Williams was no Ted Williams—although, like the Splinter, he got a hit at Fenway Park in his final major league at-bat. But where Ted homered and the Red Sox won, Dick got a pinch-hit single in a last-raps rally that fell a run short.

His days in the majors done, Dick planned to become a player/coach in the Red Sox system with the Pacific Coast League's Seattle Rainiers in 1965. But when Boston transferred its Triple-A affiliation to Toronto, the incumbent manager stayed in Seattle. So Williams got the job by default.

Which is pretty much how he got the Red Sox job, too.

Not that he hadn't proved himself in Toronto. He had won back-to-back International League championships. He'd also been ejected eight times in two years.

Williams brought his hard nose with him to Boston. Aware that the Red Sox' moody young left fielder, Carl Yastrzemski, had feuded with his managers in the past, Williams immediately revoked Yaz's captaincy. ("I don't see any need of having another chief on the team.") Williams also made a promise in spring training: "We'll win more games than we lose."

Las Vegas wasn't impressed. Preseason odds had the Red Sox at 100–1 to make the World Series. Boston wasn't impressed, either. Members of the Red Sox press corps started a pool on how many days Williams would last. And only 8,324 fans came out to Fenway on Opening Day.

It's probably just as well that expectations were so low. The young team was able to jell slowly, with little pressure. At the All-Star break the Red Sox were on pace to meet Williams's goal—if barely. They were 41–39, in fifth place.

Everything changed in a week and a half. The Red Sox won ten straight in mid-July, concluding with a doubleheader sweep at Cleveland. They returned to Boston just a half-game out of first. A crowd of 10,000 greeted them at Logan.

Boston was contending thanks in large part to career years from two key players. Third-year right-hander Jim Lonborg, just 19–27 before that season, went 22–9 and won the Cy Young Award. Yastrzemski, who had never hit more than twenty home runs in any of his first six seasons, had 44 in 1967 to lead the American League. He won the Triple Crown and was named MVP.

But it wasn't just Lonborg and Yaz ("Arm & Hammer," the *Globe* called them) who came through. Williams shuffled and reshuffled the lineup, and the right guy came up at the right time with uncanny frequency. In June, the Red Sox trailed the first-place White Sox 1–0 with two outs and no one on in the last of the eleventh. Third baseman Joe Foy singled and right fielder Tony Conigliaro followed with a walk-off homer. In July, Foy and Conigliaro teamed up on another comeback. Trailing the Angels 5–2 in the bottom of the ninth, Foy hit a two-run homer and Conigliaro tied it with a solo shot. The Red Sox won in ten, as Sparky Lyle picked up his first career win.

In August Boston had to rally in a different way after Conigliaro's cheek was shattered by a Jack Hamilton fastball. The Red Sox shook off the trauma to win that game and the six that followed, a streak that included a comeback from an 8–1 deficit.

All these unlikely events generated a feeling that had been mostly absent from Fenway Park for two decades: a sense of possibility. For the first time since 1949, the Red Sox were still alive on the final weekend. Boston, trailing Minnesota by one game, hosted the Twins for two. The math was simple: *Minus one plus two equals plus one* ... pending the outcome in Detroit. The Tigers also trailed by a game but had played two fewer; they hosted the Angels in back-to-back doubleheaders. On Saturday, as was their custom, the Red Sox spotted the Twins the lead, on a first-inning run. Starter Jose Santiago (12–4 that season; a combined 22–25 in seven others) looked unsteady. Twins starter Jim Kaat looked awesome—until he injured himself in the third. The Red Sox scored six runs off the Minnesota bullpen to win, 6–4. (The last three Sox runs came on Yastrzemski's 44th homer. Along with all the other drama, Yaz was battling Minnesota's Harmon Killebrew for the league lead in home runs. His seventh-inning bomb put him one ahead—but Killebrew matched it with a two-run shot in the ninth. That's the way it ended.) Later that day, the Angels scored six runs in the eighth to stun the Tigers and gain a split in their doubleheader. The Red Sox and Twins were now tied for first, with the Tigers a half-game back. Just one day remained.

Lonborg started the finale for Boston against fellow twenty-game winner Dean Chance. Again Minnesota struck early, with single runs in the first and third. It remained 2–0 into the bottom of the sixth. The Red Sox had just twelve outs left. And, in those pre-DH days, Lonborg was leading off. With Twins third baseman Cesar Tovar playing deep, Lonborg decided to see if he could disrupt Chance's rhythm with a bunt.

It worked. Lonborg reached, and the next three batters—second baseman Jerry Adair, third baseman Dalton Jones, and Yastrzemski—all followed with singles. The game was tied, and the Red Sox had runners at first and third with no outs. The next batter, right fielder Ken Harrelson, hit a grounder to short. Rather than take a sure out, Twins shortstop Zoilo Versalles threw home. Too late. Jones scored to give Boston the lead. The Red Sox added two more runs, on a wild pitch and an error, to make it 5–2.

The desperate Twins tried to rally in the eighth. Pinch hitter Rich Reese led off with a single. Tovar grounded into a double play. Killebrew singled. Right fielder Tony Oliva singled, sending Killebrew to third. Left fielder Bob Allison singled to left, scoring Killebrew and sending Oliva to third. But Allison was thrown out trying for a double, on a perfect throw from Yastrzemski.

To review:

Each team had bunched four singles in an inning. Thanks to Minnesota's defense, the four Boston singles had produced five runs. Thanks to Boston's defense, the four Minnesota singles had produced one run.

In the ninth, a final twin killing killed the Twins' final hope. Center fielder Ted Uhlaender led off with a single. Second baseman Rod Carew grounded into a double play, and pinch hitter Rich Rollins lofted one to Rico Petrocelli at short to end it. Lonborg, who had escaped the last two innings despite yielding hits to five of the eight batters he faced, showed a similar instinct for survival as he fled the horde that swarmed the field. In a final bit of Houdini magic, Lonborg somehow lost his inner uniform jersey to a fan but not his outer one.

Meanwhile, the Tigers had won the first game of their doubleheader with the Angels and could still tie with a sweep. Finally, came word out of Detroit: Angels 8, Tigers 5. It was official: The Red Sox had won the pennant. 1967 was the best regular season they had ever had—or ever would.

In 2011 Boston fans endured the negative of that picture-perfect 1967 season. Dick Williams died in July, then a Sox team that was projected to win 100 games concluded a September collapse with a season finale in which everything that had to go wrong for them to miss the postseason did.

61

Patriots 41, Steelers 27
January 23, 2005

By throttling the Steelers and their precocious rookie quarterback,
Ben Roethlisberger, in Pittsburgh the Patriots returned to the
Super Bowl for the third time in four years

Y ou know the story. Team loses the game, its starting quarterback, and all hope for the season in week two. Unproven youngster takes over at QB and shocks everyone by rallying the team to a division title. Veteran loses his job. Team enters the playoffs amid a quarterback controversy.

But this narrative had an alternative ending. Because this was the story not of the 2001 Patriots but of the 2004 Steelers.

Since taking over for injured veteran Tommy Maddox in September, rookie Ben Roethlisberger had gone undefeated as a starter. Pittsburgh had become the first team in AFC history to finish 15–1. En route to that record-setting record, the Steelers had flattened the Patriots 34–20 on Halloween, ending New England's record 21-game winning streak.

And yet, with the Patriots returning to town for a rematch in the AFC Championship Game, the Pittsburgh faithful were nervous. So nervous, in fact, that some among the local sports-talk radio set urged Steelers coach Bill Cowher to replace the unbeaten wunderkind with Maddox, a journeyman that no one would ever mistake for Drew Bledsoe.

That's how bad Roethlisberger had looked against the Jets in the divisional round. Roethlisberger had thrown a pick-six late in the third quarter that had given New York the lead. Then, with the score tied in the final two minutes, he threw another interception that gave the Jets a great chance to win. But kicker Doug Brien, who had missed from 47 yards just before the Roethlisberger pick, missed again from 43 on the final play of regulation. The Steelers survived in overtime.

And then there was the not-so-small matter of the Patriots themselves. This was not the same team that the Steelers had manhandled on Halloween. In that game, the Patriots had been without leading rusher Corey Dillon. In his absence, the Patriots' ground game had picked up just five yards in six attempts. The Pats had also been without one of Tom Brady's favorite targets, Deion Branch, and lost starting corner Ty Law to a season-ending foot injury during the game.

Dillon and Branch were back for the playoffs. And the Patriots had just destroyed Peyton Manning and the Indianapolis Colts in the divisional round, 20–3. It all added up to a vote of no confidence in Ben Roethlisberger and the Steelers—not just among a large segment of Pittsburgh's fan base, but also in Las Vegas. The Steelers, a 16–1 team playing at home, were the underdog.

They played like one. Roethlisberger's first pass was intercepted. The Patriots converted that into a 3–0 lead. On Pittsburgh's next possession, Jerome Bettis fumbled on fourth-and-one. On the very next play, Brady hit Branch with a deep ball for a 60-yard touchdown to make it 10–0.

But it was the Patriots' defense, exploiting Roethlisberger's inexperience, that made the decisive play. Trailing 17–3, Pittsburgh was driving late in the first half. Roethlisberger had led the Steelers from their own 23 to the New England red zone as the two-minute warning approached. The rookie was 2-of-2 on the drive, for 36 yards, and had also picked up a first down with a quarterback draw. If he could get the ball into the end zone before the half, it would not only make it a one-score game, but it would also give the whole team a huge boost of confidence.

But on second-and-six from the nineteen, Roethlisberger made an ugly throw with an even uglier result. He planted his left foot awkwardly and aimed a pass toward the right sideline, intended for tight end Jermane Truman. Pats safety Rodney Harrison jumped the route, made the interception at the thirteen-yard line, and took off. Linebacker Mike Vrabel flattened Roethlisberger—the only Steeler who even bothered to pursue the play—and Harrison was gone. So was Pittsburgh's last hope.

After avenging their Halloween loss to the Steelers, the Patriots defended their hold on the Vince Lombardi Trophy with a just-good-enough-to-win performance against the Eagles in Super Bowl XXXIX (see Game No 16).

60

Bruins 2, Rangers 1
March 29, 1929

Thanks to a gritty third period at Madison Square Garden,
the Bruins claimed their first Stanley Cup

The Boston Bruins, a fifth-year franchise, couldn't have done much more to prove themselves during the 1928–29 National Hockey League season. Boston had the highest-scoring offense and the second-stingiest defense. That added up to the league's best record, and first place in the American Division. Still, to win the Stanley Cup, the Bruins had to beat the Montreal Canadiens, top team in the Canadian Division, in a best-of-five championship series. It figured to be a grind. Montreal goalie George Hainsworth had set an NHL record that still stands: 22 shutouts. And he'd done it in a 44-game schedule. The Bruins, with rookie goalie Tiny Thompson, had logged a mind-bending stat of their own: Not once all season had they allowed more than three goals in a game.

The Bruins started the series with a pair of 1–0 wins at sold-out Boston Garden, which had opened just four months earlier. They further demonstrated their championship grit in Game 3, at the Montreal Forum. After spotting the Canadiens a 2–0 first-period lead, the Bruins responded with three unanswered goals in the second. Tenacious defenseman Eddie Shore got the game-winner as Boston completed a sweep. A huge crowd overran North Station (which also was new) to welcome the team's train back from Montreal.

But the playoffs weren't over. To claim the Stanley Cup, the Bruins had to win a "challenge series" against the Rangers. New York had earned this honor by winning a parallel tournament among the NHL's also-rans. It was a ludicrous playoff format—the equivalent of playing the Division Series after the World Series. Even more absurd, the challenge round was best-of-*three*, which gave the underdog a puncher's chance. As a *Globe* columnist identified only as Sportsman wrote, "The activities still to come have a decided savor of bunk."

In Game 1, at Boston Garden, the Bruins built a 2–0 lead behind goals from Dit Clapper and Dutch Gainor. From there they suffocated the Rangers with defense as Thompson recorded his third shutout in four playoff games. In Game 2, an 8:45 start on Good Friday at Madison Square Garden, even the elements contributed to the sense of anticlimax. It was unseasonably warm and the playing surface suffered. The ice, wrote the *Globe*'s John J. Hallahan, "was a dirty white and appeared soft in spots."

The game remained scoreless until fourteen minutes into the second period. The Bruins' leading scorer, right winger Harry Oliver, put Boston on the board with a determined rush from his own end around and through several Rangers. The Bruins then went for the kill, pressing the attack in the final six minutes of the second period. Clapper hit the post twice, but Boston couldn't pad their lead. Still, they were up 1–0, with just one scoreless period left to play to claim the Stanley Cup.

Early in the third period, the game changed in a New York minute. Thompson allowed the tying goal on left wing Butch Keeling's slap shot from the blue line. Shortly after that, Shore was sent to the penalty box for interference. Despite having dominated the Stanley Cup Playoffs, the Bruins suddenly found themselves shorthanded, minus their best defenseman, one Rangers goal away from being forced into a winner-take-all game back in Boston.

The Bruins' defense hunkered down and killed the penalty. Thompson survived thirteen shots in the third period. The game remained 1–1 as the two-minute mark approached. Then Oliver mounted another determined rush. Joining him this time was the Bruins' center, Dr. Bill Carson. The Rangers' defenders, Bun Cook and Ching Johnson, committed to stopping Oliver. So Oliver flicked a pass to Dr. Carson, who wound up and blasted the puck past Rangers goalie John Ross Roach.

Oh—about Carson's handle, "doctor." It was legitimate. Carson was a graduate of the University of Toronto's dental school. That was fitting. At a time when scoring goals was like pulling teeth, the Bruins turned to a dentist for the goal that made Boston Stanley Cup champions for the first time.

The NHL's nonsensical playoff format bit the Bruins big time the next year. Boston ran away with the NHL's regular season race with a 38–5–1 record, which remains the highest winning percentage in league history. Then they beat the Canadian Division winners, the Montreal Maroons, in the best-of-five "championship" round. But they still had to get by the Montreal Canadians—and goalie George Hainsworth—in the best-of-three "challenge" round. Wrote Sportsman in the Globe: "A rank injustice will have been done if, by any chance, they lose in the remaining series." Well, what followed was an injustice that ranks as the worst in hockey history. The Bruins hadn't lost back-to-back games all season—until they played the Canadiens. After dominating the NHL for a year, Boston lost the Stanley Cup in a span of 48 hours.

59

Celtics 117, Pistons 114
May 30, 1987

A brutal seven-game series for the NBA's Eastern Conference title concluded with a Garden classic

The seven-game scrum for the NBA's 1987 Eastern Conference title was both a physical series and a metaphysical one. It showed what happened when two groups of proud, stubborn men tried to occupy the same space at the same time. The Larry Bird Celtics had won three NBA championships and thought they had at least one more in them. The Isiah Thomas Pistons were NBA-champions-in-waiting who didn't want to wait. The overlap of their prime years may have cost each of these great teams—five future Hall of Famers for Boston, four for Detroit—a title.

But that's big-picture stuff. Of more immediate importance, there were an alarming number of episodes in which various Celtics and Pistons tried to *literally* occupy the same space at the same time. The man at the center of the two most violent clashes was Pistons center Bill Laimbeer, a 6'11", 245-pound swarm of black flies. Laimbeer was a proficient rebounder and scorer—he averaged a double-double in the series—but his primary contribution appeared to be irritating the Celtics to the point of distraction. ("The consummate provocateur," Celtics GM Jan Volk called him.)

Take what happened in Game 3.

The Pistons had returned to Detroit trailing two games to none. Their home floor was the Silverdome, a football stadium masquerading as a basketball court, which seemed to have influenced their style. Running on emotion and adrenalin—and just plain *running*—Detroit bolted to a twenty-point halftime lead. At that point the Celtics essentially conceded, resting the ailing Robert Parish (sprained ankle) the rest of the way. Still, the Pistons continued at full throttle into the fourth quarter.

Bird was attempting a layup when Laimbeer took him down with a forearm across the throat. Bird immediately started swinging, and it appeared that everyone connected in any way with either organization poured onto the floor to either break up the fight or get involved in it. (Laimbeer later claimed that Celtics coach K.C. Jones belted him during the confusion.)

Then, just as things were settling down, Bird stirred them up again by throwing the ball at Laimbeer. (Bird being Bird, he nailed his target, even though he had to fire the ball through a crowd from about ten feet away.) Bird then got into it with Pistons rookie Dennis Rodman (in his pre-hair-dye days.) Laimbeer and Bird were both ejected—not that it affected the outcome.

The true repercussions came later. With Detroit having squared the series, and the teams locked in another ferocious battle back at Boston Garden in Game 5, Parish and Laimbeer got tangled in the paint just before halftime. Having seen enough of Laimbeer, Parish clubbed him to the parquet floor. Somehow officials Jack Madden and Jess Kersey missed it. Parish not only was not ejected—he wasn't even whistled for a foul. (Even so, it took a miraculous play by Bird to steal this one; see Game No. 58.) Parish could not escape an NBA review, however, and he was suspended for Game 6—which the Celtics lost in Detroit.

The point is: This was not a matter of which team "wanted it more."

The battle of equivalent wills concluded on a wilting 93-degree Saturday afternoon at the Garden. Detroit led by one at the half. Boston led by one after three quarters. And as the third quarter ended, the Celtics actually benefitted from an overabundance of Detroit desire. Two Pistons, Adrian Dantley and Vinnie Johnson, slammed heads while diving for a loose ball. Dantley, knocked unconscious with a concussion, had to be carried off on a stretcher. His absence in the fourth quarter was crucial. He had slashed through the Celtics defense the entire series, averaging twenty points per game on 58% shooting, and earning 60 free throws.

But even after Dantley left, Boston couldn't shake Detroit. With 4:13 remaining, the score was knotted at 99—the fourteenth tie of the afternoon. Games this close often came down to which way the ball bounced.

And on the critical possession it bounced the Celtics' way not once but five times.

After Thomas almost stole the ball from Danny Ainge, who may or may not have pushed off after regaining control, Ainge launched a three. No good, rebound by Bird. The ball rotated around and back to Bird, who put up another three. No good, rebound by Kevin McHale, who passed to Dennis Johnson, who reset. After three more passes, Bird put up a long two. No good, rebound by McHale, putback, no good, rebound by Parish, putback, no good, rebound by Bird. Four passes later, Ainge put up another three—and nailed it. The game was untied for good.

On that decisive possession Boston controlled the ball for more than a minute, grabbed five offensive rebounds, and executed thirteen passes. Every Celtic touched the ball at least once and everyone but Johnson took at least one shot. "That was probably the biggest sequence," said Bird. "After you miss three or four shots in a row, you definitely think the next one is going in."

Bird didn't miss many in this one. He was 13-of-24 for 37 points, and he added nine assists, nine rebounds, and a couple of blocks. But the most telling figures were these: In 90-degree heat, with Game 7 on the line, No. 33 was the only player on either side to go the full 48 minutes.

Drained by the Pistons series, the Celtics lost the NBA Finals to the Showtime Lakers in six games. A year later, after finally dethroning the Celtics in the East, the Pistons lost to LA in seven games before winning back-to-back titles in 1989 and '90.

58

Celtics 108, Pistons 107
May 26, 1987

"There's a steal by Bird!"

"**H**avlicek stole the ball!" (see Game No. 29) might be the more famous play, partly because it had steeped in sepia-toned replays and a gravelly sound bite for 22 years before this play happened. And yes, the Havlicek steal sealed a Game 7 win. And that playoff run ended in a title.

On the other hand, Havlicek's sleight of hand merely protected a one-point lead for the last five seconds. Had Havlicek not stolen the ball, there's a decent chance that the Celtics still would have won.

"There's a steal by Bird!" is different. Without this play, the Celtics would almost certainly have lost Game 5 of the 1987 Eastern Conference Finals. And they probably would have lost the series, too, because a Game 5 defeat would have put them in a must-win situation for Game 6 in Detroit—where they had lost games 3 and 4 by scores of 122–104 and 145–119, respectively. Further, the Celtics would have had to win Game 6 without Robert Parish, who was to receive a one-game suspension for a TKO of Pistons überpest Bill Laimbeer. (For a more detailed backstory of this series, see Game No. 59.)

Like "Havlicek stole the ball!", "There's a steal by Bird!" happened on an inbounds play with five seconds left in a one-point game. The big difference was that the Celtics were trailing.

It was 107–106, Detroit. Game 5 had progressed like the series: The aging, ailing Celtics got an early jump (a two-games-to-none lead in the series; a twelve-point first-half lead in Game 5) but couldn't hold off the younger, fresher Pistons. One reason for this was Detroit's deeper bench. The Pistons' primary reserves were Vinnie Johnson, Dennis Rodman, and John Salley. The Celtics' were Darren Daye, Sam Vincent, and Jerry Sichting.

Rodman had just swatted Bird's attempt at the go-ahead shot away and Sichting was last to touch the ball before it went out of bounds.

Everyone on both sides knew what that meant. "They've gotta foul," Detroit's Isiah Thomas said later. "We go to the free throw line and win the game."

This seemed a virtual certainty. And Thomas could have pushed Detroit's odds even higher by calling timeout, which would have allowed the Pistons to advance the ball out of their backcourt for the throw-in. But Thomas was so eager to thrust the dagger that he acted impulsively—and missed his target. Thomas lofted a soft pass toward Laimbeer, who stood like a statue on the left baseline near his own basket. Bird, who had been guarding Pistons guard Joe Dumars, reacted.

Put yourself in Bird's black Converse sneakers for a moment. You have every right to feel frustrated. You've missed two shots from within ten feet in the final minute. After the second one, the Rodman block, Rodman had sprinted up the court doing that annoying dance that had already made him one of Boston's most-hated opponents, in just his rookie season. Now, like everyone else in the Garden, you know you have to foul Laimbeer—an even more hated opponent. Two games earlier, Laimbeer had clotheslined you with a vicious takedown that had triggered a brawl. Here's the perfect opportunity for payback. You have to foul him anyway, so why not get your money's worth?

But Bird put all that out of his mind—presuming that it had ever entered it in the first place, which is unlikely. Instead, he focused on the ball—and he realized he had a chance to beat Laimbeer to it.

Bird got a hand on the ball, but his momentum carried him to the end line, almost out of bounds, before he gathered it up. He turned and simultaneously realized two things: 1) He didn't have a good angle for a shot; and 2) Dennis Johnson, who'd had the presence of mind to sprint toward the basket from beyond the three-point arc, did. So, to complete Johnny Most's famous call, Bird fed the ball "underneath to DJ, who lays it in!"

In a series in which home-court advantage meant everything, Larry Bird had just stolen it back from Detroit. And it had happened so fast—a flash of lightning that triggered deafening thunder inside the Garden.

The Pistons won Game 6 in Detroit (of course) before the Celtics eked out another squeaker in Boston (of course) in Game 7 (see Game No. 59). Unfortunately, the Lakers had home-court advantage in the NBA Finals. LA went 3–0 at the Forum and beat the Celtics in six games.

57

Red Sox 11, Cardinals 9
October 23, 2004

After shocking the Yankees in the ALCS, the Red Sox opened the 2004 World Series with one of their wildest postseason wins

Tempting as it was, the Red Sox couldn't afford to treat the 2004 World Series as an anticlimax. Yes, the historic comeback against the Yankees in the American League Championship Series had provided an unprecedented emotional release—not just for the organization but also for all of New England. But unless the Sox followed up by ending their 86-year World Series drought, beating the Yankees would be just another cruel tease.

Opening at Fenway helped. Boston had home-field advantage in the World Series thanks to the American League's 9–4 rout of the National League in the All-Star Game back in July. (In another almost-too-good-to-be-true twist, the man most responsible for this outcome was Roger Clemens, now with the Houston Astros, who had started the All-Star Game for the National League—and surrendered six runs in the first inning.) The Red Sox took full advantage of home-field advantage in Game 1, with four runs in the bottom of the first. Three came on a home run by David Ortiz, who solidified his claim as the greatest big-game hitter in Sox history. After three innings the Red Sox had extended their lead to 7–2 and chased St. Louis starter Woody Williams. From there it was just a matter of Tim Wakefield harnessing his knuckleball well enough to consume some innings. But on this blustery, 49-degree night the knuckler refused to cooperate. Four walks in the fourth inning, along with a dreadful throwing error by first baseman Kevin Millar, led to three St. Louis runs and ended Wakefield's night. Wakefield's replacement, Bronson Arroyo, committed another error in the sixth as St. Louis scored two more times to tie the game at seven. The Sox retook the lead in the seventh on RBI singles from Manny Ramirez and Ortiz (of course). Then the Cardinals tied it again with an eighth-inning rally that featured not one Manny moment but two. First, Ramirez overran Edgar Renteria's single, allowing Jason Marquis to score. (The Cards' overthinking manager, Tony LaRussa, had inserted Marquis, a pitcher, as a pinch runner for Mike Matheny, an overthinking-Cards-manager-in-the-making. It almost cost him—twice. Marquis stumbled on his way to second base on Roger Cedeno's pinch-hit single, and then barely beat Manny's throw to the plate despite a generous head start.) Next, Ramirez went full-on slapstick. He inexplicably decided to slide while making a play on Larry Walker's shallow fly. He caught his spikes and dropped the ball. Cedeno scored the tying run.

No worries—Mark Bellhorn to the rescue. Bellhorn, a Boston native, had provided the difference in Curt Schilling's "bloody sock" game at Yankee Stadium with a three-run homer (see games 2–5). The Sox second baseman came through again against St. Louis. He banged a 1–2 slider from Julian Tavarez off Pesky's Pole in the last of the eighth for the decisive two-run homer.

The Red Sox hadn't so much beaten the Cardinals as escaped from them. There were two ways to look at that. You could conclude that any team capable of allowing eleven hits and eight walks in a World Series game while committing four errors couldn't be trusted. Or you could conclude that any team capable of overcoming so much bad baseball couldn't be stopped.

It was the latter, of course. Behind Curt Schilling, Pedro Martinez, and Derek Lowe, the Red Sox shut St. Louis down for the duration. After squandering nine runs in the opener, the Cardinals traveled in ever-decreasing circles in the next three games until they disappeared up their own Pujols (see Game No. 21).

56

Red Sox 12, Indians 8
October 11, 1999

An ailing Pedro Martinez came out of the bullpen to save the Sox'
season in the deciding game of the ALDS

No pitcher ever made a more convincing case for MVP than
Pedro Martinez in 1999. He won the ERA title by more than a
full run. He won the strikeout title by more than 100. More to
the point, the Red Sox made the playoffs as a wild card at 94–68. Martinez
accounted for 23 of those wins (a career high), against just four losses.
It took a combined *eighteen* pitchers to cobble together the other 71
wins—many of which were Stone Age slugfests. The contrast between a
Pedro start and the kind of game the Red Sox played the rest of the time
was never more apparent than on consecutive days at Yankee Stadium
in September. On Friday, Martinez pitched his career masterpiece. He
struck out seventeen while allowing just one hit, as Boston won 3–1. On
Saturday it took six Sox pitchers and five Sox homers to subdue the first-
place Yankees 11–10.

A month later, the best-of-five American League Division Series
between the Red Sox and Indians exaggerated these tendencies to car-
toonish proportions. Martinez started Game 1, of course. He shut out
the potent Indians—the first team since the 1950 Red Sox to score more
than 1,000 runs in a season—through four innings. Then he left the
game with a back injury, with the Red Sox leading 2–0. Cleveland rallied
to win 3–2, as Travis Fryman singled home Manny Ramirez with the
winning run in the bottom of the ninth. In Game 2 Sox starter Bret
Saberhagen failed to make it out of the third inning as the Indians ham-
mered Boston 11–1.

But the Red Sox could string hits together, too—especially at Fenway Park. In Game 3 Boston scored six runs with two outs in the seventh to break a 3–3 tie. In Game 4 the Indians bounced back to score seven runs—and lost by *sixteen*. Boston's 23 runs and 24 hits set postseason records.

Back in Cleveland the next night, with both staffs in shambles, the deciding game of this 1999 ALDS matchup was 8–8 after just 3½ innings. Where was Pedro when you needed him?

In the bullpen, it turned out. "We thought maybe [he could go] a couple of innings, tops," Red Sox manager Jimy Williams said later.

Martinez, who had taken a few warm-up tosses late that afternoon, said he wanted to "just throw the ball over the plate and see what I could do."

What he did was remarkable. He not only finished the game, but he also reduced the imposing Cleveland lineup to nine little Indians. An offense that had produced eight runs in three innings suddenly fell silent. In the top of the seventh, Jacobs Field did, too. Troy O'Leary—who had become the first Sox player ever to hit a grand slam in a post-season game back in the third inning—drilled a three-run shot off Paul Shuey to make it 11–8, Boston. Unlike every other Sox pitcher in the series, Martinez had no trouble holding a lead. Over the last six innings Cleveland didn't even get a hit, let alone a run. Only one batter (Fryman) even got the ball out of the infield. Martinez got eight strikeouts in his short night's work, including Omar Vizquel on three pitches to end it. He picked up a win in the game and the save of the season.

The pattern continued in the ALCS against the Yankees. Because he had pitched in Game 5 at Cleveland, Martinez was available for just one start against New York. That was the only game the Red Sox won (see Game No. 92). In November, Martinez picked up the most first-place votes of any MVP candidate—but failed to win the award because two voters left him off the ballot entirely.

55

Bruins 4, Canucks 0
June 15, 2011

The Bruins completed their first Stanley Cup title run in 39 years
by throttling the favored Canucks in Vancouver

Who would you rather have in goal for Game 7 with the
Stanley Cup on the line? A 37-year-old Flint, Michigan na-
tive a year removed from hip surgery? Or a 32-year-old
Montreal native a year removed from a gold-medal performance in the
Winter Olympics?

One of the great things about playoff hockey is that hypotheticals,
abstractions, and actuarial tables mean nothing. The only relevant question is: Which goalie is hotter *right now*? And in the 2011 Stanley Cup
Final, the answer, hands down, was Tim Thomas. The Bruins' goalie had
saved 201 of 209 shots through the first six games, against the NHL's top
seed.

It was a remarkable resurrection. In 2009, at age 35, Thomas had
morphed from journeyman to Vezina Trophy winner. But after that career year Thomas regressed toward the mean. And a mean regression it
was: a 17–18 record during the 2009–10 season and not a minute of ice
time in the postseason. Rookie Tuukka Rask played all thirteen unlucky
playoff games as the Bruins lost to the Flyers in the second round after
leading 3–0 in both the series and Game 7.

Same old Bruins—only more so. A week after the season ended,
Thomas had surgery to repair a torn labrum in his left hip. Great. Now,
on top of everything else that had gone so horribly wrong, the Bruins
were saddled with a damaged $5-million–a-year backup goalie with a
no-trade clause.

It turned out to be the best non-trade the Bruins ever made.

Far from damaged goods, Thomas was good as new. With his free-dom of movement restored, he was able to resume playing the butterfly style effectively again. He supplanted Rask as the number-one goalie in October and turned in another Vezina-worthy season. But even Thomas wasn't perfect, which was why the Stanley Cup Final was even after six games. Thomas had allowed just five goals in three games at Vancouver —but his opposite number, gold-medal goalie Roberto Luongo, had allowed just two goals in those three games, all Vancouver victories.

Even so, Luongo lacked Thomas's consistency—or *any* consistency. In the three games in Boston, the Bruins had pounded the Canucks by a combined score of 17–3. Twice Luongo had been pulled—including just 8½ minutes into Game 6, when he had allowed three goals on just eight shots, none particularly difficult.

So, while Game 7 was at Vancouver's Rogers Arena, there was every reason to believe that Luongo would be more likely to burst under the pressure than Thomas. And that's just the way it played out—although Luongo's Game 7 collapse was more of a slow leak than the kind of cat-astrophic rupture of confidence that he'd suffered in Boston. Luongo surrendered three goals in the first two periods, each worse than the one before. The out-and-out disaster occurred with the Canucks on a power play, desperate to cut the margin in half before the second inter-mission. Bruins center Patrice Bergeron grabbed the puck off a faceoff in the Bruins' end and started up ice. It wasn't a true breakaway; Canucks defenseman Christian Ehrhoff matched Bergeron stride for stride. And as Bergeron closed on net, Ehrhoff hauled him down. Better to commit a penalty than allow a backbreaking shorthanded goal.

Luongo allowed it anyway—even though Bergeron never actually pulled the trigger. As Bergeron slid along the ice, the puck trickled in off his stick handle with all the speed of a curling stone. Luongo sim-ply sidestepped contact. It was such a stunning goal that NBC's Mike Emrick didn't use the standard call—*He scores!*—to describe it. Instead, he employed a passive construction befitting Luongo's effort: "Bergeron protects ... and down to the ice he goes. The puck wound up going into the net."

Meanwhile, Thomas was impenetrable, despite facing nearly twice as many shots as Luongo (37–20). The shutout cemented his hold on the Conn Smythe MVP trophy. An aging, injured, overpaid backup had done what no other Boston goalie had done since Gerry Cheevers in 1972: bring home the Stanley Cup.

The 2010–11 Boston Bruins became the first team in NHL history to win three Game 7s (see games 17 and 7) en route to the Stanley Cup. But all those high-stress series took their toll on the 2011–12 Bruins—and Tim Thomas in particular. Thomas endured a backlash when he skipped a White House ceremony honoring the Bruins in January, and he was in net when the Bruins lost to the Capitals in the opening round of the playoffs. Shortly after that, Thomas announced that he was taking a sabbatical of indeterminate length—and the NHL did likewise, with a lockout that lasted until January. When the shortened season got under way, the Bruins reinstated Tuukka Rask as the number-one goalie and quietly traded Thomas to the New York Islanders in a salary-cap maneuver.

54

Celtics 130, Nationals 125
April 1, 1959

The greatest Game 7 comeback in Celtics history

The Celtics' first great rivalry was not with the Lakers but with the St. Louis Hawks. Boston beat St. Louis for their first NBA championship in 1957 (see Game No. 8). St. Louis flipped the script the following year. In 1959, when the Celtics won the Eastern Division by twelve games and the Hawks won the Western Division by sixteen games, a third straight NBA Finals matchup seemed assured.

A sore loser ruined the reunion. The Minneapolis Lakers, who had finished the regular season 33–39, shocked the Hawks in the Western Division Finals, ousting St. Louis in six games. Back east, the Celtics struggled to avoid a similar fate. After six games they were even with the Syracuse Nationals. Syracuse, which had finished 35–37 during the season, had no business taking the Celtics to a seventh game—never mind winning it. But with 4½ minutes left in the second quarter, Syracuse led 58–42 and sold-out Boston Garden had fallen into a moody silence. Syracuse's outstanding forward, 6' 7" Dolph Schayes, was having a monster game that would leave him an assist shy of a triple double (35 points, sixteen rebounds).

The Celtics, meanwhile, were entombing themselves with bricks. Boston hoisted 40 shots in the first quarter, but hit just eleven. "We had good shots but the ball wasn't going in," Bob Cousy said later. "There's nothing you can do—just feel helpless."

Coach Red Auerbach's response: Try to keep up, with the Joneses. But which one? "Should I put in Sam Jones to get some points," he said later, "or should I put in K.C. Jones to do a defensive job and hope we could creep back?"

Red went with Sam, who triggered a 9–0 run to help Boston close to within eight at the half. But still Syracuse wouldn't wilt. Six minutes into the third quarter, the Nats had the lead back up to twelve, at 83–71.

Finally the Celtics found a hot hand. It was the one with the sprained finger. Frank Ramsey, playing with a splint on his right index finger, scored eleven points in the third quarter. The Celtics closed with a 24–11 run to take a one-point lead into the fourth. When Boston extended the lead to eight, it appeared that the NBA's eastern hemisphere had recovered its equilibrium. The league would be spared the embarrassment of having two sub-.500 teams meet in the Finals.

Or perhaps not. Syracuse answered with a 10–0 run to take a three-point lead with 3½ minutes left.

Boston leaned on Cousy, the veteran point guard, and Bill Russell, the young center, to save the season. Cousy hit two free throws, Russell followed with a steal, and Cousy hit from the floor to regain the lead. After a stop, Russell had a put-back plus one to make it 124–120, Boston.

When Russell committed his sixth foul, the responsibility to protect the lead fell almost entirely on Cousy. He did so spectacularly. With the Celtics up three in the final minute, Cousy dribbled the 24-second clock all the way down before nailing a running one-hander from the right of the lane to make it a five-point game. When it was over, jubilant Boston fans carried him off the parquet floor.

The Celtics were as relieved to leave Syracuse behind as they were excited about reaching the NBA Finals. Puffing on one of Boston's trademark victory cigars, burly forward Jim Loscutoff declared, "Bring on the Lakers!"

No wonder Jungle Jim was so eager to face Minneapolis. The Celtics had beaten the Lakers eighteen straight times over the past two seasons. Boston stretched the streak to 22 in sweeping Minneapolis in the first Celtics–Lakers NBA Finals matchup.

53

Red Sox 5, Phillies 4
October 13, 1915

After hitting just fourteen home runs all season, the Red Sox crushed three in one game to outslug the potent Phillies and close out the 1915 World Series in five games

Don't try to do too much. Stay within yourself. Stick to your identity. ... Ah, screw that. To win Game 5 of the 1915 World Series, the Red Sox would have to beat the Phillies at their own game. And that meant playing a different kind of baseball than they had played all year.

Rarely has there been a greater contrast between World Series opponents. The 1915 Red Sox were a classic dead-ball era team, built around pitching (Boston had five fifteen-game winners), defense, and speed. Despite having Babe Ruth on their roster, the Sox had no power to speak of. They finished next-to-last in the American League in home runs, with fourteen. (Ruth, strictly a pitcher at that stage of his career, led the team with four, in 103 plate appearances.)

Philadelphia, on the other hand, had one bona fide ace (31-game winner Grover Cleveland Alexander) and a certified slugger. The Phillies belted 58 home runs in 1915, led by outfielder Gavvy Cravath with 24—three short of Ned Williamson's dubious National League record (which had been set at a park where the fences were less than 200 feet from home plate down the lines).

Moreover, each team's owner turned up the contrast with a little home cooking just for the World Series. Sox owner Joseph Lannin decided to use the brand-new Braves Field, which had opened in August, rather than Fenway Park for Boston's home games. Although the decision was based on economics—Braves Field held about 10,000 more fans than Fenway—it also appeared to give the Red Sox a strategic advantage. The new field was, unquestionably, a pitcher's park. It had generous foul territory and fences more than 400 feet down the lines and 500 to straightway center. Still, the move was not without risk. The Red Sox were in the unique position of hosting a team that had more experience on their home field than they did. With several Sox players scouting from the stands, the Phillies had clinched the NL pennant at Braves Field on September 29. That was also "Pat Moran Day," held in honor of the Phillies manager, a Fitchburg native. The Sox' only experience at Braves Field was an intrasquad game in which the outfielders had difficulty judging fly balls and the infielders took time to adjust to the livelier turf.

There was no question that the Red Sox would feel out of place at Philadelphia's Baker Bowl, an asymmetric oddity nicknamed the Cigar Box: 341 feet to left field, 408 to center, 400 to right center, and just 280 to right. And as if that weren't cozy enough, Phillies owner William Baker had ordered temporary bleachers built in the outfield, behind a fence that was just four feet high. Again, the move was motivated ostensibly by economics—Baker Bowl held barely 20,000 fans. But it also appeared to give the home team a strategic edge. That low fence was an inviting target for Philadelphia's sluggers, particularly at a time when a ball that bounced over the fence counted as a home run rather than a ground-rule double.

Baker Bowl's short fences weren't a factor in the first two games, which the teams split. But Boston benefitted greatly from Braves Field in a pair of 2–1 victories in games 3 and 4. Trailing three games to one, and no doubt frustrated by their lack of production, the Phillies came out swinging against Sox starter Rube Foster in Game 5 back at Baker Bowl. They scored two runs in the bottom of the first—a rally that could have been much bigger had Cravath not grounded into a double play with the bases loaded and no outs. With Boston averaging less than two runs a game in the series, it was obvious that the offense would have to step things up.

That short temporary fence helped immeasurably. Sox third baseman Larry Gardner banged a triple off of it in the second and second baseman Jack Barry drove him in to cut Philadelphia's lead in half. Right fielder Harry Hooper then tied the game with a one-hop homer over the center-field fence in the third. The Phillies got their two-run lead back in the fourth, thanks in part to the only legitimate long ball of the entire series. First baseman Fred Luderus blasted one over the right-field wall onto Broad Street. Although Philadelphia was hitting Foster hard, Sox manager Bill Carrigan stuck with his starter—unlike Moran, who had already yanked his starter, Erskine Mayer. Moran's reliever was a 6'5" southpaw from Virginia with a name that sounded like a Confederate general's: Eppa Jephtha Rixey.

For a while it looked like the move might save the series for Philadelphia. The Phillies clung to a 4–2 lead as Rixey shut Boston out on one hit over 4⅔ innings.

Sox first baseman Del Gainer got the second hit off Rixey, an infield single, leading off the eighth. Boston left fielder Duffy Lewis then tied the game by driving the ball into the temporary bleachers in center.

It was still 4–4 when Harry Hooper came up with one out in the top of the ninth. After singling and homering off of Mayer, a righty, the left-handed-hitting Hooper had been plunked by Rixey in the fifth and grounded out in the seventh. Rixey took immediate command of their third encounter, with two quick strikes. But his 0–2 pitch was too fat. Hooper drove the ball to deep right center, where it landed on the grass and bounded over William Baker's temporary four-foot fence. In a single afternoon Hooper had equaled his home run total for the entire season—and in the process became the first player ever to go deep twice in a World Series game. Most important, his second homer gave the Sox their first lead and allowed them to close out the Phillies in five games.

The *New York Times* called Hooper a "highbrow slugger" (he was one of four graduates of California's St. Mary's College to play in the 1915 World Series) who betrayed no emotion as he rounded the bases after his decisive homer. But if Hooper didn't fully grasp the magnitude of his accomplishment, his teammate, Tris Speaker, did. "Wake up, Harry!" said Speaker, slapping Hooper on the back as he crossed the plate. "You just won the World Series!"

It was more of the same for the Sox in 1916. Once again they hit just fourteen home runs all season. Once again they rode their pitching to the World Series. Once again they played their World Series home games at Braves Field. And once again they brushed aside a harder-hitting National League team (Brooklyn) in five games (see Game No. 44).

52

Celtics 97, Cavaliers 92
May 18, 2008

With Game 7 of the 2008 Eastern Conference Semifinals on the line,
Paul Pierce one-upped LeBron James

Paul Pierce didn't have to take his talents anywhere. He became a contender simply by staying put and waiting for Kevin Garnett and Ray Allen (along with some key role players) to come to him. No longer forced to carry so much of the load alone, Pierce averaged fewer than twenty points a game for the first time in eight years—and the Celtics improved from 24–58 to 66–16. But then, in the 2008 Eastern Conference Semifinals against the Cavaliers, the Celtics scored just 69 points in a Game 6 loss. So Pierce reverted to outta-my-way mode in Game 7.

LeBron James, of course, was *always* in outta-my-way mode—at least during his Cavs days. Which made this a great individual shootout as well as a no-tomorrows playoff game. LeBron scored 45 points. Pierce scored 41. But the Celtics won, 97–92.

There were several critical differences between Pierce's performance and LeBron's. One, Boston's go-to guy was hot from the get-go while Cleveland's took a while to get going. Pierce scored nine of the Celtics' first fourteen points, and Boston opened a ten-point lead less than six minutes into the game. After that, James never could draw Cleveland even.

Pierce was also far more efficient than LeBron. Pierce made thirteen of 23 shots, including 4-of-6 on three-point attempts. He was 11-of-12 from the line. LeBron was 14-of-29 from the floor—just 3-of-11 on threes. He missed five free throws in nineteen attempts.

Finally, Pierce had more help. Garnett had thirteen rebounds to go with his thirteen points as the Celtics dominated on the boards. And although Allen struggled from the floor (just 1-of-6), he hit two critical free throws with just 18.8 seconds left to make it a two-possession game. This was shortly after P.J. Brown—who was perfect both from the floor (4-of-4) and from the line (2-of-2)—had nailed a cold-blooded twenty-footer to extend the Celtics lead from one to three. Those critical plays allowed Pierce to seal the game with a pair from the line after the Cavs hit a late three.

Afterward LeBron acknowledged Pierce's individual performance and at the same time seemed not to grasp its full meaning. "He played extremely well," said James, "and that's the reason why they're going to the next round and we're not."

Pierce was a big reason that the Celtics were on their way to a title (see games 20 and 69)—but he was hardly the only one. James of all people should have realized that no one player can win an NBA game, much less a championship, all by himself.

James finally appeared resigned to that conclusion two years later, after losing another elimination game at the TD Garden. "It's all about winning for me," he said. "The Cavs are committed to doing that. But at the same time I've given myself options...."

51

Red Sox 6, Angels 3
October 5, 2007

With a dramatic walk-off win against the Angels in the ALDS,
the Red Sox reprised the spirit of 2004

I f at times John Henry & Co. have behaved less like baseball execu-
tives than movie moguls, this was probably inevitable. The 2004 Red
Sox season, a cinematic melding of drama and triumph, was the
biggest blockbuster in baseball history. But it also created a monster. Or
a Monster®—a compulsion to promote Red Sox baseball as a "brand,"
and to package each succeeding season as *2004: The Sequel*. 2005 was
rightly panned for its jump-the-shark plot. (Theo escapes Fenway in a
gorilla suit? Come on.) And 2006 was a straight-to-video disaster.

Boston's brass needed a new twist for 2007, and they got one: Make
Red Sox Nation international! Grab that overseas box office! So what if
it costs $51 million just for the right to *negotiate* with the best pitcher
in Japan? It'll be worth it!

And for one night, at least, the idea paid off. Just not in the way Sox
execs had envisioned.

The Angels were in town for the American League Division Series.
Just like 2004. Fenway was a cauldron of tension. Just like 2004. And it
simmered for more than four hours, bubble-bubble-toil-and-troubling
straight past the witching hour. Just like 2004.

And the person most responsible for creating this high drama was
Red Sox starter Daisuke Matsuzaka, Boston's high-priced Japanese import. Had anyone else in the Boston rotation been given a 2–0 first-inning lead, as Dice-K had, it's likely that the Red Sox' Game 2 victory

would have been short and tidy. (Exhibit A: Handed a 1–0 first-inning lead in Game 1, Josh Beckett had pitched a complete-game shutout in just two hours, 27 minutes.)

But Dice-K didn't do short and tidy. He pitched *his* game. That meant never giving in. Not to the hitter, not to the situation, not to the frustrations of fans, teammates, pitching coaches, or managers. It meant lots of innings like the top of the first against the Angels, which required 27 pitches to navigate, including two full counts.

Dice-K wriggled out of that mess. But after starting the second with that two-run lead, Dice-K ended it trailing 3–2 (appropriately), having used up 28 more pitches and gone to two more full counts. By the top of the fifth, Sox manager Terry Francona had seen enough. Dice-K's last offering of the night was both ball four *and* a wild pitch, putting runners on first and third with two outs.

Javier Lopez got out of the jam, and the Red Sox tied the game at three in the last of the fifth. That's the way it stayed until the ninth. The Sox bullpen had held the Angels hitless. Now the stage was set for the ultimate just-like-2004 moment.

The parallel was uncanny. Three years earlier, on another October Friday night at Fenway, the Red Sox had beaten the Angels on a walk-off home run (see Game No. 49). That rally started with a leadoff single, and David Ortiz was due up fourth. Tonight, with Ortiz again due up fourth, Sox shortstop Julio Lugo led off the last of the ninth with a single.

As in 2004, Angels manager Mike Scioscia faced some agonizing choices regarding his bullpen. In '04, with setup man Francisco Rodriguez tiring in the last of the tenth, Scioscia brought in lefty Jarrod Washburn— normally a starter—to face Ortiz with a runner at first and two outs.

Wrong move. Ortiz blasted Washburn's first pitch over the Monster—another in his seemingly endless string of clutch postseason hits.

Tonight, with Lugo at second and two outs, Scioscia decided to leave Rodriguez, who was now his closer, in the game. But he had him walk Ortiz to bring up Manny Ramirez.

Wrong move—although it was easy to understand Scioscia's thinking. Rodriguez had struck Ramirez out twice in that '04 game. Further, Ramirez had had a subpar (for him) season, with his lowest home run total (twenty) since the strike-shortened 1994 season, his rookie year, and his first sub-100 RBI season in a decade.

But, as Ramirez noted afterward, ending a vow of silence with the press: "When you don't feel good and still get hits, that's when you know you're a bad man."

This was Manny being a bad Manny. His three-run blast landed somewhere on Lansdowne Street and essentially ended the series. And if the script wasn't exactly 2004 all over again, it was certainly a faithful adaptation.

The parallels to 2004 continued throughout the 2007 postseason: After dispatching the Angels in three games, the Red Sox staged a serious comeback to win the ALCS in seven games, then swept an overmatched National League team in the World Series (see Game No. 66).

50

Red Sox 7, Angels 6, 11 innings
October 12, 1986

This was one of the most dramatic postseason comebacks in baseball history—and it would rank much higher if not for what followed

Bill Buckner started the rally. With the Red Sox trailing the California Angels 3–1 in the ALCS, and 5–2 in Game 5, Bucker led off the top of the ninth by grounding a single up the middle against Angels starter Mike Witt. Then he took a seat.

It was the obvious strategic move. Jayson Stark, then with the Philadelphia *Inquirer*, wrote that Buckner was "so hobbled by his myriad leg injuries that he could barely walk." Sox manager John McNamara sent in Dave Stapleton to pinch run and take over for Buckner at first base.

The latter consideration—Stapleton's defensive position—appeared moot. Buckner's single looked like too little too late. Jim Rice, Boston's cleanup hitter and leading RBI man during the season, followed by striking out for the seventh time in the series. Rice, now hitting just .190 in the ALCS after collecting 200 hits during the year, embodied the bitter disappointment of this postseason. By any objective forecast, the Red Sox should have won the series. They had the better regular season record. They had home field advantage. Most important of all, they had Roger Clemens. He'd had a monster of a year: 24–4, best record since the Yankees' Ron Guidry in 1978. And he'd done it with glower and power—including a record-setting twenty-strikeout performance (see Game No. 68). True, the Angels had a solid No. 1 in Witt (18–10, 2.84 ERA, 208 strikeouts). But Clemens vs. Witt in Game 1 at Fenway? That should've been no contest. It wasn't; the Angels won 8–1.

And yes, in his next start, in Game 4, Clemens had returned to form. To a point. The Rocket struck out nine and shut the Angels out through eight. Meanwhile the Sox scratched out three runs against California's number-four starter, 41-year-old Don Sutton.

Then came the ninth. Clemens gave up a leadoff homer and a pair of one-out singles. Twenty-four-year-old Calvin Schiraldi, youngest of the Boston bullpen's closer committee, allowed the tying runs on a double, an intentional walk, and a hit batsman. Angels second baseman Bobby Grich completed the comeback with a game-winning single in the eleventh.

In Game 5, with the season on the line, the Sox were in desperation mode. Lefty Bruce Hurst started on three days' rest for the first time all year. He wasn't terrible—but he wasn't terribly sharp, either. He gave up three runs in six innings. The last two had an only-the-Red-Sox twist. Boston's starting center fielder, Tony Armas, had left the game in the fifth inning with a sprained ankle. His replacement, Dave Henderson, might not have been as good at the plate, but he was an upgrade in the outfield. In fact, when the Red Sox had acquired him from Seattle in August, it was mostly to shore up their defense. And for an instant, with Boston ahead 2–1 in the last of the sixth, it looked like Henderson's insertion into the game would pay a serendipitous dividend. With a runner on second and two outs, Grich hit a long drive to center that Armas likely never would have reached. Henderson did. But instead of snaring the ball for a brilliant catch that would have preserved the lead, Henderson actually knocked the ball over the wall for a two-run homer that put the Angels ahead. When the Angels added two more runs off Bob Stanley in the seventh, the game, and the season, seemed over. Witt had been as dominant in Game 5 as he'd been in Game 1. He'd allowed just six hits through eight innings. Rich Gedman, Boston's left-handed-hitting catcher, had three of them, including a two-run homer in the second that had provided all of the Sox' scoring.

After Rice fanned for the first out in the ninth, Boston's DH, Don Baylor, stepped in. The crowd of 64,223 at Anaheim Stadium was in a delirious buzz. The Angels were just two outs away from their first trip to the World Series.

Baylor battled Witt to the limit, working the count full. Then he drilled a two-run homer over the left-field wall, cutting the Angels' lead to 5–4. But the glimmer quickly dimmed. Witt got right fielder Dwight

Evans to pop weakly to third for the second out.

Angels manager Gene Mauch would have left Witt in had anybody but Gedman been up next. But the matchup scared him—with good reason. Gedman was just a triple short of hitting for the cycle. "If I had let Gedman get another extra-base hit off Witt, I could never have lived with it," Mauch said years later. So he summoned lefty Gary Lucas, who had struck Gedman out in two previous encounters. Lucas's first pitch was a breaking ball that failed to break. It stayed inside and plunked Gedman. For the first time since May 30, 1982—a stretch of 243 appearances over more than four years—Gary Lucas had hit a batter. The Sox had the tying run on. Mauch immediately made another switch, bringing in his closer, Donnie Moore.

Up next was Dave Henderson, the substitute center fielder. McNamara had already used his best left-handed-hitting pinch hitter, Mike Greenwell, in the eighth. So Boston's last hope rested on a replacement outfielder who was in the game only because of an injury, in a seemingly unfavorable righty-righty matchup.

But the situation wasn't as bleak as it might have appeared. Moore had struggled with injuries all season. He wasn't nearly as effective as he'd been in 1985, when he had received Cy Young votes on the strength of his 1.92 ERA and 31 saves in 39 opportunities.

One of Moore's blown saves in 1985 had come against the Seattle Mariners, when Dave Henderson had taken him deep. And now, exactly fourteen months later, came a rematch. Moore was once again trying to protect a 5–4 lead; Henderson was again trying to erase it. More got ahead 1–2, then wasted one. Henderson barely got his bat on the next pitch, a splitter. Moore's next pitch was straight heat, and this time Henderson was on it, fouling it straight back. So the Angels veteran catcher, Bob Boone, signaled for another splitter. It stayed up over the plate, nice and fat. Henderson jumped on it. The ball landed eight rows deep in the left-field bleachers. Boston had a 6–5 lead, and Anaheim Stadium was suddenly so quiet that you could hear a pennant drop.

But the game wasn't over yet. Bob Stanley and lefty Joe Sambito couldn't hold the lead in the last of the ninth. With the score 6–6, Sox righty Steve Crawford, making his only appearance of the series, then loaded the bases with one out. When Crawford escaped the jam, the shifting tide was simply too strong for the Angels to overcome. The Red Sox loaded the bases with no outs in the eleventh, and Henderson came up again—against Moore, who, remarkably, was still in the game. Henderson delivered again, this time with a sacrifice fly that made it 7–6, Red Sox.

Calvin Schiraldi, who had blown a save less than 24 hours earlier, overpowered the Angels in the home half. The game ended when California left fielder Brian Downing fouled out to first baseman Dave Stapleton. So much had happened over the last three innings, it was easy to forget that Stapleton had entered the game in the ninth inning as a pinch runner for the man who had triggered the rally that had saved the 1986 Red Sox' season: Bill Buckner.

Although they still led the series 3–2, the Angels were done. They lost games 5 and 6 at Fenway by a combined score of 18–5. That put them right at the top of the list of baseball's most notorious postseason collapses. But once again, thanks to the '86 Red Sox, the Angels didn't stay on top for long.

49

Red Sox 8, Angels 6
October 8, 2004

David Ortiz's tenth-inning bomb propelled the 2004 Red Sox
into an ALCS rematch with the Yankees

T he ghosts of postseasons past still haunted the Red Sox. It was
getting just plain spooky, the way the nightmare recurred. It
always happened all at once, in the late innings. The Sox would
be ahead, a handful of outs from a victory that would end the other
team's season. And then, within just a few minutes, a few pitches would
transmogrify an imminent triumph into a grisly defeat.

2003: Pedro Martinez had a 5–2 lead with one out and nobody on in
the eighth.

1986: Calvin Schiraldi had a 5–3 lead with two outs and nobody on in
the tenth.

1978: Mike Torrez had a 2–0 lead with one out and nobody on in the
seventh.

And now *this*. 2004. Bronson Arroyo had a 6–1 lead starting the top of
the seventh against the Anaheim Angels in Game 3 of the 2004 American
League Division Series. The Sox led two games to none, meaning they
were nine outs from sweeping the series.

By the time the inning ended, the Red Sox had become the first
team in major league history to blow a five-run lead in a home playoff
game. Worse, the damage was largely self-inflicted. The Angels had

scored those five runs on just two hits. Arroyo and relievers Mike Myers and Mike Timlin had each issued a walk. Then Timlin caught too much of the plate against Anaheim's best hitter, Vladimir Guerrero, who drilled a game-tying grand slam.

In years past, the shell-shocked Sox would have curled up in the fetal position. But the 2004 Red Sox used the historic blown lead as an opportunity to demonstrate that they were made of different stuff. This group had no fear of ghosts or curses or recurring nightmares. In fact, said Johnny Damon, Boston's somnolent center fielder, the only thing worth losing sleep over was the thought of losing sleep itself. Noting that the "if necessary" Game 4 on Saturday was scheduled for the ungodly hour of 1:00 p.m., Damon said, "We would have to wake up early and play again, and we're not morning people."

Better to just take care of business on Friday night. So closer Keith Foulke escaped a bases-loaded, one-out jam in the ninth by striking out Anaheim's four and five hitters, Garret Anderson and Troy Glaus. Derek Lowe stranded two more runners in the tenth. And that brought up Damon, leading off the home half. He did his part to avoid an early wake-up call by grounding a single to center. But he was erased at second on Mark Bellhorn's sacrifice bunt attempt.

Maybe it was just as well that the sacrifice failed. Had Damon made it to second, leaving first base open, maybe Angels manager Mike Scioscia would have pitched around David Ortiz. Instead, Scioscia let lefty Jarrod Washburn challenge him.

Ortiz met the challenge. He lofted Washburn's first pitch over the Monster in left, creating a wild celebration throughout New England— and a good night's sleep for Johnny Damon.

For most players, a series-clinching walk-off home run would have been a career pinnacle. For David Ortiz, that two-run blast against the Angels was only his third- or fourth-biggest hit of the month (see games 2–5).

48

Celtics 89, Lakers 88
April 29, 1969

In Game 4 of Bill Russell's final trip to the NBA Finals, a clutch steal and a lucky shot in the waning seconds helped the Celtics even the series

B ecause it wasn't a seventh game this lacks the legendary status of other Celtics–Lakers classics from the 1960s. But it might have been the most dramatic Boston win in the rivalry's history—and the most devastating LA loss.

For starters, it was a swing game. For the fist time in seven playoff meetings, the Lakers had home-court advantage. It had already paid off. Behind crowds of 17,500 at the Forum, the Lakers had won the first two games by a total of eight points. The Celtics bounced back to win Game 3 at Boston Garden. So Game 4 was crucial. Either the Celtics would square the series, or the Lakers would head back to LA with a 3–1 lead and a chance to close out the series at home in Game 5. A record Boston Garden basketball crowd—15,128—turned out, knowing that it might be their last chance to see the great Celtics dynasty in person.

From LA's perspective Game 4 was ripe for the taking. The Celtics practically boxed it up and overnighted it to the Forum for them. Boston shot just 32% from the floor. At one point in the first half they went ten minutes without a field goal. They had another dry spell of more than four minutes late in the fourth quarter. To put the Celtics' offensive struggles in context: In 38 previous Celtics–Lakers playoff games, Boston had scored fewer than 100 points only twice—and never fewer than 95. But on a night when Boston hit rock bottom with only 89 points, Los Angeles was even worse. Two of LA's top three scorers, Wilt Chamberlain and Elgin Baylor, shot a combined 3-of-17 … from the *free-throw line*.

For all that, the Lakers were in command at crunch time. They had a one-point lead and the ball with just fourteen seconds left. And they had Jerry West, who seemed determined to win the game all by himself. West had poured in 40 points, including 10-of-10 from the line. If LA could just put the ball in his hands one more time, the game would be theirs.

They couldn't do it.

Baylor inbounded the ball to the second option, guard Johnny Egan, a deadly free-throw shooter. Egan was either stripped of the ball—Boston's version—or fouled—LA's version—by Celtics guard Emmette Bryant. Apparently Boston was right because there was no whistle. (And considering its importance, Bryant's steal ought to rank alongside those by Havlicek, Bird, and Henderson in Celtics lore.)

Bryant grabbed the loose ball, started to drive, and saw Chamberlain looming. So he dished to Sam Jones, still the Celtics' best pure shooter at age 35, for an open fifteen-footer. Jones missed. Chamberlain tapped the rebound toward the sideline, where Baylor either saved it—LA's version—or stepped out of bounds—Boston's version. Apparently Boston was right again because the whistle blew. The Celtics had a reprieve with seven seconds left.

Boston's player/coach, Bill Russell, called another play for Jones, off a screen at the top of the key. But Jones slipped as he started to shoot. He ended up shot-putting an awkward seventeen-footer in the general direction of the basket. Jones later said that on his follow-through he was less concerned with making the shot than with simply hitting the rim so that "Russell had a chance for the rebound."

The only problem with that stratagem was that Russell had removed himself from the game. "For me to rebound from where I was would have been some rebound," Russell said later.

But the rebounding issue became moot. The ball caught the front of the rim and began a series of indecisive hops. Russell: "It looked like the ball had fingers and was saying, 'I'd better crawl in.' "

And that's just what it did, to put Boston up 89–88 with one second left. Said Bryant, "Four-leaf clovers were flying all over the place."

If this was indeed the farewell tour for the Celtics dynasty, they were rolling out all the greatest hits for the home folks. On the game's final play, West tried a lob to Chamberlain, but Celtics forward Satch Sanders got a hand on the pass à la "Havlicek stole the ball!" and tipped it to Havlicek himself.

West, who had played a near-perfect game, was abject in defeat. "I must be a loser," he said.

Said Russell, the incredulous winner, "We'll take it. We're not proud."

Both were wrong.

Motivated in part by a loser move from Lakers owner Jack Kent Cooke, the Celtics summoned all their pride in an epic Game 7 at the Forum (see Game No. 14).

47

Celtics 119, Warriors 117
March 24, 1960

Bill Russell played rookie sensation Wilt Chamberlain to a standoff
and the Celtics overtook the Warriors to advance to the NBA Finals
for the fourth straight year

I n his first three NBA seasons Bill Russell revolutionized the center
position. In his fourth season he encountered a counter-revolution-
ary. Along came Wilt Chamberlain, who would serve as a 7'1" meas-
uring stick for the rest of Russell's career. In his NBA debut with the
Philadelphia Warriors on October 24, 1959, Chamberlain had 43 points
and 28 rebounds against the Knicks. That prompted a prediction from
New York coach Fuzzy Levane that, outlandish as it seemed, actually sold
the prodigy's potential short: "Some night in this league Chamberlain
will score 90 points."

Upon hearing that, Celtics coach Red Auerbach declared: "He will
never do it against Bill Russell."

Then, using a peculiar mash-up of tenses, Auerbach offered a prediction of his own: "Some of the most memorable man-to-man engagements
you sportswriters have ever seen will occur any time when Bill Russell
plays Wilt Chamberlain."

But with just eight franchises and a 75-game schedule, there were too
many man-to-man engagements to remember. Boston and Philadelphia
squared off thirteen times during the 1959–60 season. And while
Chamberlain did plenty of damage—he averaged 40 points a game against
Boston, including a 53-point eruption in February—the Celtics won the
season series, 8–5. Boston also won the Eastern Division by ten games
over the Warriors.

Still, it was obvious that it would take more than Russell to contain Chamberlain in the best-of-seven Eastern Division Finals. Chamberlain had shattered both the NBA scoring (37.6 points per game) and rebounding (27 boards per game) records. He was Most Valuable Player as well as Rookie of the Year. (He was also almost singlehandedly responsible for a 23% increase in NBA attendance.) As the season wore on, teams had become increasingly physical with Chamberlain. The Celtics took a similar, if somewhat more subtle, approach in the playoffs. In Game 1 at the Garden, Russell fouled out for the first time all year in a 111–105 Celtics win. Although Chamberlain had 42 points, the Warriors also had 27 turnovers—ten of which occurred as Chamberlain's teammates tried to feed him the ball.

Also, to prevent the speedy Chamberlain—he had starred in track and field in both high school and college—from beating the Celtics up the floor on offense, Boston forward Tom Heinsohn repeatedly stepped in front of him. That led to several collisions, and to Chamberlain's doing a slow burn. In Game 2, a 115–110 Warriors win at Philadelphia's Convention Hall, Chamberlain became so frustrated that he threw a punch at Heinsohn, triggering a brawl that required police intervention. Chamberlain wasn't ejected ("I didn't see who started it," referee Arnie Heft explained), but he hurt his right hand in the fight. Worse, from the Warriors' perspective, he had no time to recover. The injury occurred in the first of a brutal three-day stretch in which the teams played in Philadelphia on Friday, Boston on Saturday, and Philadelphia on Sunday. Playing hurt, Chamberlain scored just twelve points in Game 3 and 24 in Game 4. By the time the swelling in his hand subsided, the Celtics had a 3–1 lead and were ready to close out the series at the Garden in Game 5. Instead, Chamberlain exploded for 50 points and the Warriors won in a rout.

That gave the Celtics—Russell in particular—a sense of urgency heading into Game 6 at Philadelphia. In a terrific individual effort, Russell played Chamberlain to a virtual draw. Chamberlain had one more point (26–25); Russell had one more rebound (25–24). Each also committed five fouls, requiring them to play cautious defense near the end. All of which meant that others had to step up—and plenty of guys did. All ten starters scored in double digits, led by Philadelphia's Guy Rodgers with 31. But the Warriors' bench contributed just two points while the Celtics' sixth man, Frank Ramsey, had fourteen.

The other critical difference was free-throw shooting. Chamberlain missed six foul shots. Rodgers missed seven (3-of-10). As a team the Celtics missed just five (25-of-30). The Warriors' ineptitude from the line was especially costly in the final minute. With Philadelphia up 117–115, Chamberlain missed a free throw that would have made it a two-possession game with 36 seconds left. (There was no three-point shot in 1960.) On Boston's ensuing possession Bill Sharman tied it with a jumper from the left baseline. Rodgers then botched a chance for Philadelphia to retake the lead by missing two more from the line. Russell grabbed the rebound and the Celtics called their last timeout with nine seconds left.

Boston ran another play for Sharman. Chamberlain slid over to double-team him, altering the shot. But that also left an opening for Heinsohn. The man whose physical play on Chamberlain had helped give the Celtics the lead in the series now ended the series by tipping in a rebound as the buzzer sounded.

Afterward, Celtics owner Walter Brown gave Chamberlain the kind of backhanded compliment that would dog him for much of his career. "He's the greatest individual I've ever seen," said Brown, "but we're the champions."

After ousting the Warriors, the Celtics beat the Hawks in the NBA Finals for their third title in four years. Chamberlain, meanwhile, was so frustrated with the NBA's rough play that he announced his retirement. He changed his mind, of course, and he and Russell went head to head six more times in the postseason.

46

Patriots 31, Dolphins 14
January 12, 1986

On a rainy Sunday in Miami, the Patriots simultaneously ended a 20-year
Orange Bowl losing streak and won their first AFC championship

How to explain the Patriots' magical run to the 1985 AFC
Championship Game? Easy. There was nothing magical about
it. In beating the Jets (see Game No. 88) and Raiders (see
Game No. 64), New England had merely exposed a couple of frauds. It
wasn't as if Pats coach Raymond Berry had to outwit Weeb Ewbank
and John Madden. He just had to game-plan better than Joe Walton
and Tom Flores. And Pats' quarterback Tony Eason didn't have to outgun Joe Namath and Ken Stabler. He just had to be a better game manager than Ken O'Brien and Marc Wilson.

Now came the real test. To put New England in the Super Bowl for
the first time, Berry and Eason would have to beat Don Shula and Dan
Marino. And they would have to do it in Miami, where the Patriots had
won only once, in 1966, when the Dolphins were a first-year expansion
team.

Forget the frozen tundra of Lambeau Field—the scorched earth of the
Orange Bowl was the NFL's greatest home-field advantage. The Dolphins
held the record for consecutive home wins, 31, from 1971 through 1974
(it still stands). Eight of those wins (including a playoff game) belonged
to the 1972 Dolphins, the only team in modern NFL history to go undefeated. Recently, members of that '72 team had looked on in glee as their
Orange Bowl brethren had ended the '85 Bears' bid for perfection.

But Miami reserved a special brand of torture for their AFC East
rivals. From 1970 through the end of the '85 regular season Miami had

a 57–8–1 record within their division at the Orange Bowl. The Pats' most recent Orange Bowl defeat—a bitter 30–27 loss less than a month earlier—had spelled the difference in the 1985 AFC East race. And that allowed the Dolphins to host the AFC Championship Game for the fifth time in fifteen years.

The Patriots, of course, had never played in an AFC Championship Game, much less hosted one. Their only other title game was in 1963, during the primordial days of the AFL. They lost at San Diego by 41 points.

In sum, the dynamic between the Patriots and Dolphins leading up to the 1985 AFC Championship Game was similar to the one between the Red Sox and Yankees heading into the 2004 American League Championship Series. Much of the pregame hype even described New England's ghastly track record in South Florida as a curse. So history wasn't on the Patriots' side when they took the field at the Orange Bowl late in the afternoon of Sunday, January 12, 1986. But meteorology was. The weather was rainy, windy, and cool. That played to the Pats' strengths on both sides of the ball. The New England offense was built from the ground up, behind fullback Craig James and running back Tony Collins. Against the Dolphins' 23rd-ranked rushing defense, the Patriots happily slogged through the muck all game long. James carried 22 times for 105 yards, Collins twelve for 61. And seldom-used Robert Weathers carried sixteen times for 87 yards, including a 45-yard sprint in the second quarter to set up the first New England touchdown. Weathers also caught a two-yard touchdown pass from Eason, who could hardly have been more economical. Eason threw just twelve times, completing ten for a mere 71 yards—but three TDs.

Just as important was what Eason *didn't* do: throw an interception. Marino threw a pair, which effectively canceled out his two touchdown passes. He also had a critical fumble, when he lost the snap at the Miami 36 just after the Patriots had taken a 10–7 lead in the second quarter. New England converted that turnover into a touchdown and a 17–7 halftime lead.

From Miami's first offensive play, when linebacker Steve Nelson jarred the ball loose from running back Tony Nathan, the Dolphins simply couldn't hang onto the ball. This was due as much to the Patriots' approach as to the wet conditions. Berry was ahead of his time in encouraging defenders to go for the strip at every opportunity. The Patriots did this to devastating effect during the postseason, forcing thirteen fumbles in three games.

Actually, they weren't all forced. A critical unforced fumble occurred early in the fourth quarter. Miami had just converted one of two Patriots fumbles (both by punt returner Roland James, subbing for the injured Irving Fryar) into a quick touchdown to cut a 24–7 deficit to 24–14. Having provided not much more than a colorful background until then, Miami's slicker-clad crowd came to life. They grew louder when the Dolphins defense forced a three-and-out. With 12:47 left, Miami had the ball and the game's most explosive quarterback. On second-and-ten from his own 37, Marino handed the ball to Joe Carter, a speedster from Alabama with breakaway potential. Carter found a seam and appeared headed for a big gain into New England territory. The Orange Bowl was in full roar.

Then Carter abruptly turned back, like a man who just realized that he'd forgotten something. He had. Although no one on the Patriots had touched him, Carter had lost the ball. Fifteen-year veteran Julius Adams—whose personal history of Orange Bowl horrors had begun with consecutive losses by a combined score of 93–3—recovered at the Miami 45.

The Dolphins' entire 45-man roster, along with the sagging, soggy crowd of 75,662, knew what the Patriots were going to do next. It worked anyway. Nine straight times over the next five minutes Eason handed off to one of his versatile assortment of backs. Only once on the drive, on third-and-seven from the 32, did New England hedge. They went into a shotgun formation with a three-receiver set. Eason then handed the ball to the lone setback, Collins, who slipped through the frustrated Miami defense for fifteen yards and spirit-breaking first down. Three plays later Mosi Tatupu, another veteran of one too many Orange Bowl beat-downs, broke a tackle and burst into the end zone from a yard out to make it a rout. The losing streak, and the Miami mystique, were history.

In hindsight it's obvious that the '85 Patriots were overachievers. Which isn't to say that they didn't belong in the Super Bowl. In another year, against another team, a tough, disciplined group such as theirs might well have gone all the way. Unfortunately, the '85 Patriots had to face the '85 Bears, who belong in any discussion of the greatest NFL teams of all time.

Worse, with a glowering defense that specialized in stuffing the run and harassing the quarterback, the Bears were an especially bad matchup for a ground-oriented team led by Tony Eason. The outcome of Super Bowl XX was as cartoonishly ugly as a Refrigerator Perry touchdown plunge. The Patriots had as many sacks allowed as rushing yards gained (seven) in a 46–10 defeat.

45

Celtics 120, Lakers 117, OT
April 30, 1968

This crucial Game 5 victory in the 1968 NBA Finals propelled
the Celtics to their ninth title in ten years

T he Lakers played the 1968 NBA Finals like they were attached
to the Celtics with a bungee cord. The Celtics won Game 1. The
Lakers snapped back to win Game 2. The Celtics won Game 3.
The Lakers snapped back to win Game 4. Now, in Game 5 at the Garden,
the same pattern played out quarter by quarter. The Celtics hit LA with
an early 10–0 run and expanded the lead to 32–13 lead in the first quarter. The Lakers contracted their deficit to just 56–54 by the half. Aided
by a 19–2 run late in the third quarter, the Celtics pulled away again to
go up by eighteen early in the fourth.

This time LA's elasticity snapped them back hard enough to leave a
mark. Led by Jerry West (35 points on the night), Elgin Baylor (24), and
former Celtic Mel Counts (20), the Lakers erased a 108–102 deficit
in the final 1:04. And they had the last shot in regulation, too, after Bill
Russell was called for traveling with three seconds left. But Baylor's
28-footer rimmed out.

The taffy pull continued in overtime. The Lakers scored first. The
Celtics retook the lead. Then, spurred by point guard Archie Clark's
three-point play, LA went up 115–113.

The Celtics had dominated the 1960s in part because their big players routinely made little plays and their little players sometimes made
big ones. This game turned on the latter variety. When the Lakers failed
to box out on consecutive Celtics possessions, Larry Siegfried and Don
Nelson scored on put-backs to make it 117–115, Boston.

149

For Nelson, a six-year veteran, that one little rebound was the culmination of a much larger one. After the Lakers released him in 1965 the Celtics grabbed him for the bargain-basement fee of $1,000. But his new teammates didn't treat him like a cast-off. "The players made me feel like a Celtic the first day I showed up," said Nelson, whose 26 points in Game 5 were a career high.

After West tied the game again, it was time for the Celtics' big players to make some big plays. John Havlicek hit from the right corner for the last of his team-high 31 points to again give Boston the lead. And then, just as he had in the closing moments of the Celtics upset of the 76ers in the Eastern Division Finals (see Game No. 31), Russell made sure they kept it. When Baylor attempted the tying jumper, Russell put up his hand like a traffic cop and redirected the ball to Nelson. After being fouled, Nelson hit the free throw that took the last bounce from LA's step.

With the regular season and playoffs combined, this was the Celtics' 100th game of the season. They were the first to hit that milestone and they were not a young team. So when Russell was asked, albeit in a joking way, if the Celtics were merely toying with LA, trying to stretch the series out, he refused to play along with the gag. "It may just be all over in Los Angeles," he declared.

It was *all over in Los Angeles. Led by John Havlicek's 40 points, the Celtics routed the Lakers in Game 6, 124–109, to regain the NBA championship and give Russell his first title as player/coach.*

44

Red Sox 2, Dodgers 1, 14 innings
October 9, 1916

Young lefty Babe Ruth set a still-standing record for innings pitched in a World Series game as the Red Sox seized control with a dramatic victory in Game 2

O ut of context, it sounds like one of the dumbest decisions in baseball history. Red Sox manager Bill Carrigan had Babe Ruth at his disposal for the 1915 World Series. But, except for a single pinch-hitting appearance, Carrigan didn't use him. *Babe Ruth*.

In context, it makes sense. Ruth, just twenty years old, was a promising left-handed pitcher. But he was just part of one of the deepest staffs ever assembled. Among the youngsters Ruth was competing with for innings were Carl Mays, who would go on to win 208 games in his career, and Herb Pennock, who would go on to win 241 games and make the Hall of Fame. The veterans included Smoky Joe Wood, who had set the Sox record for wins in a season in 1912, with 34.

None of *those* guys pitched in the 1915 World Series either. Instead, Carrigan went with a three-man rotation of pitchers in their prime: righties Ernie Shore and Rube Foster, and lefty Dutch Leonard. Hard to argue with the results; the Red Sox beat the Phillies in five games (see Game No. 53).

A year later, the Sox returned to the Series, this time against the Brooklyn Dodgers. Boston opened at home—which, as in 1915, meant Braves Field rather than Fenway Park. Shore was still the number-one starter. But Ruth had taken over the number-two spot on the strength of his 23–12 regular-season record, which included a league-leading nine shutouts.

Ruth's bid for a World Series shutout ended in the top of the first in Game 2. With two outs and no one on, Brooklyn center fielder Hi Myers squared up a 1–0 off-speed pitch and drilled it to deep right center. Sox center fielder Tillie Walker slipped, leaving right fielder Harry Hooper to chase the ball down as it rolled toward the fence, some 500 feet from home. Myers easily circled the bases for an inside-the-park home run.

This was a disconcerting start. In Game 1, a 6–5 Sox win, Shore had held the Dodgers in check until the ninth, when they staged a four-run rally. (Mays, who came on for the save, got out of a bases-loaded jam to end it.) If Brooklyn, which led the National League in hitting, got their offense going early, it could be a long day for Boston.

Well, it was a long day for Boston—but also for Brooklyn. And it proved beyond any doubt that, at 21, Ruth was ready for prime time (which, in 1916, meant the lengthening October shadows of late afternoon). After that first-inning hiccup, Ruth shut the Dodgers down for the next 13⅓ innings. He also tied the game in the third, with an RBI groundout against fellow lefty Sherry Smith.

Not that he wasn't tested. Brooklyn ran itself out of a potential big inning in the third, with two runners thrown out on the bases. And the potential go-ahead run was thrown out at the plate in the top of the eighth. Ruth then had to overcome a huge letdown, when Boston failed to break the tie in the ninth, despite putting runners on first and third with no outs.

But Ruth held the Dodgers hitless in extra innings. It looked like he could go forever. It also looked like he might have to; in the tenth, for the second straight inning, the Red Sox had the potential winning run thrown out at the plate.

At last, in the last of the fourteenth, with the sky nearly too dark to continue play, the Red Sox won the game with some paint-by-numbers small ball. Smith, Ruth's left-handed counterpart, was still pitching for Brooklyn. Sox first baseman Dick Hobitzell led off with a walk, his fourth of the day. Left fielder Duffy Lewis bunted him to second. Carrigan sent in Mike McNally, a fleet rookie infielder, to pinch run. And he sent the right-handed hitting Del Gainer in to pinch-hit for lefty-hitting third baseman Larry Gardner. On a 1–1 pitch, Gainer poked the ball into left field and McNally sprinted home. After several excruciating false endings, the longest World Series game in history was abruptly over.

The great Christy Mathewson, having just concluded his brilliant pitching career, covered the game for the Globe. He was duly impressed with Boston's young left-hander. But he added this: "This guy Ruth is a sucker ever to pitch a ball. He is a natural hitter, especially against southpaws, and should be in there every day."

43

Bruins 2, Canadiens 1, 2 OT
April 23, 2011

Tim Thomas's spectacular save gave the Bruins a second life
in sudden-death overtime, and they took full advantage

A psychological shift occurs during sudden-death overtime in a
Stanley Cup Playoff game. At first, each side is eager for a quick
strike: *Let's end this now*. But the longer overtime grinds on, the
more the dread of losing overtakes the desire to win.

That was certainly the case for Boston in this game. After squandering home-ice advantage in the first two games of the 2011 Stanley
Cup Quarterfinal, the Bruins had squared the series with two gritty wins
in Montreal. Now, with a chance to regain control back at the TD
Garden in Game 5, the Bruins had battled the Canadiens to a scoreless
standstill through two periods. Then Brad Marchand poked home a
rebound at 4:33 of the third period to put the Bruins up—only to see
Montreal tie the game six minutes from the end. It remained that way
through one full overtime period and into a second. For the Bruins to
lose after all that hard work would have inflicted a Sisyphean devastation.

After 85½ minutes of hockey, that tipping point loomed. As Montreal's
pair of wings, Brian Gionta and Travis Moen, streaked across center ice
on a textbook two-on-one rush, the Garden crowd felt gravity's pull.

The Bruins' lone defender, Andrew Ference, committed early, just
as Moen carried the puck to the top of left faceoff circle. Goalie Tim
Thomas lined up behind Ference to seal the strong side of the net. Then,
before Ference could make a play, Moen rifled the puck across the ice.
Gionta was wide open, and so was the back door to the Bs' goal.

And then it wasn't. As Gionta delivered the shot, right on target, Thomas reared back across the goalmouth as if spring-loaded and got a leg pad in front of the puck.

The spectacular save rejuvenated the home team and its fans. As Bruins right wing Nathan Horton said afterward, "That definitely gave us a big lift and gave us a little bit more momentum to carry on."

The skate was on the other foot, and less than four minutes later it was Montreal's turn to watch helplessly as a long night of effort came to nothing. Ference, a defenseman now on the offensive, fired a shot from the left faceoff circle, with center David Krejci screening Montreal goalie Carey Price. Price blocked the puck but couldn't contain it. Neither could Canadiens defenseman Roman Hamrlik, who allowed Horton to get inside position. The puck skittered through their skates and wound up on the blade of Horton's stick, as if drawn by a magnet. The net was wide open—and this time it stayed that way as Horton flicked the puck home before Price could react. The goal triggered an explosive release in the Garden—as much a rejoicing over not losing as a celebration of winning.

That goal was a career high point for Horton, a seven-year veteran seeing his first playoff action after the Bruins had picked him up from the Florida Panthers the previous summer. But he needed just four days to top it (see Game No. 7).

42

Braves 5, A's 4, 12 innings
October 12, 1914

After rallying from last place on the Fourth of July to win the National League pennant, the Miracle Braves rallied from two runs down in extra innings to beat the Athletics en route to a World Series sweep

Boston has been a Red Sox town for as long as the Red Sox have been around. Despite a 25-year head start (and eight National League pennants), the Boston Braves became the Boston Bridesmaids as soon as their American League rival arrived in 1901. That first season, the Red Sox drew nearly twice as many fans as the Braves. Over the next dozen years, as the Red Sox won three titles before record crowds, the Braves languished.

The disparity between the two franchises was never more apparent than in 1912. Playing in their new state-of-the-art stadium, Fenway Park, the Red Sox won 105 games (and the World Series) while drawing almost 600,000 fans. The Braves, playing in a nineteenth-century relic called the South End Grounds, lost 100 games and drew just 121,000 fans.

Braves owner James Gaffney tried to shake things up in 1914. He went to considerable lengths to lure second baseman Johnny Evers, a future Hall of Famer, from the Cubs. Evers and Boston's incumbent shortstop, Rabbit Maranville—another future Hall of Famer—comprised the best middle infield in baseball, to support a couple of promising second-year pitchers, Dick Rudolph and Bill James.

For all that, the 1914 Braves lost sixteen of their first nineteen games to once again settle into the basement.

They were reborn on the Fourth of July. Despite losing a doubleheader to Brooklyn to fall fourteen games under .500 and a season-worst fifteen games out of first, Boston had reason for optimism. That day's papers carried the news that Gaffney had signed eight players, including Evers, Maranville, Rudolph, James, first baseman Butch Schmidt, and catcher Hank Gowdy, to multi-year contracts. He wasn't quitting on them—and they didn't quit on him. Over the rest of July the Braves went 18–5.

Two significant events occurred on August 1. Weary of his obsolete stadium, Gaffney had made an arrangement with Red Sox owner Joseph Lannin to transfer that day's Braves–Cardinals game to Fenway Park. The Braves won, 4–3, in ten innings, before 20,000 fans—a Braves' record. Wrote the *Globe*'s J.C. O'Leary, "Many of the spectators in the grandstand saw the Boston National League team play for the first time in years."

The win also put the Braves at .500 for the first time all season.

Two days later, Lannin offered to let the Braves play at Fenway for the rest of the year, free of charge. His motives weren't strictly altruistic. In other cities, such as Chicago and St. Louis, postseason exhibitions between the local AL and NL teams had been a lucrative draw. With the Red Sox 7½ games behind the first-place Philadelphia A's and fading, a postseason series at Fenway with the suddenly respectable Braves had become an attractive possibility for Lannin.

The "Miracle Braves" ruined that plan by qualifying for the World Series. They climbed from last to first in 38 days, and then won the National League pennant going away, by 10½ games over the Giants.

Still, not many experts gave them much chance against Connie Mack's A's. Philadelphia had won the World Series three times in four years.

Again the Braves pulled a stunner, winning the first two games on the road. Boston was fully smitten with the Braves when they returned. A crowd of 35,520—greater than any that had watched the Red Sox in the 1912 World Series—jammed Fenway Park for Game 3. The Braves rewarded them with their best comeback yet.

Over nine intense innings, Braves starter Lefty Tyler battled 21-year-old Bullet Joe Bush to a 2–2 draw. A's catcher Wally Schang led off the tenth with a single. After Bush struck out on a failed bunt attempt, right fielder Eddie Murphy hit a comebacker to Tyler. Rather than take the sure out at first, Tyler tried to get Schang at second. Schang, who had been running on the pitch, beat the throw. A groundout advanced the runners to second and third, and a walk loaded the bases with two outs. That brought up Philadelphia third baseman John Franklin Baker, a.k.a. "Home Run." It was an intimidating nickname in the dead-ball era.

Baker didn't hit a home run, but he did hit the ball very hard, toward second. It stunned Evers, who knocked the ball down but had no play. Schang scored the go-ahead run. Then Evers, who was still collecting himself, held the ball while Murphy ran home as well. With one ringing infield hit, the A's led 4–2. The Braves had just three outs left to try to recoup those two runs.

Gowdy got one run back before Bush could get even one out, with a home run leading off the last of the tenth. Right fielder Herbie Moran walked with one out. Evers then atoned for his mental error by advancing the tying run to third with a single. Left fielder Joe Connolly brought Moran home with a sacrifice fly to tie the game at four, triggering a five-minute ovation from the Fenway fans.

Braves manager George Stallings summoned righty Bill James in the eleventh. Like Rudolph, James had won 26 games during the regular season. And just two days earlier he had held the A's to two hits in a complete-game, 1–0 victory. Now he shut the A's out for two more innings in relief.

Because of the growing darkness, the umpires had announced that the twelfth inning would be the last, regardless of what happened. Hank Gowdy led off again. He was five-for-eight in the series and had already walked, doubled, and homered off Bush. And yet Connie Mack left Bush in the game. Mistake; Gowdy lined a ground-rule double to left. Stallings sent in backup outfielder Les Mann to pinch run for Gowdy, and rookie Larry Gilbert to pinch-hit for James. Bush intentionally walked Gilbert to set up both a potential double play and a force-out at third.

Moran then bunted up the third-base line. Bush fielded the ball, turned, and threw wildly past Baker, trying to force Mann. And so, as "the purple haze of eventide was gathering over Fenway Park" (to use the purple prose of the *New York Times*), Mann was home free in the new home of the Braves.

The next day, behind Dick Rudolph and another large, noisy throng at Fenway Park (34,365), the Miracle Braves completed the first four-game sweep in World Series history. Owner James Gaffney parlayed that success into a new ballpark, Braves Field, in 1915. But all Braves Field really accomplished for the Braves was to give them more seats that they couldn't sell. The franchise quickly backslid to irrelevance. When they won their next World Series, in 1957, they were playing in Milwaukee.

41

Boston College 47, Miami 45
November 23, 1984

Boston's most memorable college game ever

As the cliché has it, no one would have dared to write a script for a scenario as implausible as this one. But the cliché is wrong. Leigh Montville *did* write the script. Doug Flutie just added some notes.

For years, Montville wrote an NFL column called "Pro Picks" in the Boston *Globe* on fall Fridays. He led each column with his prediction for that Sunday's Patriots game. But because the Patriots had played in Dallas on Thanksgiving Day in 1984, Montville led the next day's "Pro Picks" column with his forecast for the BC–Miami game, a Black Friday matinee in the Orange Bowl. There was keen local interest in the game, which pitted a pair of Heisman Trophy contenders at quarterback: Flutie for the No. 10 Eagles and sophomore sensation Bernie Kosar for the Hurricanes, the defending national champions.

This was Montville's prediction:

BOSTON COLLEGE 44, MIAMI 43—Night is arriving. The Orange Bowl lights are on. The game has gone forever with all of those passes. Flutie takes the Eagles down the field and scores with zero seconds left. The Eagles go for the two-point conversion. Flutie scores on a rollout.

Flutie's notes:
The score is about right. And I love the "zero seconds left" part.

But instead of rolling out for two points, how about if I throw for six? (Remember, I'm still trying to convince the doubters that I'm a "real" quarterback.) And it can't be a short pass—there has to be a believable explanation for why the Miami defense would leave a receiver open in the end zone. So how about if I heave it farther than anybody thinks I can—say, 65 yards into the rain and wind? It will be the perfect answer to all those critics who think I'm too small and don't have enough arm strength. (Oh, and for that "Hollywood" touch, let's have my roomie, Gerard Phelan, catch it.)

The Miracle in Miami sealed the deal for the 1984 Heisman Trophy, with Flutie winning by a comfortable margin over Ohio State running back Keith Byars. (Kosar was a distant fourth.) Flutie then closed his brilliant college career with a 45–28 victory over Houston in the 1985 Cotton Bowl.

40

Patriots 24, Colts 14
January 18, 2004

In their first postseason encounter, Tom Brady got the better of
Peyton Manning—with a huge assist from Bill Belichick's defense

A t some point the Indianapolis–New England rivalry turned into
a popularity contest between Peyton Manning and Tom Brady,
at least on the national stage. It was a competition based as much
on Q Rating as QB rating. Who was the funnier host on *Saturday Night
Live*? Who was the better pitchman? Who was the bigger *star*?

It didn't start out that way. When Brady and Manning first faced
each other, on September 30, 2001, it was just another one o'clock game
on CBS. Despite two Pro Bowl selections in his first four years, Manning
was still trying to justify his status as the first pick of the 1998 draft.
Brady was an anonymous backup making his first NFL start, in place of
the injured Drew Bledsoe. Manning's Colts, 2–0 and averaging more
than twenty points per *half*, seemed destined for the playoffs. Brady's
Patriots, 0–2 and having scored twenty points, period, were headed
straight for oblivion.

Brady's Patriots proceeded to obliterate Manning's Colts 44–13.

Afterward Manning received more blame than Brady received
credit. Manning had thrown two more touchdown passes to the Patriots
(a pair of pick-sixes) than Brady had. And anyway, Manning wasn't
competing against the Patriots' offense—he was competing against Bill
Belichick and the Patriots' defense. And failing miserably.

That game set a trajectory for each team and its young quarterback.
Toward the end of the year, Colts coach Jim Mora became so frustrated
with Manning's interceptions (23 that season) that he threw Manning

under the bus during his infamous "Playoffs? You kidding me? *Playoffs?*" meltdown. ("We've thrown four interceptions for touchdowns this year," Mora said. "That might be an NFL record!")

Mora was fired in January—just as Brady, now permanently installed as Belichick's starter, was beginning a precocious run through those same Playoffs? *Playoffs!* to the Patriots' first Super Bowl win.

When Brady and Manning reached the postseason together for the first time, at the end of the 2003 season, each quarterback's reputation was essentially unchanged. Brady, the consummate game manager, extended his playoff record to 4–0 with a gritty victory over Tennessee in the bitter cold (see Game No. 67). Manning, on the other hand, entered the 2003 postseason with a playoff record of 0–3, and each defeat had been worse than the last. But in just two weeks Manning rewrote his résumé. In wins over Denver and Kansas City, he threw eight touchdown passes and no interceptions while completing nearly 80% of his attempts. Of course, there was still the question of whether he could maintain that level of performance against Belichick and the Patriots, in cold and snowy Foxboro. But at least now the question was legitimate, not merely rhetorical.

The answer came quickly. On the game's first possession, the Patriots mounted a seven-minute drive that concluded with Brady's seven-yard touchdown pass to David Givens. Manning answered with a drive that, at first, appeared to be a continuation of the brilliance he'd displayed in reaching the AFC Championship Game. But on third-and-three from the New England five, Manning backtracked, stutter-stepped, then floated a terrible pass into the end zone to Pats safety Rodney Harrison, who looked more like his intended receiver than his intended receiver (tight end Marcus Pollard) did. Manning was left to stew on the sidelines while Brady led the Patriots on a thirteen-play drive for a field goal. By the time Manning returned to the field, for just his second series, it was already the second quarter. That drive lasted all of one play, as cornerback Ty Law made a diving, one-handed interception of a pass intended for Marvin Harrison.

That essentially settled things in a classic not-as-close-as-the-score-indicated game. It should have been a blowout; five New England drives ended in field goals. Another ended when Brady, showing uncharacteristic impatience, threw an interception in the end zone. But, once again, this was more about Manning and the Colts versus the Patriots' defense—and it was another mismatch. Along with four interceptions (three by Law) and a fumble recovery, the Patriots battered the Colts all day, sacking Manning four times and harassing his receivers to disrupt their patterns. Several vicious hits would have drawn unnecessary-roughness flags today. And the Colts complained bitterly that the Patriots were violating the existing illegal-contact rule.

But that amounted to so much sour grapes. There was no doubt as to which was the better team. On this day Manning backslid all the way to the Mora era. In fact, you could pluck another line from Mora's 2001 meltdown, apply it to the Colts' performance in the 2003 AFC Championship Game, and it fit perfectly: "I don't care who you play—whether it's a high school team, a junior college team, a college team, much less an NFL team—when you turn the ball over five times, [including] four interceptions ... you ain't going to beat anybody."

If you can't beat 'em, enjoin 'em. Prompted, at least in part, by the Colts' complaints, the NFL's competition committee tightened the language on illegal-contact penalties before the 2004 season. And it helped Manning and the Colts not one bit in their next playoff game at Foxboro, a 20–3 loss in that season's divisional round. Two years later, however, Manning achieved some redemption by leading the Colts back from a 21–3 deficit to beat New England 38–34 in the AFC Championship Game en route to his first (and so far, only) Super Bowl title.

39

Celtics 135, Bulls 131, 2OT
April 20, 1986

In the finest individual performance in NBA playoff history, 23-year-old Michael Jordan almost beat the great '86 Celtics all by himself. But not quite

The 1985–86 Boston Celtics finished 67–15, the best record in franchise history. They were 37–1 at Boston Garden, the best home record in NBA history. (They also won three "home" games in Hartford.) In the opening round of the playoffs, Boston faced a Chicago Bulls team that had finished 30–52. That was (and still is) the worst record of any playoff team since 1968.

And yet the Bulls were a tough draw. Forty-three of Chicago's losses had happened while Michael Jordan was sidelined with a broken bone in his left foot. But Jordan had returned a month before the playoffs. He was healthy. He was hungry. And the challenge of facing the greatest Celtics team ever, on their home floor, inspired the first sustained display of his legendary competitive fire.

Chicago coach Stan Albeck's strategy was obvious in Game 1— maybe too obvious. Isolate Jordan and let him do his thing. Jordan scored 30 first-half points and the Bulls built an early twelve-point lead. But in the second half Boston clamped down on Jordan (he still finished with 49 points) and pulled away for a 123–104 win.

In Game 2, Albeck again gave Jordan the green light—but within a more conventional offensive structure. The result was a revelation. Jordan again came out firing, scoring seventeen first-quarter points as the Bulls again built an early lead. This time, Chicago sustained that lead for most of the game. When at last the Celtics surged ahead, in the opening minute of the fourth quarter, it happened on a play that would have broken the average player's will. With the shot clock about to expire, Larry Bird nailed a long three that put the Celtics up 93–92 and took the roof off the Garden.

Instead of wilting, Jordan got better. He collected a pair of free throws on a drive to the hoop to regain the lead. Those were the first of eighteen fourth-quarter points. Five times Jordan's shots either tied the game or gave Chicago back the lead. Only one other Bull, Dave Corzine, hit a field goal in the fourth quarter—and that was on a feed from Jordan with three minutes left.

Almost as telling as Jordan's point total were the Celtics foul totals, which climbed in direct proportion. Bill Walton and Dennis Johnson fouled out. Bird, Robert Parish, and Danny Ainge each had five. So it's not as if the Celtics weren't trying to stop Jordan. They just couldn't do it. Said Bird, "I didn't think anyone was capable of doing what Michael has done to us the past two games."

The clearest sign that Jordan had already achieved a rarefied status among NBA players came at the end of regulation. With the Bulls down 116–114, Jordan attempted the last shot just before the buzzer. He didn't take the ball into the paint to go for the tie. He pulled up for a three, going for the win. It was his first attempt from beyond the arc all day.

It was no good. But referee Ed Middleton whistled Kevin McHale for a foul, on what could generously be termed a borderline call.

To review: With a playoff game on the line, an official gave a 23-year-old second-year player on a 30–52 team the benefit of a critical call over a veteran team with a 40–1 home record playing on their own floor.

Still, Jordan needed to deliver under intense pressure. At the time, a shooter was awarded just two free throws when fouled on a three-point attempt. Jordan, all alone at the foul line, with all zeroes on the clock and 14,890 Boston Garden fans trying to rattle him, needed to sink both to send the game into overtime.

The first one nearly rolled out before dropping. The second one was all net. It was Jordan's 54th point of the game.

The game seesawed through the first overtime and into the second. With 1:12 left, Jordan again tied the game, 131–131, with a short jumper. That gave him 63 points, breaking Elgin Baylor's playoff record of 61.

Baylor had set the record at Boston Garden 24 years earlier. The Lakers had won that game, but the Celtics won the 1962 NBA Finals (see Game No. 11). Even paired with the great Jerry West, Baylor couldn't overcome a balanced Celtics team that featured seven future Hall of Famers.

And so it was with Michael Jordan in 1986. The Celtics had five future Hall of Famers, and it took every one of them to overcome Jordan's singular performance. Bird had 36 points, twelve rebounds, eight assists and two blocks. McHale had 27 points and fifteen rebounds. Johnson had fifteen points and eight assists. Parish had thirteen points and nine rebounds. Walton had ten points and fifteen rebounds.

Two guys who were not destined for the Hall also came through at crunch time. Danny Ainge had 24 points, all after halftime, as Boston battled back from a double-digit deficit. And when the Celtics needed one last answer for Jordan, it came from backup guard Jerry Sichting, who hit a jumper from the top of the key to break the final tie.

Afterward Jordan professed to be unimpressed with his performance. "I wanted to win the game so badly that the points don't even mean anything to me," he said. "Maybe fifteen years down the line I can look back and be happy about it. But not now."

The Celtics completed a first-round sweep of the best-of-five series with a 122–104 win at Chicago. (Jordan fouled out of that game with just nineteen points.) Boston coasted to the 1986 NBA championship with a 15–3 playoff record, including 10–0 at the Garden. No other team pushed them as hard on their home floor as Jordan's Bulls did.

38

Red Sox 5, Tigers 2
October 19, 2013

Six days after David Ortiz hit the most electrifying grand slam in Fenway history (see Game No. 15), Shane Victorino matched it to send the Sox to the 2013 World Series

Baseball's postseason exposes one-dimensional players. Feasting on the mistakes of number-five starters and bad middle relievers, even the most sluggish of sluggers can pile up impressive numbers over 162 games. But against top-tier pitchers armed with exhaustive scouting reports, those same hitters are often reduced to haplessness. On the other hand, unsung scrappers who have spent their careers relentlessly figuring out ways to succeed often take over in October.

Take Prince Fielder as an example of the former and Shane Victorino as an example of the latter.

Fielder is clearly the more gifted player, or at least the more advantaged one. He's the son of "Big Daddy" Cecil Fielder, a prototypical first baseman/DH who hit 319 home runs in a thirteen-year major league career. At age twelve, during batting practice at the old Tiger Stadium, Big Daddy's little boy put one into the seats. That's the kind of thing major league scouts salivate over. From the time he was a Little Leaguer, Fielder was focused on a singular, lucrative skill: hitting the ball out of major league parks.

There were no big-league parks anywhere near Wailuku, Hawaii, where Shane Victorino grew up. He was a good ballplayer and a high school track star. He was also on the small side. So scouts tended to focus on his limitations rather than his potential. As Victorino recalled: "A scout told my mom in high school, 'He'll never be a major league player. He'll never get there.' "

But he did, at roughly the same time as Fielder. Entering the 2013 American league Championship Series between Fielder's Tigers and Victorino's Red Sox, each had played eight full seasons. A superficial statistical comparison suggested that Fielder was superior. He was a career .286 hitter who averaged 35 homers and 108 RBI a season, versus a .277/13/57 line for Victorino.

But a comparison of their postseason numbers was more revealing. Victorino's playoff stats were better than his regular season stats. In 50 postseason games he was hitting .280 with six homers and 31 RBI.

Fielder's postseason numbers were much worse. In 33 games, he was hitting .197 with five home runs and just eleven RBI.

They had faced each other in the playoffs once before, in a 2008 NL Division Series matchup. Victorino's Phillies had dispatched Fielder's Brewers in four games. Fielder hit .071. Victorino hit .357. He also supplied the biggest hit of the series: a momentum-swinging grand slam off C.C. Sabathia with the score tied early in Game 2.

In the 2013 ALCS, both struggled. Entering Game 6, Fielder was 4-for-19 with four strikeouts; Victorino was 2-for-21 with nine strikeouts. This was due in part to the extraordinarily high level of pitching on both sides. But in Victorino's case there were extenuating circumstances. Although he was a natural righty, he'd taught himself to switch-hit in the minors. Along with his speed, his hustle, and his great defense, hitting left-handed gave him a complete package of skills that helped him to overcome what he lacked in size.

But nagging injuries—injuries that had resulted in part from his damn-the-torpedoes outfield play—led Victorino to abandon his lefty swing in August and go back to hitting almost exclusively from the right side. This wasn't a liability in the division series; against Tampa Bay's lefty-laden staff, he had hit .429. But against Detroit's succession of right-handed fireballers, who also mixed in an array of breaking stuff down and away, Victorino looked lost.

In Game 6, as so often happens to guys battling horrific slumps in the postseason, Fielder and Victorino each batted in a critical spot.

Fielder first. With his team trailing in the series 3–2 and in the game 1–0, Fielder came up with runners on first and second and no outs in the top of the sixth. Red Sox manager John Farrell pulled starter Clay Buchholz and brought in lefty Franklin Morales.

Morales took all the pressure off of Fielder by walking him on four pitches, all well out of the strike zone.

Farrell left Morales in to face switch-hitting DH Victor Martinez, Detroit's best hitter in the series. (In doing so, Farrell risked flushing a season's worth of goodwill that he had built up among a jaded Red Sox Nation.) Martinez blasted a 2–1 fastball off the wall in left-center. The hit scored two runs—but *only* two runs. The ball caromed right to Sox left fielder Jonny Gomes, who held Martinez to a single while the plodding Fielder stopped at third. Still, as righty Brandon Workman came in to face Jhonny Peralta, it looked like the Tigers were on the verge of a big inning. But they failed to even get an insurance run, due to a shocking absence of basic base-running instincts.

Peralta grounded to second. At that point Martinez and Fielder each did what the other should have done. Fielder, who should have dashed for home, instead moved tentatively off third. Martinez, who should have lingered near first, instead dashed toward second. That took all the pressure off Sox second baseman Dustin Pedroia, who otherwise would have had to make a split-second decision which of three bases to throw to (home to get Fielder, second to try to start a double play, or first to take the sure out). By running right into a tag, Martinez allowed Pedroia —another undersized overachiever—to double up the indecisive Fielder by throwing home. As Fielder tried to retreat to third, he belly-flopped into the dirt well short of the bag. Catcher Jarrod Saltalamacchia ran him down and tagged him out. In the span of two batters the Tigers had managed to seize the lead but lose the momentum.

Victorino's nowhere-to-hide moment came in the last of the seventh, when he came up with the bases loaded and one out. Detroit still led 2–1. Boston's sense of urgency was growing. If they lost Game 6, they would have to face 2011 MVP/Cy Young Award winner Justin Verlander on full rest in Game 7.

Victorino's skid now stood at 2-for-23 with nine strikeouts. He had failed even to get a bunt down with two on and no outs in the third, against Cy-Young-winner-in-waiting Max Scherzer. That wasn't like him. Victorino prided himself on fundamentals—on being the type of player who was willing to take one for the team. In fact, he had taken the art of taking one for the team to record-setting heights in the 2013 postseason, getting hit by pitches six times. Earlier in the series, Verlander had claimed that Victorino was leaning so far over the plate that he was getting hit with pitches that should have been called strikes.

"But you can't think about not hitting a guy," Verlander said. "You've got to think about executing your pitches and not changing anything because of that."

But with the bases loaded in a one-run game, how could Detroit pitcher Jose Veras and catcher Alex Avila *not* think about that? There was no way they could risk running anything in on Victorino's hands. Unlike many other hitters, who would instinctively jackknife out of the way, Victorino would happily stand there and trade a bruise for the tying run.

In effect, Veras had to concede the inside corner, even when the count reached 0–2. That freed up Victorino to lean out and protect the outer half. And Veras had to be careful not to go *too* far outside, because if he skipped one to the backstop, that also would result in a tie game.

So despite being in command of the count, Veras worked as if he were trying to aim the ball through a narrow window. His next pitch was a breaking ball that hung over the plate—"a pitch I could handle," Victorino said.

But just as important was *how* he handled it. He put a compact, uppercut swing on the ball. "The first thought," said Victorino afterward, "was [to] get enough air to tie the game [with a sacrifice fly]."

He wasn't trying to crush the ball, and in fact he didn't—"a glorified pop fly," *Sports Illustrated*'s Ted Keith called it. It wasn't hit nearly as hard as Victor Martinez's bases-loaded single in the sixth. But it was far more effective, because it went over the Green Monster instead of off of it. There could hardly have been a tidier summary of the 2013 Red Sox: guy tries to make a productive out and ends up with a grand slam.

And the image of Shane Victorino jubilantly circling the bases, contrasted with the image of Prince Fielder dog-paddling in the dirt, summed up the 2013 American League Championship Series. The Tigers might have had more raw talent. But the Red Sox had better baseball players.

Another of Boston's unsung scrappers, closer Koji Uehara, closed out the Tigers to win the ALCS MVP Award and send the Red Sox to the World Series (see Game No. 32).

37

Celtics 112, Lakers 109
April 24, 1963

An aging Bob Cousy summoned the strength to end his career
with a flourish as the Celtics beat the Lakers for their fifth straight
NBA championship

O f the thirteen players on the 1962–63 Boston Celtics, eight are
now in the Hall of Fame. That raises a chicken-or-the-egg question. Did the Celtics win eight straight NBA championships
because they had a roster full of Hall of Famers? Or did the Celtics send
so many players to the Hall of Fame because they won eight straight
NBA championships?

The answer is: both, at least according to a formula developed by
Basketball–Reference.com.

The formula uses seven variables, including individual stats like
points per game, to determine the probability that a player's career was
Hall of Fame worthy. But the metric, which is 96.7% accurate, also places
significant value on the number of championships a given player won.

Three of the Hall of Famers on the 1962–63 Celtics—K.C. Jones,
Frank Ramsey, and Clyde Lovellette—were borderline candidates who
benefitted from having played on multiple title-winning teams. The remaining five, however, rank among the top nineteen NBA Hall of
Famers of all time. Further, those five comprised a legitimate *team* rather
than a collection of ill-matched stars: center Bill Russell, forwards Tom
Heinsohn and John Havlicek, point guard Bob Cousy, and shooting
guard Sam Jones.

That raises another question: Why did one of the greatest assem-
blages of talent in history have such a hard time winning the 1963 NBA
championship? The Celtics needed seven games to get by the Cincinnati

Royals in the Eastern Division Finals and six hard-fought battles to beat the Lakers in the title round (Boston's average margin of victory: four points).

Well, for one thing, those other teams were *good*. The Lakers' Jerry West and Elgin Baylor, along with Cincinnati's Oscar Robertson, were top-fifteen Hall of Famers. Further, they were all in their prime. Robertson came within a nickel of averaging a triple double that season: 28.3 points per game, 10.5 rebounds, 9.5 assists. Baylor (29.0/12.2/4.1) and West (27.1/7.0/5.6) weren't far behind, and they were on the same team.

The Celtics' Hall of Fame contingent, on the other hand, ran the gamut. Havlicek was a rookie—and a wounded one at that. He missed two games of the Finals with a sprained ankle. Lovellette was an add-on. He had won his first NBA championship in 1954, as a rookie with the Minneapolis Lakers. Now he provided an occasional breather for Russell.

And then there was Bob Cousy.

Cousy had announced that his thirteenth season with the Celtics would be his last. He was 34, when 34 felt a lot older than it does now. He had career lows for minutes played, points and rebounds per game, and free-throw percentage, among other things. That presented a challenge for coach Red Auerbach. The Celtics, four-time defending NBA champions, wanted to win *now*, while also showing the proper respect for the most popular player the franchise had ever known—and planning for a future without the dynamic point guard who had always set the table for all those other Hall of Famers.

The result was some wildly uneven performances through the playoffs—from both Cousy and the Celtics. In a desultory 109–99 loss at Cincinnati in Game 6 of the Eastern Division Finals, Cousy (five points) went to the bench with 5:06 left in the third quarter and didn't return. "He just wasn't playing well," was Auerbach's terse explanation. But Cousy bounced back with a huge Game 7, scoring 21 points and dishing out sixteen assists—many to backcourt mate Sam Jones, whose career-high 47 points helped the Celtics blitz the Royals 142–131.

The NBA Finals brought more of the same. Cousy, who fouled out just twenty times in his career, fouled out of both Boston losses—each of which occurred after a cross-country flight. His legs just weren't there anymore. The Celtics had to fly across the country again for Game 6 in LA—but fortunately there was an extra off day built in. With additional rest, not to mention the incentive to end his career on a high note, Cousy finished strong. He scored sixteen first-half points as the Celtics built a 66–52 lead. In the second half Cousy had just two points, which came on a beautiful left-handed hook shot, but Boston was still up by twelve after three.

The fourth quarter was a near disaster. As the Lakers mounted a comeback, Cousy twisted his left ankle, spraining it so severely that he was unable to put any weight on his foot as he was helped from the floor. The LA crowd, assuming that they had just watched the final act of a great career, saluted Cousy with a standing ovation.

Six minutes later, his ankle taped and shot full of novocaine, Cousy returned. LA had clawed to within one. But Cousy recorded his final assist, on a feed to Satch Sanders, to make it a three-point lead. LA never did catch up. Down the stretch It was Cousy's fellow Holy Cross alum, Heinsohn, who made most of the key plays, including a steal with the score 104–102 and LA looking for the tying bucket. Heinsohn added four clutch free throws, the last of his team-high 22 points, to put it away at 112–107. But he shifted the attention to his retiring teammate at game's end. "It was a great team victory," said Heinsohn, "and Bob Cousy played absolutely his finest game of the playoffs."

The Cousy Era had ended, but there was no time for reflection. Auerbach cajoled the Celtics to hurry and get dressed so they could catch the red-eye back to Boston. "Here we win five titles in a row," said Heinsohn, "and we can't even stay for a beer."

Asked how he thought the Celtics would manage without him, Cousy said, "They'll do all right. Nobody is indispensible."

The Celtics did more than all right in 1964, breezing through the playoffs with an 8–2 mark to match the 1961 team as the most dominating of the Russell Era.

36

Red Sox 3, Cubs 2
September 9, 1918

Despite hurting his pitching hand with some off-field hijinks,
Babe Ruth extended his scoreless streak to 29⅔ innings to liven up
a gloomy World Series

For generations, New Englanders were jealous of their forebears who had been around in 1918. Which no doubt would have made those forebears laugh.

There was a war on, you morons! There was a flu pandemic! Everybody and their uncle was either staging a strike or threatening to!

Yeah, but the Red Sox won the World Series!

So? The Red Sox always win the World Series!

Yes, Boston baseball fans had become somewhat jaded by 1918. And with a world war still raging, a World Series struck many Americans as inappropriate. In July, Secretary of War Newton Baker had ruled that baseball players had to abide by his work-or-fight decree. All able-bodied American males of draft age in "nonessential" occupations had to either join the military or take a job in a war-related industry. Most minor leagues suspended operations immediately and indefinitely. (Who knew how long the war would last?) The major leagues completed a truncated season, with teams playing anywhere from 122 to 129 games. Initial plans called for starting the World Series on August 20, but Secretary Baker granted the leagues an extension until September. In gratitude the leagues agreed to slash ticket prices and contribute a portion of World Series receipts to the war effort.

It didn't help. Crowds for the Red Sox–Cubs World Series were only about 50% of capacity in both Boston and Chicago. Players and management did themselves no favors by bickering over how to divide the reduced profits. (Game 5 was delayed an hour because of a threatened players' strike.)

Fortunately, Babe Ruth was around to liven things up.

In 1918, for the first time, the Red Sox had given Ruth (and his prodigious bat) more starts as a position player than as a pitcher. He responded with a league-high eleven homers. But he was still Boston's best left-hander, so he also made nineteen starts on the mound. And in the opening game of the World Series in Chicago, manager Ed Barrow chose him over Carl Mays (21–13) and Sad Sam Jones (16–5). Ruth went out carousing the night before—then pitched a complete-game 1–0 victory. That extended his postseason scoreless streak to 22⅓ innings, dating to Game 2 of the 1916 World Series (see Game No. 44). But it merely set the stage for his performance in Game 4, which added to the Ruthian legend.

To cut costs, the 1918 World Series was played as a pair of home-stands. The first three games were in Chicago. The rest were in Boston. Having taken two of three on the road, the Red Sox were in great position heading into Game 4. But discerning observers among the Fenway crowd of 22,183 might have noticed that the middle finger on the Babe's pitching hand was a ghastly yellow. Ruth had injured it "during some sugarhouse fun" on the long train ride from Chicago, according to the *Globe*'s Edward F. Martin. The trainer had applied iodine, affecting Ruth's grip and "causing the ball to shine and sail."

Whatever the reason, Ruth had no command. He issued six walks. He threw a wild pitch. He made a bad throw to second. He gave up seven hits. He put runners on in every inning but the fourth. And yet, despite all that, he managed to stretch his scoreless-innings streak to 29⅔ (a record that stood until 1961). In addition, batting sixth in the order, à la Little League, the Sox pitcher drove in the game's first two runs with a long triple to right-center in the fourth. (In a World Series in which the two teams combined to score just nineteen runs in six games, this constituted a major rally.)

But in this game, as in his life, Ruth's wildness eventually caught up with him. A leadoff walk in the top of the eighth followed by a single followed by a wild pitch led to two runs that tied the game.

But in the last of the eighth Chicago gave the lead right back with a surpassing display of sloppiness. Pitcher Phil Douglas, on in relief of Lefty Tyler, gave up a leadoff single to Sox pinch hitter Wally Schang.

Schang advanced to second on a passed ball charged to Cubs catcher Bill Killefer. Sox right fielder Harry Hooper laid down a bunt, which Douglas fielded and threw wildly past first, allowing Schang to score.

The Red Sox had the lead back. Ruth didn't seem to want it. He gave up a single and a walk in the ninth before Barrow finally yanked him. Sox righty Leslie Ambrose Bush, a.k.a. "Bullet Joe," entered with runners on first and second and no outs. Cubs second baseman Chuck Wortman bunted up the first base line. Sox first baseman Stuffy McInnis, playing in, made a great hustle play, grabbing the ball and firing to third. The lead runner, Fred Merkle—infamous for his baserunning "boner" a decade earlier—failed to beat the throw. The tying run remained at second and the force remained in order. This turned out to be of huge importance; pinch hitter Turner Barber grounded to Sox shortstop Everett Scott, who started a game-ending double play.

Ruth had escaped with his perfect World Series record (3–0) and his growing legend intact.

After dropping Game 5, the Red Sox closed out the earliest World Series in history by beating the Cubs 2–1 on September 11, 1918. Just 15,238 people were at Fenway to see it. A considerably larger and more enthusiastic crowd was on hand the next time the Sox won the World Series at home (see Game No. 32).

35

Bruins 5, Maple Leafs 4, OT
May 13, 2013

In the opening round of the 2013 Stanley Cup Playoffs, the Bruins
pulled off the greatest Game 7 comeback in hockey history

Could the Bruins win a tight playoff series with Tuukka Rask in
goal instead of 2011 Conn Smythe Trophy winner Tim Thomas?
That was a major question heading into the 2013 Stanley Cup
Playoffs. After their first-round series with the Toronto Maple Leafs it
essentially remained unanswered, even though the Bruins had executed
the most electrifying Game 7 win in hockey history. Because for most
of the crucial sequence, a 31-second span late in the third period, the
Bruins had no goaltender at all.

Funny thing was, it was almost predictable—both that they found
themselves in such a predicament and that they escaped from it. The
2013 Bruins were as difficult to read as *Finnegans Wake* (powerplay, still
anemic, passing from curve of blade to bend of board, brings us by re-
circulation of blackish discus back to point of nevercoming triggerpull).
This was due, in part, to the lockout-shortened season, which limited the
sample size to 48 games. The Bruins began by winning eight of ten. They
ended by losing six of eight, squandering an opportunity to win the
Northeast Division. Even so, there seemed little reason to fear the Maple
Leafs, Canada's answer to the Chicago Cubs. After Game 4, which David
Krejci won by completing the hat trick in overtime to put the Bruins up
3–1, the series seemed as good as done. Then the Leafs ground out consecutive 2–1 decisions to even the series at three each. Still the Bruins
rated a significant edge, based on experience alone. This was Boston's
fifth Game 7 in little more than two years. It was Toronto's first Game 7

since 2004. And the Leafs hadn't won a seventh game on the road in twenty years.

Yes, the Bruins were banged up. They started Game 7 minus a pair of defensemen, Andrew Ference and Wade Redden, and lost Dennis Seidenberg after just 37 seconds. But when Matt Bartkowski stepped in and scored his first career goal just 5:39 into the first period, the Bruins appeared ready to break out of their offensive funk.

Instead, it was Toronto that found a rhythm. With Zdeno Chara off for high sticking, Cody Franson tied the game halfway through the first period. Franson scored again at 5:48 of the second. Phil Kessel made it 3–1 early in the third. And when Nazem Kadri stuck in a rebound 3½ minutes later, he also appeared to have stuck a fork in the Bruins. NESN play-by-play man Jack Edwards, noted for his outpourings of black-and-gold bombast, offered a clear-eyed appraisal: "The Toronto Maple Leafs, unless they suffer a colossal collapse, are going to eliminate the Boston Bruins."

One colossal collapse, coming up.

The first cracks in the Toronto facade formed at 9:18 of the third period, when Milan Lucic fed Nathan Horton from behind the Leafs net. Horton buried it. It was 4–2.

According to a mildewed hockey adage, a two-goal lead is the most difficult to protect. That sounds absurd; obviously a one-goal lead is more difficult to protect. (PuckScene.com actually went to the trouble of analyzing an entire season's worth of NHL games to confirm this.) But safeguarding a two-goal lead *can* present a psychological challenge, depending on how much time remains. A team that goes up two goals in the first minute of the game won't try to sit on the lead for the rest of the night. A team that's up two goals in the last minute of the game will.

But what should a team that's up by two goals with 10:42 remaining in Game 7 of a playoff series do—in particular, a young team playing on the road, which has just allowed a confident team and a hostile crowd to come to life? It would be foolish to try to sit on a one-goal lead for that long—but a two-goal lead? That might be doable.

Consciously or otherwise, the Leafs started playing like an NFL team in a prevent defense. (Toronto forward Matt Frattin did manage a breakaway with about 3½ minutes left, but Rask denied him.) And although they maintained that two-goal lead for more than nine minutes, they did so knowing that the worst stress was yet to come. That was because of a stratagem unique to hockey: the extra skater. By the time Bruins coach Claude Julien called Rask to the bench, with two minutes left, the Leafs were wilting. The Bruins, on the other hand, had their sense of urgency reinforced by that extra attacker. And hockey players, perhaps more than any other athletes, are adrenalin-driven.

For the Bruins, this was the ultimate high-wire rush. They were working without a net—or at least without anybody to guard it. After a Toronto dump-in, the goalmouth gaped as Chara gathered the puck in his own end with just 1:45 on the clock. All the Leafs had to do was execute a simple poke check, and they could have iced the game with an empty-netter. But by then Toronto had become so tentative—not risking any penalties or turnovers—that they were having difficulty even getting a blade on the puck. They looked like stand-ins, just occupying space while the Bruins ran a drill designed to overcome a two-goal deficit with less than 90 seconds left.

Once he reached the offensive zone, Chara camped out at the right point. He lurked unguarded, stick cocked, as Patrice Bergeron fed him the puck from across the ice. No Leaf was within twenty feet of Chara as he one-timed a shot. Toronto goalie James Reimer stopped the puck but couldn't contain it. Lucic pounced on the rebound and flicked it in with 1:22 left.

Toronto no longer had to worry about protecting a two-goal lead.

Boston now completely controlled the flow. Bergeron won the ensuing faceoff, which allowed Rask to immediately retreat to the bench again. The Bruins carried the puck into the offensive zone with no resistance. With just under a minute left, Leafs winger James van Riemsdyk had a shot at a loose puck along the boards, but he pulled up and Lucic beat him to it. Moments later, with Chara providing a screen the size of a drive-in theater, Bergeron drilled the puck just under the crossbar from just inside the blue line to tie the game.

Rask, having joined the TD Garden's 17,565 spectators for that historic two-goal flurry, did his part less than two minutes into overtime by stoning Joffrey Lupul twice in five seconds. Meanwhile his Toronto counterpart, Reimer, couldn't contain the puck—he could only hope to stop it. Add his teammates' sudden inability to outskate the Bruins to loose pucks, and you had a terminal combination. Six minutes into overtime, Bergeron collected yet another puck that squirted out of the crease and drilled it past Reimer to complete the most dramatic Game 7 comeback ever.

After advancing to the Stanley Cup Final and taking a two-games-to-one lead over the Chicago Blackhawks, the Bruins dropped three straight, culminating in a Game 6 loss in which a 2–1 lead with 1:17 left became a 3–2 deficit a mere eighteen seconds later. Despite this dispiriting end, the 2013 Bruins will undoubtedly be remembered as one of Boston's all-time favorite teams. In addition to the Game 7 miracle against the Leafs, there was also the inspiring image of Gregory Campbell finishing a shift against the Pittsburgh Penguins on a broken leg in the Eastern Conference Final, and the revelations that Patrice Bergeron had played Game 6 against Chicago with multiple injuries that should have kept him in the hospital, including a collapsed lung.

34

Bruins 2, Maple Leafs 1
April 3, 1941

After losing the NHL's leading scorer, Bill Cowley, to an injury in Game 1 of the Stanley Cup Semifinal, the Bruins clawed back to win the series with a late goal in Game 7, en route to their third championship

No team ever entered the postseason hotter than the Bruins in March of 1941. First-place Boston had lost just once in their last 32 games. But once again, using the inverted pyramid scheme that was the Stanley Cup Playoffs during the Pre-Common Sense Period (1928–1942), the NHL put its best skate forward during the preliminaries and saved the worst for last. The Bruins had to play the second-place Toronto Maple Leafs, who'd finished just five points back, in a best-of-seven semifinal for the privilege of facing the Detroit Red Wings, who had finished a distant third, in the Stanley Cup Final. (For a complete explanation of this absurd playoff format, see games 60 and 10.)

Boston kept its momentum rolling for most of Game 1, a 3–0 Bruins victory at Boston Garden. In the third period, however, Maple Leafs left winger Sweeney Schriner changed the tenor of the series. He took out Bruins center Bill Cowley, the NHL's top scorer, with an illegal leg check that injured Cowley's knee. With Cowley sidelined, Toronto evened the series with a 5–3 win in Game 2, then blew the Bruins off the ice, 7–2, at Maple Leaf Gardens in Game 3.

But really, all the first three games accomplished was to work the slop out of the series. After that came three straight high-tension games. Each ended with the visiting team winning by the same score, 2–1. A berth in the Stanley Cup Final came down to Game 7, at Boston Garden.

With Cowley still out, Bruins coach Cooney Weiland had to reinvent his offense in midflight. He was rewarded with clutch performances from unlikely candidates. Flash Hollett, for instance. Hollett, a defenseman, had come up with Toronto. Leafs owner Conn Smythe became disenchanted with his cockiness (and his salary demands) and unloaded him on the Bruins in 1936 for a reported $16,500 in Depression-era dollars. At the time a lot of hockey experts thought the Bruins had wildly overpaid. And while Hollett had yet to realize his full potential during a full season, he always gave the Bruins their money's worth against Smythe and the Leafs. When Boston had beaten Toronto in the Stanley Cup Final two years earlier, four games to one, Hollett had scored the dagger goal. And barely a minute after Bucko McDonald had put Toronto ahead 1–0 in the first period of Game 7 of the '41 semifinal, Hollett haunted Smythe again by scoring the tying goal.

Assisting was Eddie Wiseman, another player that the Bruins had paid a steep price for. Boston had acquired Wiseman the year before from the New York Americans in a trade for local icon Eddie Shore. For a time many Bruins fans booed whenever poor Wiseman was on the ice.

They weren't booing anymore.

But the most surprising development in Cowley's absence was the resurrection of Mel Hill. Since scoring three sudden-death goals against the Rangers in the 1939 Stanley Cup Semifinal (see Game No. 10) Hill had dropped into a valley. He'd scored just five goals in the entire 1940–41 season. In fact, after Cowley's injury, Weiland had relied more on Pat McReavy, a recent call-up from the minor-league Hershey Bears, than Hill. But in Game 6, Weiland switched Hill from right wing to center and installed him on the first line, hoping to recapture some of that old offensive magic. What he hadn't counted on was Hill's stifling defense on Billy Taylor, Toronto's assists leader.

On top of that, Hill, the "Sudden Death Kid," did indeed rediscover his magic scoring touch—although he didn't quite wait for sudden death to do it. When he blasted the game- (and series-) winning goal past Toronto goalie Turk Broda—off another assist from Wiseman—5:43 was left on the clock.

Hill, who understood the vagaries of success in professional sports as well as anyone, was self-effacing about his return to hero status. This was his take on the dramatic goal that had won Game 7: "I looked around to see who was going to check me, then looked for somebody to pass to. I couldn't see either, so I decided to let Broda have it. I guess he didn't want it either."

The Bruins swept the Red Wings in the final to win their second Stanley Cup in three years. It took 29 years to win the next one (see Game No. 22).

33

Celtics 109, Warriors 107
April 5, 1962

To reach the NBA Finals for the sixth straight year, the Celtics had to get by the Philadelphia Warriors in Game 7 of the Eastern Division Finals. And that meant they had to contain Wilt Chamberlain, who had averaged a remarkable 50.4 points per game that season

R eally, what more did they need to do? Boston had proved they were the better team. Over and over again. For the third straight year Bill Russell's Celtics had finished at least ten games ahead of Wilt Chamberlain's Warriors in the NBA's Eastern Division. Boston beat Philadelphia eight times in twelve tries during the regular season. And in three meetings at Boston Garden during the 1962 Eastern Division Finals, the Celtics had blown the Warriors off the floor, winning the first one by 26 and the next two by fifteen points apiece. But Philadelphia was able to compensate for each blowout loss on the road with a close, hard-fought win in their own building, Convention Hall. So in order to advance to the NBA Finals for the sixth straight year, the Celtics faced a Game 7 in which they had to beat the Warriors at Boston Garden. *Again.*

The dynamic was bound to breed hostility. The Celtics were as weary of repeatedly proving the same point as the Warriors were of having the same point repeatedly proved at their expense. In Game 5 at the Garden, the simmering tensions erupted into the type of violence that would require days to adjudicate in today's NBA, with its video reviews and Flagrant 1 fouls and Flagrant 2 fouls and double technicals. The ugliness began in the second quarter, when Warriors guard Ed Conlin drove Bob Cousy into the basket support. It ended in the fourth, when Tom Heinsohn decked Philadelphia forward Ted Luckenbill and was tossed from the game. In between were two episodes in which players brandished courtside stools for protection (the first was Boston's 6'4" guard Sam Jones in a confrontation with the 7'1" Chamberlain; the second was Philadelphia's 6'0", 185-pound guard Guy Rodgers, who had riled the Celtics' 6'5", 250-pound enforcer, Jim Loscutoff).

So there was plenty of burn at work in Game 7. But there was no room for sideshows or distractions. Too much was at stake, and neither team could build a big enough lead for the players to take things personally. All the emotion poured into the game itself.

Chamberlain, at that stage of his career, was a force beyond all reckoning. He had averaged 50.4 points and 25.7 rebounds per game for the season and was barely a month removed from his record 100-point game against the Knicks. But, as in their first elimination-game encounter two years earlier (see Game No. 47), Russell played him to a stalemate. He held Chamberlain to 22 points while scoring nineteen (including five from the line in five attempts). Each had 22 rebounds.

With Russell and Chamberlain devoting so much energy to containing each other, the game became a four-on-four battle among their teammates. Cousy gave Boston the edge with nine fourth-quarter points as the Celtics rallied from an 81–80 deficit to a 102–91 lead six minutes in. But led by Tom Meschery (who had a game-high 32 points) and Tom Gola (who had 16 points playing on an injured ankle) Philadelphia went on a 10–1 run to cut the deficit to just two with three minutes to go. A Jones jumper and a controversial goaltending call against Chamberlain on a Heinsohn shot made it 107–102 with 1:24 to go. But again the Warriors fought back—and this time it was Chamberlain doing all the damage. A notoriously shaky free throw-shooter, he hit a pair after being fouled by Jones and then an and-one after being hacked by Heinsohn on a put-back. The game was tied at 107 with eleven seconds left.

The Celtics left it up to Jones, their high scorer in the game (28 points). With two seconds left he floated a fifteen-footer up and over Chamberlain and straight down into the net. The evidence might have been less convincing this time, but once again the Celtics had proved they were the better team.

Among those in the Garden crowd that night was Lakers guard Jerry West, who was waiting to see which team he would face in the NBA Finals (see Game No. 11). West called it "the greatest game I've ever seen."

32

Red Sox 6, Cardinals 1
October 30, 2013

This win triggered a Fenway celebration that was 95 years in the making

Pick a moment. Any moment. From John Lackey's first pitch to Koji Uehara's last, Game 6 of the 2013 World Series was replete with revealing glimpses of the "Boston Strong" Red Sox.

There was Jonny Gomes, at the plate in a scoreless game with two on and two out in the third. With his signature combat helmet (a gift from an Iraq war veteran), Gomes had given new meaning to the term "platoon player." He was supposed to have sat in Game 4 at St. Louis, but wound up in the lineup when Shane Victorino's back acted up. Given an unexpected start, Gomes (0-for-10 to that point) delivered the biggest hit of the Series, a tie-breaking three-run homer as the Sox drew even. After that, manager John Farrell decided to stick with him for the duration. So he was in the lineup tonight against the Cards' flame-throwing young righty Michael Wacha—who hit him to load the bases.

That brought up Victorino, whose back had recovered sufficiently for him to return to the lineup. And he continued an uncanny trend. In the ALCS against Detroit, each of the Sox' two wins at Fenway had turned on a grand slam—one from David Ortiz (see Game No. 15) and one from Victorino (see Game No. 38). In the World Series, the Sox grabbed 3–0 leads in each on their two Fenway wins on the strength of bases-loaded doubles. Mike Napoli had delivered the first, in Game 1. And Victorino (like Gomes, 0-for-10 at the time of his key hit) delivered the second, lofting a 2–1 pitch off the left-field wall.

In twelve games against Detroit and St. Louis, the Red Sox hit just

.207 overall. But in eleven plate appearances with the bases loaded, the Red Sox were 6-for-9 with two doubles, two homers, two sacrifice flies, a run-scoring groundout, and nineteen RBI. The Sox squeezed more than 40% of their total run production in the ALCS and World Series out of just *nine* official at-bats.

Ortiz, a big part of those bases-loaded rallies, won World Series MVP on the strength of his own outsized stats. He reached base nineteen times in 25 plate appearances for an absurd .760 on-base percentage. Ortiz was such a presence in the lineup that Farrell was forced to sit Napoli (who had provided Gold Glove-caliber defense along with a fistful of clutch hits) for the three games in St. Louis and move Ortiz from DH to first base. Napoli didn't sulk, nor did his performance suffer; upon his return to the lineup at Fenway in Game 6, he contributed an RBI single.

But the most unlikely offensive contribution happened in the last of the fourth, when Sox shortstop Stephen Drew led off against Wacha. You'll rarely see a bigger mismatch—on paper. Wacha's 2013 postseason numbers entering the game: a 1.00 ERA in 27 innings with 28 strikeouts. Drew's 2013 postseason numbers entering the game: 4-for-50 with nineteen strikeouts. But Drew went all Ortiz on Wacha's first pitch and drove it into the bullpen, a blow that seemed to drain whatever starch St. Louis had left.

Lackey, the Sox starter, wasn't as sharp as he had been in outdueling Justin Verlander in Boston's 1–0 win over the Tigers in Game 3 of the ALCS. But with the Sox building a 6–0 lead, he didn't have to be. When he left, with the score 6–1 and the bases loaded in the seventh, the Fenway crowd gave him an ovation that would have been unimaginable in the dark days of September 2011. He and Jon Lester (2–0 in the World Series, with just one earned run, one walk, and fifteen strikeouts in 15⅓ innings) had been two of the primary targets of fans' wrath during the collapse of the Terry Francona regime. But Farrell, their old pitching coach, had restored both confidence and accountability.

Junichi Tazawa stepped in to end the St. Louis threat in the seventh before handing the ball to rookie Brandon Workman, who worked a perfect eighth, before handing the ball to Koji Uehara in the ninth. He was perfect, too, of course. And after striking out Matt Carpenter to end it, Uehara leapt into the arms of David Ross.

A 34-year-old middle reliever converted to a closer, and a 36-year-old backup catcher. That was Boston's battery at the end.

It was harder to say which feat was more impressive: the way GM Ben Cherington had created the roster or the way Farrell had used it. Uehara, for instance. Of all the components of the 2013 Red Sox out-of-the-blue title run, Uehara's emergence as baseball's best closer was the out-of-the-bluest. He was one of seven midlevel free agents added to a 93-loss team the previous winter. And although he had put up some eye-popping numbers as a setup man with the Rangers in 2012—a 1.75 ERA, with just three walks and 43 strikeouts in 36 innings—there was nothing in his background to suggest he could handle the pressure of closing. In fact, the numbers screamed the exact opposite: In three post-season appearances, Uehara had allowed five earned runs, including three homers, in just 2⅓ innings.

But Uehara was pressed into service when the Red Sox lost not one closer but two—Joel Hanrahan and Andrew Baily—by the All-Star break. This on a team whose best starter, Clay Buchholz, had gone on the shelf after a 9–0 start—and this during a season in which *Sports Illustrated* had forecasted a 77–85 record and another last-place finish. Red Sox Return to Winning Formula, if Not Winning Ways, the headline read.

Well, SI was half right.

The Uehara deal was part of an organization-wide *mea culpa*. Under Cherington, the Red Sox steered away from the kind of splashy signings (Carl Crawford, Adrian Gonzalez) designed, among other things, to perpetuate a contrived sellout streak at Fenway Park that had begun in 2003. On April 10, 2013, with the Baltimore Orioles in town, the streak quietly ended, ridding the organization of another albatross.

The reboot worked better than anyone could have expected. Gradually, the energy returned to Fenway Park, until it reached a new peak. Six-and-a-half months after the Sox failed to sell out Fenway for the first time in a decade, they commanded the highest scalpers' prices in the park's 102-year history, for the climactic game of the World Series.

With their grinding hitters and efficient pitchers, the 2013 Red Sox weren't as flashy or as talented as the '04 or '07 teams, each of which had won the World Series in a sweep. But that turned out to be a hidden blessing. By taking six games to finish the job, the 2013 Red Sox became the first Boston team since 1918 to share the final out of the World Series with the home folks.

31

Celtics 100, 76ers 96
April 19, 1968

The Celtics got their first Game 7 road victory while avenging the previous year's Eastern Division Finals loss to the Philadelphia 76ers, who had ended Boston's eight-year reign as NBA champions

T he celebration was laced with schadenfreude. The Philadelphia 76ers had just won the NBA Eastern Division Finals. And for the first time in eleven years the Boston Celtics had *not* won the NBA Eastern Division Finals. Further, it was no fluke. Philadelphia had finished eight games ahead of Boston in the 1966–67 season. Then the 76ers needed just five games to brush the Celtics aside in the playoffs, closing with a 140–116 blowout. Best of all from the home crowd's perspective, native son Wilt Chamberlain had out-Russelled Bill Russell. Chamberlain scored 29 points to Russell's four. He also had 36 rebounds. But the most telling stat was his thirteen assists. In this series Chamberlain had proved that he could be a team player. He hadn't led Philadelphia in scoring in any of the five games, and his ball distribution had provided the kind of balance that could turn Red Auerbach green.

It was as humbling an end to the Celtics' dominance as any Bostonian could have imagined. The crowd at Convention Hall savored the occasion by lighting up cigars en masse, making a mockery of Auerbach's signature celebration. They also began a chant: "Boston is dead!"

It sure seemed that way. The 76ers went on to beat the Warriors for the 1967 NBA championship and brought back essentially the same team the next season. The Celtics didn't change much either. Guard K.C. Jones retired—the first Boston player since 1958 to end his career as anything other than an NBA champion. But Russell remained, as did shooting guard Sam Jones. Those two—the only players to have been along for the entire eight-year reign—were in their mid-thirties. Russell was saddled with the added burden of being the Celtics' coach as well as their center. Auerbach had stepped down as coach after the '66 title. It was natural to deduce that the loss of his leadership had contributed to Boston's decline.

Even the Celtics' home court seemed like a musty relic. Boston Garden was built in 1928. Meanwhile, the Celtics' two greatest rivals, the 76ers and the Lakers, unveiled new state-of-the-art arenas for the 1967–68 season—the Spectrum and the Forum, respectively. It all added up to a palpable sense that the NBA's future was in Philadelphia and LA, and that its past was buried in Boston.

So it was a shock to the basketball world when the Celtics reclaimed the NBA title in 1968—and they did so by winning Game 7 of the Eastern Division Finals at the Spectrum and Game 6 of the NBA Finals at the Forum.

The Game 7 victory over the Sixers was particularly stunning—not to mention satisfying. There was little indication that it was coming. Once again, Philadelphia had finished eight games ahead of Boston in the East. Once again, Philadelphia had taken a 3–1 lead in the series. They had everything going for them. They had Chamberlain. They had Alex Hannum, the only coach to have beaten Boston in the playoffs since 1957. (Hannum had also coached the 1958 St. Louis Hawks team that had beaten Boston.) They also had history on their side. No NBA team had ever blown a 3–1 series lead.

But Boston still had Bill Russell. And he had found his coaching voice, which was softer than Auerbach's. His low-key approach helped the Celtics relax, focus, and win Game 5 at the Spectrum and Game 6 at the Garden to even the series at 3–3. That forced an improbable Game 7 back at the Spectrum. It was the first Game 7 that Boston had ever played on the road.

Again Russell tried to downplay the difficulty. "Before the game we were loose in our dressing room," he said later. "We just sat around and told jokes. You can't get up and give a pep talk because it would make things more tense."

Instead, all the tension ran through Chamberlain and the heavily favored 76ers. They didn't respond well. Philadelphia shot just 29% in the first half as the Celtics took a 46–40 lead. In the second half, Russell limited Chamberlain to just two points (he had only fourteen for the game) and a single field goal attempt. And although Russell had just twelve points himself, he picked his spots. When the Sixers rallied to take an 81–79 lead with 8½ minutes left, Russell quieted the crowd with a hook shot to tie it. He also hit a late free throw to give the Celtics a three-point lead.

And then, fittingly, it was his defense that iced it. With Boston leading 98–95 and the shot clock off, Philadelphia's Chet Walker drove for a layup that would have cut the deficit to one. Instead Russell recorded his tenth block of the game. When Hal Greer missed the put-back, Russell grabbed his 26th rebound. Knowing that the 76ers had to foul, he quickly got the ball to Jones, an 80% free-throw shooter. Jones sank the pair (he and fellow veteran John Havlicek were a combined 11-of-11 from the line) to put it away.

Afterward Russell received the highest compliment imaginable. Said Auerbach, "You want two reasons why we beat Philly? Russell the player and Russell the coach."

After leading the Celtics over the Lakers in the NBA Finals (see Game No. 45), Russell returned for one more season—and his greatest challenge yet (see games 48 and 14).

30

Red Sox 7, Reds 6, 12 innings
October 21, 1975

During the 86-year championship drought from 1918 to 2004, Carlton Fisk's Game 6 pole dance in the 1975 World Series was the Red Sox' apogee

I t was *not* a no-doubter. How could it have been? After four hours of emotional flux—of one what-the-flux moment after another—how could Game 6 of the 1975 World Series have ended any way other than this? The home team down three games to two, batting in extra innings, the score tied, the ball launched with home-run distance right down the leftfield line, a fair ball curving toward the foul pole....

The tension of this moment had been building for days. The Red Sox had lost Game 5 to the Reds on a Thursday night in Cincinnati. They didn't play again until the following Tuesday night, at Fenway, because of a biblical New England storm. (Some perspective: The 2004 Red Sox' historic comeback against the Yankees, all four games, took less time than the delay between games 5 and 6 of the 1975 World Series.)

The rain allowed Red Sox manager Darrell Johnson to use staff ace Luis Tiant for a third World Series start, on full rest. And when Fred Lynn, Boston's combination RoY and MVP, staked El Tiante to a 3–0 lead with a first-inning homer, Sox fans could exhale for the first time in almost a week.

But inning by inning the cottonmouth returned. Boston left the bases loaded in the third. They failed to score after putting runners on second and third with one out in the fourth. Cincinnati made them pay by tying it in the fifth. Then the Reds took the lead with two runs in the seventh and chased Tiant (*Why is he still in there when there's a full staff available?*) with Caesar Geronimo's leadoff homer in the eighth.

And then the real turbulence began. In the last of the eighth, pinch hitter Bernie Carbo's two-out, two-on, 2-and-2 liner into the center-field bleachers squared the score. By the last of the ninth the Red Sox had morphed from almost certain losers into seemingly sure winners. Bases loaded, no outs. Then: *No! No! No!* At least that's what third-base coach Don Zimmer claimed he yelled at Denny Doyle as Doyle tagged up on Lynn's pop fly down the left-field line. But Doyle heard *Go! Go! Go!* And he went. George Foster made the catch and threw Doyle out at the plate.

In the top of the eleventh it was Cincinnati's turn to see the potential winning rally die with a shocking double play. With one out and the speedy Ken Griffey Sr. at first, Reds second baseman Joe Morgan launched a drive toward the low wall in deep right. Dwight Evans turned, sprinted toward the wall, and blindly stuck out his gloved left hand. The ball landed in the webbing. Griffey, who ran on the play, was doubled off first. And then in the top of the twelfth, there was Sox righty Rick Wise, a starter who had won a career-high nineteen games that season, wriggling out of a two-on-and-one-out jam, striking out Geronimo to end yet another threat.

And now Carlton Fisk was leading off the last of the twelfth against Pat Darcy, who had retired six straight. Fisk had struggled a bit in Cincinnati, in games 3, 4, and 5. After homering in his first at-bat at Riverfront Stadium, he had gone 2-for-11 with three strikeouts and a rally-killing double play.

When Game 6 was washed out in its original time slot on Saturday afternoon, Fisk was the only Sox player to stick around Fenway for BP. Maybe he had found his swing again.

The first pitch from Darcy was a ball. The next one was a meatball. Fisk jumped all over it and drove the ball to deep left, toward the foul pole and the climax that this game deserved. The ball was fair—and so was the ending.

Although Fisk's heroics allowed the Red Sox to walk off—dance off, actually—with the win, the drama wasn't over. The next night, in Game 7, Boston again jumped to a three-run lead. Again the Reds tied it. And again Darrell Johnson made a curious move with his pitching staff. In Game 6 he'd stuck with the veteran, Tiant, a little too long. In Game 7 he entrusted the Sox season to a rookie, Jim Burton, with the game still tied in the ninth. Morgan's two-out bloop single scored Griffey with the go-ahead run. No dancing this time; when Carl Yastrzemski flied to center to end it, Fisk was in the on-deck circle.

29

Celtics 110, 76ers 109
April 15, 1965

"Havlicek stole the ball!"

B ill Russell played ten Game 7s in his NBA career and won them all. Eight were at home. This has left the impression that Russell was an infallible big-game player, and that Boston Garden—with its parquet floor and the prison ward that passed for the visitors' locker room and all manner of unseen leprechauns poised to tip the ball in the Celtics' direction—was a sort of supernatural ally.

Which was nonsense, of course.

Take perhaps the most famous Game 7 win in Celtics history, in the 1965 NBA Eastern Division Finals. It was immortalized in Johnny Most's euphoric croak: "Havlicek stole the ball!" But if not for an architectural quirk at Boston Garden and a Bill Russell blunder, Havlicek wouldn't have needed to steal the ball in the first place.

Boston, six-time defending NBA champions, had cruised to first place in the East with a 62–18 record. That gave them home-court advantage over the Philadelphia 76ers, a .500 team during the regular season—but one that had improved its odds immeasurably by acquiring Wilt Chamberlain from the Warriors in mid-January.

Chamberlain's reputation, like Russell's, has been grossly oversimplified. Chamberlain was en route to his sixth straight scoring title that season, but he had never won a championship. A common theory held that Chamberlain's gravity was such that he upset the orbit of any other star who came near him. Philadelphia coach Dolph Schayes, no Chamberlain fan in the past, vowed to change that. "I expect him to play differently for me," Schayes said. "I want him to play more defense, get the ball off the boards, lead the fast break. Hustle."

Chamberlain did. When the Sixers upset Oscar Robertson, Jerry Lucas, and the Cincinnati Royals in the first round, Chamberlain wasn't even Philadelphia's leading scorer. Smooth-shooting guard Hal Greer was. And while Chamberlain was an efficient offensive machine in the Eastern Division Finals—he averaged 30 points a game and hit exactly that number four times—it was Greer who drove the Celtics to distraction. He averaged 24 points per game as Boston and Philadelphia split the first six games. Two of those points came on one of the most dramatic hoops in NBA history—a 35-foot prayer with one second left in Game 4 to force overtime, in a game that the 76ers eventually won.

Greer was such a force that Celtics guard K.C. Jones abandoned any thought of playing help defense in Game 7. He focused on containing Greer at all costs. And he largely succeeded; Greer got just twelve points. And with the raucous Boston Garden crowd behind them, the Celtics raced to a 35–17 first-quarter lead.

But Philadelphia closed the quarter with a 9–0 run, and by halftime they were ahead. Even more disconcerting for the home folks, the 76ers had mounted their comeback in a very Celtics-like way. It wasn't Chamberlain or Greer who was killing them—it was Philadelphia's sixth man, forward Dave Gambee, who had scored nineteen first-half points.

But the Celtics had invented the sixth man concept, and they still had the league's best: John Havlicek. After a cold start, Havlicek scored fifteen of his 26 points in the third quarter as the Celtics countered the Philadelphia comeback. The Boston lead was eight at the end of three quarters, and it still stood at seven with just under two minutes remaining.

Then two Celtics stars almost blew it. Boston had a three-point lead, and Sam Jones, who had scored a game-high 37 points, had the ball as the clock ticked down under ten seconds. One more hoop would ice it. And even if Jones missed, it would be almost impossible for Philadelphia to secure the rebound, advance the ball, score, get the ball back, and score again. But Jones let the 24-second clock expire before getting a shot off. After the stoppage, Philadelphia lobbed the ball to Chamberlain, who scored on an uncontested dunk. Suddenly it was a one-point game with five seconds left.

Bill Russell took charge. He would inbound the ball from under the Boston basket. He trusted no one else with the responsibility. Besides, his height gave him the best chance of getting the ball over the Philadelphia defenders. But it also put him perilously close to the guy wires that extended from the Garden balcony to the bottom of the backboard, just ten feet above the floor. The wires were one of the Boston Garden's tumbledown touches that drove Celtics opponents crazy. But in this case the Garden handed the Celtics' opponent an almost inconceivably lucky break. On Russell's throw-in the ball hit a guy wire and dropped straight down. At first the Celtics thought the ruling would be a dead ball and a do-over.

But no. It was a violation. 76ers ball. Under the Celtics basket. With five full seconds left. And multiple offensive options.

Greer took the ball under the basket and prepared to inbound it. Would he try an alley-oop to Chamberlain? If so, should the Celtics foul and send Chamberlain, a notoriously poor free-throw shooter, to the line? Or would Philadelphia run a screen to try to get the ball back in the hands of Greer, who had already proved once that he could be a cold-blooded jump shooter with the game on the line?

As Greer held the ball out of bounds, everyone in the Garden was anxiously mulling these various scenarios—including John Havlicek. Havlicek was guarding forward Chet Walker on the perimeter. With 24 points on the night, Walker was yet another offensive weapon to account for.

Havlicek, who had his back to Greer, knew that Philadelphia had five seconds to inbound. He counted the time in his head. When the play still hadn't started at the three-second mark, Havlicek stole a glance at Greer and read his intentions. "I had both the man passing in and Walker pretty much in sight," Havlicek said later. "So now I sense that something fast is going to happen. And it does."

With the play designed for the ball to come back to him, Greer tried to make a perfect lob pass for Walker to catch and return. "I didn't put enough on the ball," Greer said later. Having anticipated the pass, Havlicek had already started moving toward the spot. And really, he didn't steal the ball per se; he batted the pass away like a defensive back. Sam Jones grabbed the ball and dribbled the other way as Most rasped, "It's all over!"

That's the description that lingers. But afterward an immensely relieved Bill Russell offered a pretty good alternative. "You might very well say that this game went right down to the wire," Russell said. "And it won't sound so corny in this instance, will it?"

There were no down-to-the-wire games in the 1965 NBA Finals. The Garden's maintenance crew moved the guy wires out of the way, and the Celtics breezed by the Lakers in five.

28

Red Sox 3, Pirates 0
October 13, 1903

This victory gave the Red Sox the first World Series title in history

When the Red Sox gathered at Macon, Georgia for spring training at the start of their third season, they didn't expect to play in the World Series that October. No team did; the World Series didn't exist yet. It wasn't until late that summer, when the Red Sox were running away with the American League and the Pittsburgh Pirates were idling atop the National League, that Pirates owner Barney Dreyfuss got in touch with Red Sox owner Henry Killilea and said, in effect, *Care to make it interesting?* So if that first World Series felt thrown-together, that's because it was.

Killilea had far less enthusiasm for the concept than Dreyfuss did. An absentee owner with a law practice in Milwaukee, Killilea haggled with his players over how to divide Boston's share of the gate receipts. He conducted negotiations through Red Sox business manager Joseph Smart via the relatively new (and cumbersome) technology of long-distance telephone. And he didn't agree to terms with his own team until less than a week before the series was supposed to start, on October 1.

The protracted negotiations seemed to undermine the Sox' enthusiasm. The day before Game 1, when informed that he would be the starter, Boston's ace pitcher, Cy Young, told reporters, "I will try to be there."

Young was physically present at Boston's Huntington Avenue Grounds the next day, but it's reasonable to wonder whether he and his teammates had mentally committed to playing a postseason series. Further, they had to play in a chaotic atmosphere, as a crowd of 16,000—

some 7,000 beyond the seating capacity—showed up. The overflow spilled across the spacious outfield (the fence in dead center was 530 feet from home plate), where ropes separated fans from the players—if just barely. Because of the SRO crowds in both Boston and Pittsburgh, the 1903 World Series had a unique ground rule: Any ball hit beyond the ropes but short of the fence was a triple. As Boston shortstop Freddy Parent said decades later of the make-it-up-as-we-go-along approach, "What a way to run a World Series!"

All those distractions added up to a disastrous opening inning for the Red Sox. The Pirates scored four runs on three hits, a walk, and three errors. Behind right-hander Deacon Phillippe, Pittsburgh coasted to a 7–3 win. And so, along with his many lifetime accolades, Cy Young has the ignominious distinction of being the losing pitcher in the first World Series game ever played.

The 1903 World Series had a best-of-nine format. The first three games were in Boston and the next four in Pittsburgh. The last two, if necessary, would be played "at Boston or some other city mutually agreed upon." The way things started, the Red Sox looked like they would have been better off playing *all* the games in some other city. They dropped two of three at home and then lost Game 4, at Pittsburgh's Exposition Park, to fall into a 3–1 hole.

But that's when the Pirates' lack of pitching depth caught up with them. During the regular season, Pittsburgh had three solid starters: Phillippe, 25-game winner Sam Leever, and sixteen-game winner Ed Doheny. But by the time the World Series began, Doheny had left the team because of mental-health issues ("DOHENY INSANE," screamed one headline). He never pitched again. In addition, Leever had developed a sore pitching shoulder, an injury that he'd aggravated in a trap-shooting competition. He started Game 2, but any hope that he might have re-gained his effectiveness vanished with his first pitch, which Boston's Patsy Dougherty blasted for the first postseason home run in Red Sox history. Leever lasted just an inning in that game, a 3–0 Boston win.

Thanks to a travel day, a rainout, and the shorter rest required in those days, Phillippe, threw complete-game victories in games 1, 3, and 4. But with Phillippe unavailable for games 5 and 6, the Red Sox pounced, scoring seventeen runs off of the Pirates' spare parts. That was more than enough support for Cy Young and number-two starter Bill Dinneen, respectively. A rainout before Game 7 bought an extra day of rest for

Phillippe—but also for Young. With Phillippe clearly wearing down, the Red Sox put up four early runs and went on to win 7–3.

Although there hadn't been a single lead change in any of the games, it had been a dramatic series nonetheless. The Red Sox had rallied from a 3–1 deficit to take a 4–3 lead back to Boston.

When rain pushed Game 8 back a day, Pittsburgh player/manager Fred Clarke decided to bring back Phillippe for a fifth start, on two days' rest. Boston's player/manager, third baseman Jimmy Collins, countered with Dinneen. The Red Sox now showed a sense of urgency that they had lacked when the series started. This was most apparent in the fourth inning. In the top half, Pittsburgh third baseman Tommy Leach worked a two-out walk for the Pirates' first baserunner. Up next was future Hall of Famer Honus Wagner.

With his performance through the first seven games, Wagner had become an unwitting archetype: the big-time player who comes up small in the postseason. After leading the National League with a .355 average during the regular season, he had morphed into A-Rod in flannel during the World Series. He was mired in an 0-for-11 slump when he stepped into the box at that critical moment, and was just 5-for-24 in the series. Then he caught the kind of break that can sometimes get a good hitter going. With Leach running, Parent, the Sox shortstop, started toward second. Wagner hit a routine grounder to short, but when Parent tried to backtrack he slipped on the wet infield. The ball leaked through to left and Leach continued to third.

The Pirates were an aggressive team that liked to run. In Game 1, under similar circumstances, Pittsburgh had immediately taken control of the game by scoring four runs with two outs in the first inning. In that inning alone, the Pirates running game had pressured Lou Criger, Boston's normally reliable catcher, into a pair of errors and made him look as uncomfortable as "a fur overcoat in July," according to the *Globe*.

Now, in Game 8, Pittsburgh tried to make Criger sweat again. Wagner, who'd led the team with 46 stolen bases, followed Leach's lead and took off for second. Criger faked a throw. Leach, whether attempting the back half of a double steal or just taking an aggressive lead, strayed off third. Criger turned and made a snap throw to Collins, who returned it to Criger, who tagged Leach out at home.

Having quashed a Pittsburgh threat in the top half of the fourth, the Red Sox immediately mounted one of their own in the last half. Boston's cleanup hitter, Buck Freeman, started it with one of those ground-rule triples past the ropes. Parent reached on an error when Pirates catcher Ed Phelps mishandled his bunt, with Freeman holding third. Freeman held third again as first baseman Candy LaChance bunted Parent to second. Then Sox second baseman Hobe Ferris singled to center to drive in two runs, which was one more than Dinneen needed.

It was almost unfair. The Pirates were holding onto their last hope with Deacon Phillippe's fraying right arm. Meanwhile, the Red Sox had 21-game winner Bill Dinneen on the mound, with Cy Young warming up just in case.

Young wasn't needed. Dinneen allowed just four hits, and retired the last seven in order. Honus Wagner struck out to end it.

T. H. Murnane, the *Globe*'s baseball editor and the Peter Gammons of the dead-ball era, called the game "a thrilling climax to the greatest sporting event ever known in this country." For all its flaws, the first Fall Classic had been a classic after all.

The Red Sox repeated as American League champions but not as World Series champions because the National League champion New York Giants refused to play them. By the time the Red Sox won the AL pennant again, in 1912 (see Game No. 12), they had a permanent new home, Fenway Park, and the World Series had become a permanent fixture.

27

Celtics 111, 76ers 109
April 29, 1981

Down 3–1 in the Eastern Conference Finals and 109–103 with
90 seconds left in Game 5, the Celtics somehow stayed alive

One reason that Magic Johnson's Lakers won five NBA championships in the '80s to three for Larry Bird's Celtics was that
Boston played in the tougher conference. Sure, the Sonics,
Rockets, Suns, and Jazz all had their moments. But with the possible
exception of the 1985–86 season (when the Hakeem Olajuwon/Ralph
Sampson Rockets took out the Lakers), the second-best team in the East
was better than the second-best team in the West throughout the
decade. After reaching their peak in 1986, with perhaps the greatest
team in NBA history, Bird's Celtics spent the back end of the '80s brawl-
ing with the Bad Boy Detroit Pistons, with Michael Jordan's Bulls calling
for next. And this was after Boston had spent the first seven seasons of
Bird's career contending with a Dr. J. 76ers team that averaged 58 wins
a year.

Here's how evenly matched that early-'80s Boston–Philadelphia
rivalry was: The Celtics entered the finale of the 1980–81 regular season
with a record of 61–20 ... and needed a 98–94 victory over a 62–19
Sixers team at Boston Garden just to win the East. (The teams had split
the season series and had the same record in the Eastern Conference,
so Boston got the top seed because of a better Atlantic Division record.)

Not that that guaranteed anything. A year earlier, the third-seeded
Sixers had bounced the top-seeded Celtics in five games before losing
to the Lakers (behind a tour de force performance from Johnson, the
MVP) in the Finals.

And it looked like more of the same in the 1981 Eastern Conference Finals. Philadelphia not only won three of the first four again, but they even won them in the same order. And when the 76ers built a ten-point halftime lead in Game 5 at the Garden, the Celtics were on the brink of another premature summer.

Boston fought back in the second half, thanks to a resolute effort from Bird (32 points, eleven rebounds, five assists) on a night when he lacked his shooting touch. But he needed help. And in the last 90 seconds he got plenty.

With Philadelphia up 109–103, Sixers rookie guard Andrew Toney tried to ice the game. Toney, who would prove to be such a matchup nightmare against the Celtics that he would earn the nickname "The Boston Strangler," brought an added dimension to a Philadelphia offense that already had the versatile Julius Erving, center Darryl Dawkins, forward Bobby Jones, and guard Lionel Hollins. Toney had earned his playoff bona fides in his first-ever postseason game. He drove the parquet lane at Boston Garden and sank a pair of free throws with two seconds left to turn a potential one-point Sixers loss into a one-point win. He followed up with 35 points in Game 2. If Philadelphia's precocious rookie scored again here, the Celtics would be finished.

But center Robert Parish, in his first season with the Celtics, got a hand on Toney's shot and triggered a fast break the other way. Boston guard Tiny Archibald finished with a slick move on Toney for the field goal plus one. That five-point swing saved the season.

Parish blocked Toney again on the next possession ("I didn't see him coming," Toney said), which turned into Bird's final hoop of the night to make it a one-point game with 47 seconds left.

With the Garden crowd now in full roar, Philadelphia had trouble even getting a shot attempt. Bird picked up an errant Erving pass and tried to convert it into the go-ahead hoop. He missed, but M.L. Carr, a guard, grabbed the rebound and was fouled. Carr sank both free throws (Boston was 35-of-39 from the line) to put the Celtics ahead. Carr then grabbed a defensive rebound on Philadelphia's next possession to bookend his huge offensive board. He sank another free throw to complete a miraculous 8–0 run over the last 80 seconds. Said the Celtics' gangly rookie Kevin McHale, who contributed a highly efficient twelve points, "It's like we were on death row and walking to the electric chair and they [told us we] have a couple more days left."

McHale's analogy was appropriate. In a couple of days the Celtics faced a must-win game at the Spectrum, where they had lost eleven straight (see Game No. 26).

26

Celtics 100, 76ers 98
May 1, 1981

The Celtics overcame a seventeen-point deficit to end an
eleven-game losing streak at Philadelphia's Spectrum
and even the Eastern Conference Finals at three games each

Having forced Game 6 in the 1981 Eastern Conference Finals
(see Game No. 27), the Celtics were now forced to do something that they hadn't done since Larry Bird was at Indiana
State: win at the Spectrum. Boston had lost eleven straight times in
Philadelphia, dating back to January 1979. Their Spectrum streak covered the spectrum. Some losses were blowouts, including a 32-point
defeat in their final visit of the 1980–81 regular season. Some were close,
including Game 4, just five days earlier. The Celtics had come within
an ill-advised Tiny Archibald pass of forcing overtime after trailing by
eighteen in the third quarter. And although there's no such thing as
a moral victory in the NBA—certainly not in the playoffs—the Game 4
comeback proved to be good practice. Because early in the second quarter of Game 6, the Celtics faced a seventeen-point deficit. But they
had enough sense not to try to get it all back at once. As Archibald said
later, "There are no seventeen-point plays in basketball."

Still, when Boston had trimmed just two points from the Philly
lead a full quarter later, a sense of urgency took hold. Larry Bird (just
2-for-10 in the first half) scored eleven points in the third quarter to
help bring Boston to within 73–70. Just as important, the Celtics defense forced eleven Philadelphia turnovers in the quarter. Forward
Cedric Maxwell was particularly effective, hounding Julius Erving into
a dreadful 5-of-17 performance. But perhaps the surest sign that the
Celtics were no longer intimidated by the Spectrum's hostile atmos-

phere was when Maxwell shoved an abusive Sixers fan during Boston's third-quarter rally.

But Philadelphia didn't fold, either. Although the Celtics caught the 76ers early in the fourth, tying the game at 80 on a three-point play from Bird, they had trouble overtaking them. The final quarter was a twelve-minute tension headache. There were eight lead changes in a little more than five minutes. The first came when Bird put Boston up 84–83 on a jumper with 7:34 remaining; the eighth came on a pair of Archibald free throws that made it 96–95 with 2:16 left.

And it wasn't as if the Celtics simply ran out the clock after that. In fact, the last two minutes might have been the toughest. When center Robert Parish (21 points, ten rebounds) fouled out at the 1:44 mark, Celtics coach Bill Fitch was forced to rely on a rookie, Kevin McHale, to preserve the lead. McHale responded with two key stops, altering a drive from Philadelphia's leading scorer, Darryl Dawkins, with 1:27 left and blocking a shot from Celtics killer Andrew Toney with just thirteen seconds remaining. In between, Bird deflated the Sixers with a "shooter's touch" bouncer reminiscent of Don Nelson's high-hopper at the LA Forum in 1969 (see Game No. 14) to make it a three-point game. But a bucket and a steal by Toney gave the 76ers one last shot at the lead—and McHale rejected it. Two free throws from Maxwell sealed one of the signature wins of the original Big Three era. Said McHale, "We may not have the eleven most flamboyant players in the league, but we have the eleven most determined players."

Games 4, 5, and 6 of the series had each come down to the final seconds. So did Game 7 (see Game No. 25).

25

Celtics 91, 76ers 90
May 3, 1981

For the third straight time, the Celtics overcame a double-digit deficit in an elimination game. And this Game 7 victory sent the original Big Three to the NBA Finals for the first time

This was the de facto NBA championship game. Ostensibly, Game 7 of the 1981 Eastern Conference Finals would determine only whether the Boston Celtics or Philadelphia 76ers advanced to the NBA Finals. But with the 40–42 Houston Rockets having won the Western Conference Finals by besting—or at least not being worse than—another 40–42 team, the Kansas City Kings, the NBA's imbalance of power was obvious. Even some of the Celtics acknowledged it. "The winner of this series will win the championship," forward Cedric Maxwell said before Game 7 with Philadelphia at Boston Garden. "I don't think there's any doubt about that."

Nor was there any doubt that Game 7 with Philadelphia would be unbearably close. There was no separation between the Celtics and Sixers. Each had finished 62–20 overall, 42–16 in the Eastern Conference. They had split six games in the regular season and six more in the postseason.

Nor were there any secrets. These teams knew each other so well that the games followed a predictable pattern. Philadelphia, with Julius Erving unleashing a variety of scoops and swoops, would start fast. In games 4, 5, and 6, the Sixers had sprinted to leads of eighteen, ten, and seventeen points, respectively.

Then, as the Sixers' legs tired, the Celtics would constrict their free-flowing offense. As Boston hounded Philadelphia's shooters and pounded the boards, the 76ers' lead would melt as quickly as a springtime snowfall. Then it was simply a matter of which team made more plays in the fourth quarter. In Game 4, the 76ers had. In games 5 and 6, the Celtics had (see games 27 and 26). The margin in each of those three games was two points.

Game 7 was closer still.

To no one's surprise, Philadelphia got the jump. The 76ers shot 64% in the first quarter, their percentage boosted by a couple of thunderous dunks by Darryl Dawkins, who had ten points in the quarter. The Philadelphia lead again hit double digits, at 47–36, with 4:42 left in the half, and at 67–56 with 7:18 left in the third.

To no one's surprise, the Celtics answered. Boston trimmed the lead to 75–71 by the end of the third and scored the first six points of the fourth to take their first lead since the opening minutes.

That's when Dr. J. responded. Erving, like Bird, led his team with 23 points. Ten of them came in a 14–5 run, capped by a reverse put-back, which made it 89–82, Philadelphia, with just 5:23 remaining.

The Sixers didn't get another field goal the rest of the way. The Celtics smothered them, recording two blocks and four steals (three by Bird) down the stretch. And while Boston's offense struggled—the Celtics shot just 38.2%, worse than any performance they had submitted during the regular season—they manufactured just enough points to get the job done. It was 89–89 with 1:10 remaining when Dawkins missed badly amid a slam dance in the paint. (Afterward Sixers coach Billy Cunningham openly lamented the lack of calls down the stretch.) Bird grabbed the rebound and took it all the way for a pull-up, using the glass on a twelve-footer for what turned out to be the game-winner.

Or at least that was the bucket that gave the Celtics enough points to come out ahead. But really the Celtics won with an accumulation of stops. One went almost unnoticed in the intense heat of the final moments. With 34 seconds left the Celtics had the ball and a chance to salt the game away. But Lionel Hollins poked the ball away from Celtics guard Gerald Henderson. Philadelphia's Maurice Cheeks grabbed the loose ball, igniting a 3-on-1 break. Henderson, attempting to atone for his error, retreated and stood his ground under the Boston basket as Cheeks charged through him. The call went against Henderson—but the contact kept the shot from dropping. Cheeks then front-rimmed the first free throw before hitting the second for the final margin. The game ended when Bobby Jones's attempted lob to Erving on a throw-in caromed off the backboard, as the noise threatened to rupture Boston Garden like an overfilled balloon.

Maxwell summed up the game and the series: "They have more physical talent than we do and their transition game is better than ours. We just executed a little better down the stretch."

Houston proved to be a tougher opponent than anticipated, extending the NBA Finals to six games. But the Celtics lived up to Maxwell's prediction and won their fourteenth championship. And while it was the first title for the original Big Three, it was Maxwell himself (17.7 points per game, 9.5 rebounds, 2.8 assists) who was named MVP.

24

Patriots 24, Steelers 17
January 27, 2002

An all-around effort from Troy Brown, and Drew Bledsoe's
last hurrah as a Patriot, sent New England to the Super Bowl

Tuck *this.* The prevailing opinion across Football America was that the Patriots didn't belong in the AFC Championship Game. Playing at home, in a snowstorm, they'd nevertheless needed a liberal interpretation of an arcane NFL statute (the Tuck Rule) to beat the Raiders in the divisional round (see Game No. 9). Now they were playing on the road against the top-seeded Pittsburgh Steelers, a team that had blasted the defending Super Bowl champion Baltimore Ravens 27–10 in the divisional round. Las Vegas put the line at ten points—the same as when Pittsburgh had hosted the 1–13 Detroit Lions the month before.

Coach Bill Belichick duly noted this.

That hardly made Belichick unique. Exploiting bulletin-board material had been a coaching staple for decades. (Besides, the yappy Steelers made this portion of the job easy.) What set Belichick apart was his alchemical ability to wring more from a collection of players than the sum of their skills. Everyone on the roster was important—but none more than the others. Belichick had made that clear during the season. He'd stuck with backup quarterback Tom Brady, even when the incumbent starter—franchise QB Drew Bledsoe—recovered from a devastating hit he'd suffered against the Jets' Mo Lewis in week two.

And when Brady suffered an ankle injury in the second quarter of the AFC Championship Game, Belichick didn't hesitate to switch back. "We were better with a healthy Drew Bledsoe," Belichick said later, "not knowing where Tom was with his injury."

This made a great storyline. Bledsoe completed his first three throws, including an eleven-yard touchdown pass to David Patten to give the Patriots a 14–3 halftime lead. But it wasn't Bledsoe who won the game. If any individual distinguished himself among New England's group of unheralded gamers, it was Troy Brown. He led the receivers with eight catches for 121 yards. He put the Patriots ahead by returning a punt 55 yards for a touchdown in the first quarter. And, serving on another special-teams unit, Brown had a key role in the most important play of the game. With the Patriots still leading 14–3, Pittsburgh had driven to the New England seventeen-yard line early in the third quarter. Pittsburgh kicker Kris Brown attempted a 34-yard field goal that would have made it a one-possession game. But Patriots defensive lineman Brandon Mitchell blocked the kick. Troy Brown scooped the ball up on the run. As he was being tackled at midfield, Brown pitched to Antwan Harris, who took it 49 yards to the end zone.

It was a ten-point swing in fifteen seconds.

The defense did the rest. The game plan centered on stopping Pittsburgh's top-rated running game. Mission accomplished. The Steelers gained just 58 yards rushing, with featured back Jerome Bettis averaging less than a yard a carry (eight yards on nine attempts). That put the game in the hands of Pittsburgh's erratic quarterback, Kordell Stewart. And although he led a pair of third-quarter touchdown drives to get the Steelers close, he also threw a pair of fourth-quarter interceptions. After the second one, which came just before the two-minute warning, the Patriots ran out the clock.

In his final play as a member of the Patriots, Bledsoe took a knee. Then he tucked the game ball safely away. No need for a review this time.

The upset did little to elevate the Patriots' status. The following week, in Super Bowl XXXVI, they were fourteen-point underdogs against the Rams. And that played right into their hands (see Game No. 1).

23

Celtics 95, Lakers 93
April 28, 1966

The Celtics hung on—barely—in Game 7 of the 1966 NBA Finals
to send Red Auerbach into retirement from coaching with his eighth
straight championship

T he further the Bill Russell Era recedes into history, the greater
the tendency to think of it in monolithic terms. It's as if those
replica early banners in the Garden rafters are prehistoric de-
posits left behind by a giant green glacier. It formed in 1956 and remained
intact for thirteen years, relentlessly scouring the NBA landscape. When
Russell retired in 1969, the glacier abruptly melted.

But to think of the Russell years in that way is to do each of those
thirteen individual teams a disservice. The Celtics of the '60s were moth-
ers of reinvention, performing at a high level year after year while adapting to a rapidly changing environment. Both the NBA and the USA were
studies in fluid dynamics at that time. The NBA expanded from eight
teams to fourteen during the decade and stretched its western boundary
from the Mississippi to the Pacific. Meanwhile, America was roiling with
social upheaval. And the two most divisive issues, the Vietnam War and
the civil rights movement, inevitably crossed over into sports. In 1966
Muhammad Ali risked his boxing career by declaring that he would
refuse to serve in the military if drafted. (As the case progressed through
the courts over the next few years, Russell would be one of the few athletes to publically support Ali's stance.)

Also in 1966, the Celtics advanced the cause of civil rights—even
if, from their perspective, they were simply acting in the best interests
of their team. In January Red Auerbach announced that he would retire
at season's end. In April, during the NBA Finals, Boston announced that

Russell would succeed him. The Celtics thus became the first major professional sports team in the US to choose a black head coach.

Russell, who would also continue as the team's center, chose not to dwell on the social implications of the move (at least not publicly). And he used a joke to deflect the question of how he would handle his dual role: "I'll be playing for a coach I love."

The day of the announcement, Russell was preoccupied with a more immediate challenge. "Right now we have to think about this year," he said. "And we haven't made a very good start in this series with Los Angeles."

No, they hadn't. In Game 1 of the NBA Finals, the Celtics had blown an eighteen-point lead and lost to the Lakers in overtime. In the process they had also lost home-court advantage. It was the latest obstacle in what was proving to be the most difficult title defense since the Celtics had begun their seven-year reign as NBA champions in 1959.

The troubles started in the regular season. With Wilt Chamberlain (acquired from the San Francisco Warriors the previous winter) aboard for the full year, the Philadelphia 76ers had ended the Celtics' nine-year run as Eastern Division champions. This meant, among other things, that the Celtics lacked a first-round bye for the first time in a decade. The scrappy Cincinnati Royals extended the Celtics to the full five games in the Eastern Division Semifinals, before Boston finally clinched with a 112–103 win at the Garden ... all while Wilt and the Sixers rested up for the Eastern Division Finals ... which the Celtics proceeded to win with surprising ease, bouncing Philadelphia in five. Even so, the graying Green had some extra miles on the odometer when they met the Lakers in the NBA Finals. It was a rematch from 1965—but the '66 Lakers were much stronger. Elgin Baylor, who had missed the '65 Finals because of a knee injury, was back. And even if he wasn't as explosive as he'd once been, he could still score; his 36 points in the Game 1 upset were proof enough of that. Meanwhile, Jerry West was as prolific as ever, and the Lakers had added another future Hall of Famer, rookie guard Gail Goodrich from UCLA.

But the Celtics were still the seven-time, defending NBA champions, and they played like it over the next three games. They blew the Lakers out by twenty points in Game 2 at the Garden and then won back-to-back games in LA to go up 3–1. Auerbach's retirement party, it appeared, would be a happy occasion.

But the Lakers were surly guests. Behind 41 points from Baylor and 31 from West, Los Angeles won Game 5 in Boston. Even more disturbing was the Lakers' Game 6 victory, in which LA unveiled the most balanced attack Boston had ever seen from them: 32 points from West, 28 from Goodrich, 25 from Baylor, and twenty from center Rudy LaRusso. "When somebody other than West or Baylor gives us a scoring lift like that," said LA coach Fred Schaus, "we're going to win."

On the other hand, when the Celtics clamped down on defense the way they were capable of, LA was going to lose. And that was Boston's mission in Game 7 at the Garden. ("Defense and dollars," Auerbach preached before the game.) The Celtics applied suffocating pressure from the opening tip, jumping to a 10–0 lead. The Lakers didn't get a field goal until more than four minutes into the game. It took them four more minutes to get another one. The Celtics harassed West (12-of-27), Baylor (6-of-22), Goodrich (2-of-9), and LaRusso (2-of-7) into a combined 22-of-65 from the floor on the night. Russell, who had been beaten to the hoop several times on Goodrich drives in Game 6, stood especially tall. He had 25 points, 32 rebounds, and an untallied number of blocks. (Blocks and steals didn't become official stats until 1973.)

The Boston lead peaked at nineteen in the third quarter. Behind West and Baylor, LA mounted a late run to cut the lead to eight. But a Russell dunk made it 95–85 with just 45 seconds left. The Garden crowd crowded the parquet floor, preparing to celebrate. Auerbach didn't even wait—he sparked his traditional cigar. But an 8–0 run by the Lakers almost made him choke on his stogie.

Part of the problem, according to John Havlicek, were the Celtics' own fans. Havlicek said that the court was slick with spilled drinks, which contributed directly to a pair of Boston turnovers. "I love the Boston fans," he said later, "but they've got to learn to keep their composure. We have to do it and so do they."

As the game ticked down to a tenser conclusion than anyone anticipated, Havlicek kept his composure long enough to receive a final pass from K.C. Jones to run out the clock—on the game and on Auerbach's coaching career. "I think he is the greatest basketball coach who ever lived," Russell said at the team's farewell dinner. "I even got to like him sometimes."

Russell's coaching career got off to a rough start as the 76ers routed the Celtics in the 1967 Eastern Division Finals, ending the Celtics streak of championships at eight. But Boston surprised everybody by regaining the title in 1968 (see games 45 and 31).

22

Bruins 4, Blues 3, OT
May 10, 1970

The Bruins' 29-year championship drought ended with
a classic Bobby Orr moment in overtime

S ports distort your sense of time, especially during the lean years.
One failed season blends into the next, until eventually the whole
experience of following a team becomes an undifferentiated funk.
(Just ask a Cubs fan.) You spend decades hoping for a moment. And
when at last that moment arrives, you want to freeze the frame as an
everlasting reminder. It serves as both an antidote to all those poisonous
years past, and a vaccination against the diseased seasons to come.

That's why Ray Lussier's image of Bobby Orr floating above the
Boston Garden ice at 5:10 p.m. on May 10, 1970, is the best sports pho-
tograph ever taken. It's the ultimate freeze frame. Orr is suspended in
space; the moment is suspended in time. It is the precise instant of
change. When Orr had begun his takeoff, the Bruins hadn't won a title
since 1941. When he landed, they were Stanley Cup champions.

For the St. Louis Blues, Orr's overtime goal, which completed a
sweep in the final, was sudden death. But for Boston, it was a moment of
eternal life.

*Success produces its own distorted sense of time—an urgency to capitalize
on a fleeting opportunity. Although that early '70s team was nicknamed
the "Big Bad Bruins," it had an underlying fragility. Boston was as
vulnerable as the ligaments in Orr's oft-injured left knee. And although
the Bruins won another Stanley Cup in 1972 (see Game No. 70), there was
also a sense, similar to the nagging feeling that attends the Brady–Belichick
Patriots, that they left at least one more title on the table.*

21

Red Sox 3, Cardinals 0
October 27, 2004

This game officially eighty-sixed 86 years of frustration

I t was routine. Had this Red Sox–Cardinals game happened during the regular season, it would quickly have slipped below the surface, into the deep pool of forgettable Major League Baseball games. No individual effort or specific play stood out. There were no dramatic twists, no shocking turns. No ebb, just flow. The Red Sox led from the game's fourth pitch, when leadoff batter Johnny Damon homered. St. Louis never even put the tying run on after the first inning. Starter Derek Lowe delivered seven rock-solid innings (no runs, three hits, one walk, four strikeouts), the bullpen built a bridge in the eighth, and Keith Foulke worked around a leadoff single in the ninth. Foulke wasn't the prototypical closer. He was a control pitcher—not a fireballer who blew people away with 99-mph heat. So there wasn't even a cathartic punch-out to end it. Instead there was a tapper to the mound and a flip to first. It was a matter of executing a routine play—in the same way that signing a historic treaty is a matter of executing a few strokes of a pen. When Red Sox first baseman Doug Mientkiewicz squeezed the ball, the achievement became indelible. Boston's World Series drought of 86 years, one month, two weeks, two days, seven hours, and 24 minutes was officially over.

Through good times (the 2007 World Series) and bad (September 2011, all of 2012), the hangover from that October night in St. Louis lasted until 2013, when the "Boston Strong" Red Sox gave the team a new identity.

20

Celtics 97, Lakers 91
June 12, 2008

The biggest comeback in NBA Finals history gave the Celtics control of the series en route to their seventeenth title

The number of lead changes isn't always an accurate indicator of how compelling a basketball game was. Game 4 of the 2008 NBA Finals, for example, had just one. It happened with 4:07 remaining, when Eddie House nailed an eighteen-footer off a pass from Paul Pierce. When that shot rattled in, it was like watching the rising tide wash away the last vestige of a sand castle. The Celtics had completed the greatest comeback in NBA Finals history, overcoming a 24-point deficit against the Lakers. It was the finest hour for the second coming of the Big Three.

Ray Allen went the full 48 minutes. He had nineteen points, nine rebounds, a couple of assists, and three steals. He had plenty of other games during his Celtics years when he had a better shooting touch, but he never submitted a better all-around effort. His key shots were not jumpers but determined drives to the hoop. With sixteen seconds left Allen delivered the coup de grâce when he sent the extravagantly annoying Sasha Vujacic into a tantrum after blowing past him for a layup.

Kevin Garnett had sixteen efficient points (50% from the floor, 2-of-2 from the line) while contributing his usual stellar defense.

And then there was Paul Pierce. He had twenty points, four rebounds, seven assists—and one key block. It happened near the end of a 7–0 Celtics run in the third quarter that chopped the Lakers' lead from twenty to thirteen in just 55 seconds. Pierce not only stuffed Kobe Bryant—on a turnaround jumper, no less—but he also controlled the rebound and hit Allen with an outlet pass that led to a pair of free throws. Pierce harassed Bryant (6-for-19, seventeen points) all night—but never more emphatically than on that possession. And with Pierce bottling up Bryant, it was only a matter of time before the rest of the Lakers wilted under Boston's defensive intensity. Five different Lakers hit threes in the first half—but LA went 0-for-7 from beyond the arc after intermission.

The best way to grasp the dramatic shift in the game's complexion is to compare the waning moments of the second quarter to the waning moments of the third. Los Angeles scored six points in the last ten seconds of the first half. The last three came at the buzzer on a 25-footer from Jordan Farmar, who brought the ball all the way up the floor with minimal resistance, for a 68–50 Lakers lead. But by the final seconds of the third quarter, the LA lead was down to four and Boston was contesting not just every shot and every pass but every step. With the shot clock winding down on LA's last possession, Farmar again hoisted a three—but this time under extreme pressure. It was an airball. The Celtics pushed the ball up the floor. When the Lakers doubled Pierce, expecting him to take the last shot, Pierce dished to P.J. Brown alone under the basket for a slam that made it a two-point game heading into the fourth. The Lakers were now playing in a perpetual flinch, the Staples Center had morphed into the Crisis Center, and Phil Jackson's Zen Master routine rang hollow. ("Momentum's a strange girl," Jackson told ABC's Michelle Tafoya between periods with a wan smile. "She really jumped on the other side of the ship.")

It was another Pierce assist, to House, that finally gave Boston the lead, which they held to the end. Afterward, as he headed to the locker room, Pierce barked, "That's how you do it!" And he would know; he had played a key role in a 26-point comeback against the Nets in 2002 (see Game No. 73). But that game was in the Eastern Conference Finals, and it was in Boston. This one was in the NBA Finals, and it was in LA.

"That's how you fight!" said Pierce. "One more! One more, C's!"

The C's failed to deliver "one more" in Game 5, even though the Lakers again coughed up a huge lead (nineteen points). This time LA managed to recover for a 103–98 win. But that simply allowed the Celtics to clinch the title at home, in a Game 6 that turned into an enormous Garden party (see Game No. 69).

19

Celtics 124, Lakers 121, OT
May 31, 1984

This was the first of two gutty overtime wins—one at home,
one on the road—that the Celtics needed to steal the 1984 NBA Finals
from the Lakers

S even times between 1959 and 1969 the Celtics and Lakers had met in the NBA Finals. Seven times the Celtics had won. But now, in their eighth meeting, in the spring of 1984, the Celtics were eighteen seconds away from making dubious NBA history: first team to open the Finals with two losses at home. This was a surrealistic nightmare—Dali's *The Persistence of Memory* rendered on a parquet canvas. The Lakers had a 113–111 lead and the ball. The shot clock was dark, taunting the Celtics like one of those melting Dali watches.

The Celtics had made their own bed with ten unmade free throws in the fourth quarter. Kevin McHale had just missed a pair with a chance to tie it. After the second miss, Magic Johnson had grabbed the rebound and called time so coach Pat Riley could map the final steps of Boston's demise.

If these Lakers had any institutional memory of past Garden disasters, there was no evidence of it at that point. A month earlier, their incomparable center, Kareem Abdul–Jabbar, had supplanted Wilt Chamberlain as the NBA's all-time leading scorer. This was a good omen for LA. Back in 1969, the last time the Celtics and Lakers had met in the NBA Finals, LA had acquired Chamberlain in a futile attempt to dethrone Bill Russell. That same year, across town, Abdul–Jabbar (still known as Lew Alcindor) had led UCLA to its third straight NCAA championship, concluding his college career with an 88–2 record.

For all his individual accomplishments, Abdul–Jabbar was more a team player in the Russell mode than a singular force like Chamberlain.

221

And it showed in the Celtics' much-anticipated showdown with the Showtime Lakers. Like their '60s forebears, these Lakers could score points in clusters. But they did so with unprecedented efficiency. Their 53.2% field goal percentage for the 1983–84 season was an NBA record. (The next year's edition of Showtime topped that with a 54.5% mark, which still stands as the highest ever.) They had bolted to a 30–12 first-quarter lead in Game 1 and held on to win 115–109.

Sufficiently alarmed by that Game 1 beatdown, the Celtics had charged to a thirteen-point lead in Game 2. They were still up three with just 1:15 to play. But they couldn't hang on against the relentless Lakers attack. Now all LA had to do to seize command of the series was take care of the ball and sink a couple of free throws—and they were 12-of-12 from the line in the fourth quarter. And unlike the '60s Lakers, whose crunch-time options were limited to Elgin Baylor and Jerry West, this team had multiple weapons, including five future Hall of Famers: Abdul–Jabbar, Johnson, James Worthy, Bob McAdoo, and Jamaal Wilkes.

But, suddenly, inexplicably, unexpectedly, purple and gold turned to black and white. The Lakers suffered a 1960s flashback.

From the left sideline in LA's backcourt, Worthy inbounded the ball to Johnson. As McHale and Larry Bird double-teamed him, Johnson immediately threw the ball back to Worthy in the corner.

To that point, Worthy had played a near-perfect game. Since missing his first shot he had hit eleven straight from the field and led all scorers with 28 points. He had tied the game with 1:12 left on an unflinching and-one drive off an Abdul–Jabbar feed, sinking the shot despite colliding with Cedric Maxwell in the paint.

Now there was no one within ten feet of Worthy when he received Johnson's pass. The Lakers still had eight seconds to advance across the timeline, two full timeouts in case of emergency, and the ball in their leading scorer's hands. There was no reason to panic. But Worthy did. As soon as Danny Ainge left his man, Byron Scott, and made a run at him, Worthy lobbed a pass over Ainge's head, through the paint, intended for Scott. Meanwhile, just beyond the three-point line, Gerald Henderson—who had entered the game with 35 seconds left after Dennis Johnson fouled out—had just left *his* man, McAdoo, and turned to watch Worthy. Like a free safety, Henderson read the pass and jumped the route. He knocked the ball down and then knocked down the tying layup in a span of two stunning seconds.

Timeout, LA. For the Lakers, this was one of those *If you had told us before the series started...* situations that should have felt better than it did. They were still up in the Finals, 1–0, having trounced the Celtics at the Garden. And with Game 2 tied, they had the ball at midcourt with thirteen seconds left. Not a bad position to be in at all.

But the Henderson steal had changed something. A Lakers team that had spent the better part of 96 minutes demonstrating that they were quicker than the Celtics was suddenly afraid of being beaten to the ball. On the Lakers final possession of regulation, Johnson became so protective that LA didn't get a shot off. As Johnson said later, "I would rather hold it and take our chances in overtime than throw it in [to the post] and have them steal it."

He had good reason to worry. With fourteen seconds left in OT, LA again had a chance to win with a last-second shot. The difference this time was that the Lakers *had* to make the shot because the Celtics had just taken a 122–121 lead on Scott Wedman's corner jumper. Twice the Lakers tried to penetrate; twice Boston center Robert Parish knocked the ball loose. The second time Parish recovered the ball and fed it to Bird, who hit the clinching free throws.

Yes, those plays were critical. But Henderson's steal is the persistent memory.

Although the series was now even, the Celtics knew they would have to find a way to win one in LA—which they did (see Game No. 18).

18

Celtics 129, Lakers 125, OT
June 6, 1984

The Lakers were running all over the Celtics—until Kevin McHale went Rambo on Kurt Rambis

Playing at home, the Celtics were lucky to salvage a split with the Lakers in the first two games of the 1984 NBA Finals. Only Gerald Henderson's sleight of hand saved them from being down 0–2 (see Game No. 19). Gaining a split in Los Angeles would require more than a well-timed finesse play. In Game 3, the Lakers ran over, around, and through the Celtics. The 137–104 thrashing was the worst loss Boston had ever suffered in the Finals. Magic Johnson dealt a Finals-record 21 assists, and LA set another Finals mark with 47 points in the third quarter.

Seven Lakers hit double figures. Kareem Abdul–Jabbar led LA with 24 points, which was no surprise. But the Lakers also got a huge contribution from power forward/cult hero Kurt Rambis. With his unruly hair and Buddy Holly glasses, Rambis looked like he had gotten lost en route to a casting call for *Slapshot II* and ended up at the Forum. He scored seventeen points and racked up the game's most damning stat from Boston's perspective: 7-of-7 from the floor, all from within five feet. Said Larry Bird, who often found himself playing the Lone Ranger on defense, "We played like sissies.… I can't believe [we] would let a team like LA go out there and punch us out like they did."

Bird's teammates got the message, but they didn't pass it on to the Lakers immediately. LA sprinted to an early fourteen-point lead in Game 4. Seventeen of their 68 first-half points came as a result of their devastating fast break. The Celtics drew to within four early in the third quarter. Then an Abdul–Jabbar skyhook made it 76–70, Lakers, and Dennis Johnson was short on a jumper on the Celtics' next possession. Abdul–Jabbar grabbed the rebound and hurled a long outlet pass to Magic, who dished to Rambis, trailing the play at full speed. For an instant it seemed as if the Lakers had been toying with the Celtics, merely gathering a second wind before blowing them away again.

Rambis launched for the layup. Two Celtics charged through the paint. Henderson slapped at Rambis's hands. Kevin McHale aimed higher, clotheslining Rambis and knocking him hard to the floor. A swelling cheer inside the Forum instantly shifted to a stunned *Ohhhhh!*

Rambis went after McHale, but the Lakers' James Worthy cut him off and inadvertently knocked him down among the photographers.

Bird, playing the good cop, helped Rambis up.

The Lakers managed just one fast-break basket the rest of the night. Boston's improved shooting was part of the reason; Henderson scored eleven third-quarter points, and each converted jumper was one less opportunity for LA to trigger their running game. But there was also little question that McHale's takedown had changed both the game's tempo and its tenor. From then on it was a testy half-court grudge fest. Abdul–Jabbar committed a number of outbursts, including throwing an elbow at Bird, that would have earned anybody but the NBA's all-time leading scorer a technical, if not an ejection. As he admitted years later, "Our reaction was too personal."

Indeed, Abdul–Jabbar put the *personal* in personal foul, particularly in the last minute of regulation. LA led by five when Abdul–Jabbar hacked Robert Parish on a putback with 39 seconds left. Parish converted the three-point play to make it 113–111. Then, when Michael Cooper missed a jumper on LA's next possession, Abdul Jabbar cleared out Bird on an attempted offensive rebound with sixteen seconds left. Not only did Abdul–Jabbar foul out on the play, but he also gave Boston a chance to tie the game from the line—with their best shooter, no less. Bird hit both shots.

As in Game 2, LA had a chance to win on the last possession of regulation. As in Game 2, they never got the shot away. With Abdul–Jabbar gone, the Lakers' half-court options were limited. Parish swiped Johnson's pass for Worthy with four seconds left. McHale just missed a putback of Bird's jumper at the buzzer. After leading by five with just 40 seconds left, LA was lucky to survive for overtime.

In OT, as in regulation, the final minute spelled the difference. With 35 seconds left and the score tied at 123, Magic back-rimmed a pair of three throws. Although Bird was just 8-of-24 from the field at that point, the Celtics were determined to get him the ball. After Bird's defensive nemesis, Michael Cooper, slipped, Cedric Maxwell immediately passed to Bird. Worthy gambled on a steal and missed. Bird ended up backing in against Magic. His fifteen-foot fall-away gave Boston the lead with sixteen seconds left. With a chance to tie it from the line, Worthy hit just one of two with ten seconds left. A pair of Dennis Johnson free throws and M.L. Carr's breakaway dunk put the game away.

Boston had crunched LA at crunch time, with five points in the last 40 seconds of regulation and six points in the last seventeen seconds of overtime. But it was a single crunching play with 6:53 left in the third quarter that had swung the game—and the series—the Celtics' way.

The NBA Finals had a 2–2–1–1–1 format in 1984 (and reinstituted in 2014), which meant Game 5 was back at Boston Garden. The game-time temperature was 97 degrees. That effectively put the brakes on LA's fast break. As the Lakers went rubber-legged in the second half, the Celtics strolled away for a 121–103 victory. LA evened the series at home in Game 6 before Boston won Game 7 at the Garden, 111–102, to run their record to 8–0 against the Lakers in the NBA Finals.

17

Bruins 1, Lightning 0
May 27, 2011

This taut classic sent the Bruins to the Stanley Cup Final
for the first time in 21 years

Through two periods of Game 7 of the 2011 Eastern Conference
Final the Boston Bruins and Tampa Bay Lightning had played to
a tie. Not just a tie but a *scoreless* tie. That created a different atmosphere than if the score had been, say, 3–3. There had been no shift of
momentum. The tension just kept building. As Tampa Bay coach Guy
Boucher said later, "It felt like overtime the entire game." Boucher knew
it was too much to expect his Lightning to strike twice on a night like this.

By then it had become clear that the officials weren't going to provide
any help. The Lightning had forced Game 7 by scoring three power-play
goals in Game 6. But Tampa Bay never got a man advantage in Game 7—
and neither did the Bruins.

Boston did, however, have the advantage of playing before 17,565
hockey-mad fans at the TD Garden. From the opening faceoff, the
crowd pegged the decibel meter. And when the Bruins finally picked
the lock on the Lightning's 1–3–1 defense—thanks to consecutive perfect passes from Andrew Ference to David Krejci and Krejci to Nathan
Horton, who flicked the puck past Tampa Bay goalie Dwayne Roloson
at 12:27 of the third period—the noise swelled to a crescendo. The crowd
remained standing for the final 7:33, and as the seconds ticked down it
was as if the Lightning were trying to penetrate not just the Bruins' defense but also a wall of sound.

The Bruins' defensive pressure was so suffocating that the Lightning
managed just two shots on net after the Bruins took the lead—none after

the three-minute mark. Tampa Bay couldn't even get Roloson off the ice for an extra attacker until just 30 seconds remained. And by then it was too late. Tonight, one little goal was enough.

But one big goal remained. For the first time in 21 years the Bruins were going to the Stanley Cup Final.

Against Vancouver in the final the Bruins were involved in two more 1–0 games and lost both. Fortunately they conjured more than enough offense in the other five games (and the Canucks committed enough ugly defense; see Game No. 55) to win four of them. And while none of those four wins was as esthetically pleasing as this purist's delight, each was still a thing of beauty to Cup-starved Bruins fans.

16

Patriots 24, Eagles 21
February 6, 2005

New England's third Super Bowl win in four years had just enough
suspense to keep Pats fans from feeling complacent

Success in the NFL requires mastering two types of time management. The macro kind involves an astute use of draft picks, trades,
free-agent signings, and the salary cap to widen a team's window
of opportunity for winning a championship. The micro kind involves
efficient use of the clock when the championship is actually on the line.

In the early aughts the Patriots were better than everybody else at
the macro kind. And in Super Bowl XXXIX they were better than the
Eagles at the micro kind. The result: The 2004 Patriots became just the
eighth team to repeat as Super Bowl champions, and just the second to
win three Super Bowls in four years.

The '04 Patriots were a great team that didn't have a lot of great
players. Of the eleven offensive starters, three were undrafted free agents,
and four others were drafted in the fifth round or later. You could argue
that the Patriots' offense worked *because* it didn't have a lot of great players. There were no prima donnas. The featured back, Corey Dillon, was
in his first year with New England after seven hard seasons in Cincinnati.
The Patriots had acquired him through a byzantine transaction only
slightly less complicated than a credit-default swap. And although Dillon's
attitude had clearly gone sour in Cincinnati, the Patriots read his discontent correctly. He was just a competitive player who had burned
most of his prime years on a team that never crested .500. New England
hoped that replacing the departed Antowain Smith, whose production
had declined, with a back of Dillon's caliber, and with Dillon's motiva-

tion, could provide just the kick the team needed to stay on top.

Like so many other moves that the Patriots made at that time, it was the perfect call. Dillon produced a Patriots-record 1,635 yards rushing in 2004 and provided a balance that the offense needed. With Dillon behind him, Tom Brady was just as happy to hand the ball off as to throw it. Brady had just two 300-yard passing games as the Patriots repeated their 14–2 mark from 2003, a stretch that included a 21-game winning streak.

The defense was of a higher pedigree than the offense. All but one defensive starter was chosen in the first three rounds of the draft—and the lone exception was Rodney Harrison, a fifth round pick from Western Illinois who had spent nine years with the Chargers. Like Dillon, Harrison was a Pro Bowl talent who had fallen out of favor with his original team but flourished when given a fresh start in New England.

With a solid defense and an efficient, clock-controlling offense, the 2004 Patriots were designed not to annihilate opponents but to outlast them. And that's just how Super Bowl XXXIX played out. The score was 0–0 after one quarter, 7–7 at the half, 14–14 after three. It wasn't until the fourth quarter that the difference between the Patriots and the Eagles showed. Up to that point New England had been uncharacteristically sloppy. Tom Brady had killed a second-quarter scoring drive by fumbling on a play-action fake to Kevin Faulk on second-and-goal from the five. And New England had committed seven penalties for 47 yards.

The drive that put the Pats up for good epitomized the offensive balance. It covered 71 yards in nine plays. Four were Brady passes—all completions, to three different receivers, none for more than fourteen yards. Kevin Faulk had two carries for twenty yards. Dillon had the other three carries, good for fourteen yards—including the last two for the touchdown. At last the game was conforming to expectations. The Patriots were favored by seven, and that was their margin early in the fourth quarter.

An Adam Vinatieri field goal extended the lead to ten points. Still, the businesslike Patriots couldn't shake the flighty Eagles. After a Patriots punt, Philadelphia took over at their own 21 with 5:40 remaining. That was plenty of time for the Eagles to come back, if they played with a sense of urgency. Inexplicably, they didn't. McNabb started the critical drive with four straight dump-off passes of five yards or less, all to receivers who stayed inbounds. And after each meager gain, the Eagles huddled up. It took nine plays, and almost three minutes, just for Philadelphia to cross midfield. And although McNabb eventually hit speedster Greg Lewis for a big strike—a 30-yard touchdown catch over rookie Dexter Reid, who had replaced the injured Eugene Wilson—Philadelphia was on the short side of the two-minute warning by then.

The Eagles followed with another curious move. With two timeouts, and needing just a field goal, Philadelphia could have kicked the ball deep. By forcing a three-and-out, they would have gotten the ball back with decent field position and about 45 seconds to work with. Instead, they tried an onside kick, which the Pats' Christian Fauria smothered at the Philadelphia 41. The Eagles still managed to force a three-and-out, but the Patriots were able to pin them deep—thanks in part to yet *another* bad decision. The Eagles sent no one back to return the kick. Or to fair-catch it. Josh Miller's pooch punt landed at the sixteen and rolled to the four before the Pats downed it.

Still, the Eagles had 46 seconds to try to get in field goal range. McNabb promptly squandered half that time with a dump-off to running back Brian Westbrook that gained all of a yard. Fittingly, McNabb's night ended with an interception, his third of the game, to Rodney Harrison. The Patriots, who prided themselves on doing all the little things right, were champions in part because their opponent had done so many little things wrong.

The Patriots were foiled in their next two Super Bowl appearances by the anti-McNabb, Eli Manning, who led the Giants on a pair of two-minute-drill touchdown drives. That raises some intriguing questions. Would the 2004 Patriots have beaten either of those two Giants teams? Possibly not. Conversely, would the 18–0 Patriots have beaten the 2004 Eagles? Almost certainly. But even a team as micromanaged as the Patriots can't control the quality of their opponent—which, as Super Bowl XXXIX demonstrated, can be a vital ingredient in a championship.

15

Red Sox 6, Tigers 5
October 13, 2013

With the grandest of grand slams, David Ortiz changed the postseason course of the 2013 Red Sox

Many of the 68,756 who had paid to watch the Pats–Saints game at Gillette Stadium on Columbus Day weekend missed the money moment. They were sitting in traffic on Route One when Tom Brady led the Patriots to an improbable 30–27 win, hitting rookie Kenbrell Thompkins with a seventeen-yard touchdown pass with five seconds left. Those who heard the call on their car radios also heard radio color man Scott Zolak call them out. "Who left the building?" Zolak bellowed. "Unicorns! Show ponies! Where's the beef?"

Pats fans had no beef. It's just that, even at their best, Tom Brady and the Patriots couldn't compete with David Ortiz and the Red Sox in October. And many fans at Gillette just wanted to get home for Game 2 of the 2013 American League Championship Series against the Tigers, which started at Fenway about half an hour after the Pats game ended.

The Sox gave them plenty of time to settle in.

Writers were practically required by law to describe the 2013 Red Sox as *resilient*. With a handful of new arrivals—Mike Napoli, Mike Carp, Shane Victorino, and Jonny Gomes in the lineup; Ryan Dempster in the rotation, and Koji Uehara in the bullpen—Boston engineered a worst-to-first turnaround in the AL East. Of course, it helped to have Ortiz and Dustin Pedroia healthy again, and to have John Lackey recovered from Tommy John surgery. But mostly it helped to have Bobby Valentine out of the manager's office and John Farrell in.

The 2013 Red Sox also showed resilience on a day-to-day basis, with

24 come-from-behind wins. Two games best summed up the team's character. On August 1, the Red Sox scored six runs in the bottom of the ninth to overcome a 7–2 deficit and stun the Mariners 8–7. A little more than a month later, it was the Red Sox who coughed up a late 7–2 lead. The Yankees scored six unanswered runs to take an 8–7 lead into the ninth. But with two outs and nobody on against Mariano Rivera, the Red Sox manufactured the tying run, then cobbled together the winning run in the tenth.

So that label—*resilient*—was both accurate and unsettling heading into the ALCS against pitching-rich Detroit. It suggested not only that the Sox were capable of climbing out of a hole, but also that they were liable to fall into one. And over most of the first two games, the Sox dug a hole of historic depths. In Game 1, a 1–0 Tigers victory, Boston's lone hit didn't come until the ninth inning. And now, in Game 2, trailing 5–0 with two outs in the bottom of the sixth, against presumptive Cy Young winner Max Scherzer, the Red Sox *still* had only one hit in the series—and 27 strikeouts.

That's when Victorino delivered a first-things-first single to left-center. That took care of the no-hitter. Pedroia followed with a wall-ball double that scored Victorino. That took care of the shutout. More than that, it allowed the Red Sox to exhale. Cutting the deficit to four runs also provided a psychological lift. If things fell together just right, Boston could now tie the game with one swing.

And that's just the way it worked out.

With Scherzer done after seven innings, Detroit manager Jim Leyland managed the bottom of the eighth like a man who was so worried about a panic attack that he induced a panic attack. Righty Jose Veras started the inning by getting Stephen Drew on a grounder to short. Then he gave up a double to Will Middlebrooks.

Next!

In came lefty Drew Smyly to face Jacoby Ellsbury. After getting ahead in the count 1–2, Smyly walked him.

Next!

Righty Al Alburquerque entered and struck out Victorino for the second out. Then he yielded a single to Pedroia that loaded the bases.

Next!

The very scenario that Leyland had been trying to avoid had materialized. Ortiz was up as the potential tying run. And after all that maneuvering, Leyland neglected the most important move of all. He forgot to remind closer Joaquin Benoit, who entered to face Ortiz, of the Tigers' predetermined strategy in that situation: Keep the ball out of the strike zone. Instead, Benoit threw a first-pitch changeup that stayed up and over the plate. And Ortiz took that hypothetical *one swing* and transformed it into something vividly, violently real. The ball rocketed toward the Red Sox bullpen in deep right.

Tigers right fielder Torii Hunter, Ortiz's old teammate on the Twins, started back. And he charged headlong into one of those moments that no one can imagine before they happen but no one can forget once they do. Hunter collided with the low wall, which flipped him into the Sox bullpen, his feet rotating into the air like an old-fashioned foosball player's. Hunter didn't catch the ball—but Mani Martinez, a Sox bullpen catcher, did. Martinez, who had been warming up Dempster, heard the roar and looked up just in time. He didn't even have to come out of his crouch to catch Ortiz's latest postseason souvenir. And, standing at the rear of the bullpen was Steve Horgan, a Boston cop who thrust his arms in the air in a gesture of triumph. *Celebrity* and *celebrate* share the same root word, and Horgan become the former simply by doing the latter.

Three people, three spontaneous movements, all now forever linked in another indelible Fenway instant.

Hunter emerged stunned—less by the physical trauma of his fall than by the sheer implausibility of what had just occurred. "The one guy you don't want to beat you," Hunter said later, "and he beat us."

Technically, Ortiz's homer didn't beat the Tigers; it merely tied them. But Hunter was right. The Tigers were done, and everyone knew it. A run in the bottom of the ninth on an infield single, an error, a wild pitch, and a single through a drawn-in infield just made it official.

Afterward, it was the Ortiz bomb that everyone was buzzing about. Said Leyland, "David's one of those guys that's been born for those magic moments."

His first great magic postseason moment had occurred a decade earlier, on another October Sunday at Fenway. That afternoon, Ortiz drilled a go-ahead two-run double off A's closer Keith Foulk in a division series elimination game (see Game No 77). That comeback inspired an incongruous cheer down at Gillette Stadium, where Titans quarterback Steve McNair had just given Tennessee a 27–24 fourth-quarter lead over the Patriots.

On that day in 2003, as on October 13, 2013, the Pats rallied to win. Not that anybody remembers it. In Boston sports, David Ortiz owns October. Not even Tom Brady at his best can change that.

Those resilient 2013 Red Sox began their ALCS comeback with a dramatic grand slam—and that's how they completed it, too (see Game No 38) before going on to claim their first World Series title at Fenway in 95 years (see Game No. 32).

14

Celtics 108, Lakers 106
May 5, 1969

In Bill Russell's swan song, the Celtics won Game 7 of the NBA Finals on the road for the first time—and spoiled the Lakers' party plans

The last one was the hardest. When Bill Russell won his first title he was 23 years old and played just 58 games. When he won his eleventh title he was 35 years old and played 95 games. He had also inherited Red Auerbach's job as coach. It would have been difficult enough to fill those shoes without also continuing to wear a Hall of Fame center's sneakers.

Further, Russell's final climb through the playoffs was the steepest. The Celtics finished 48–34 in 1969, their worst record during Russell's career. They received the Eastern Division's fourth and final seed, denying them home-court advantage throughout the playoffs. A first-round win over second-seeded Philadelphia wasn't terribly surprising. The Sixers had looked scary good when they had dethroned the Celtics in '67; now they just looked scattered. But Boston's opponent in the Eastern Division Finals was the ascendant New York Knicks, a team with four future Hall of Famers (Bill Bradley, Dave DeBusschere, Walt Frazier, and Willis Reed), along with a young Phil Jackson. The Knicks had beaten the Celtics six times in seven regular-season meetings. "New York is ready to have a ticker-tape parade for its basketball team," the *Globe*'s Clif Keane reported.

It would have to wait a year. The Celtics stole Game 1 at Madison Square Garden and gutted out one-point wins at home in games 4 and 6 to advance to the NBA Finals for the tenth time in eleven years. And there they faced the toughest challenge yet. After losing the title to

Boston in 1968, the Los Angeles Lakers had reloaded by trading for Wilt Chamberlain. And the Lakers held home-court advantage for the first time in seven playoff meetings with the Celtics.

In a classic home-cooked series, it appeared that that would make all the difference. After six games each team had won three times on their own floor. The Lakers expected the trend to continue in Game 7. "We should win," said Chamberlain. Jerry West, who was averaging 37 points a game, was even cockier. "We're going to beat them," he said.

But Lakers owner Jack Kent Cooke took the overconfidence over the top. Before Game 7 he distributed an itinerary for the victory celebration. Bags of balloons nested in the Forum rafters.

Russell got hold of the itinerary. He read it to his team in the locker room. It provided the proud, aging Celtics the energy they needed to make one last push. Boston ran LA ragged in building a 59–56 halftime lead, then applied smothering defense in the third quarter, forcing sixteen straight missed shots. The Boston lead peaked at 100–83 with ten minutes left in the game.

Sam Jones, the oldest Celtic, played like the youngest. Jones, who had announced that the 1968–69 season would be his last, scored 24 points and was also the only Celtic who was perfect from the line (4-of-4). But he developed foul trouble pursuing the relentless West (who was playing through a hamstring injury). There were still seven minutes left when Jones picked up his sixth foul, and by then the lead had shrunk to twelve. (Lakers fans, atoning somewhat for Cooke's lack of class, gave Jones a standing O when he left.)

With Russell and John Havlicek playing with five fouls each, and with the Celts uncharacteristically cold from the line (20-of-31), and with West still possessed, LA clawed back. West scored thirteen points during a 19–3 run that trimmed Boston's margin to a single skinny point, 103–102, with three minutes left. It stayed that way through several tense exchanges of possession. And then, although they were almost 3,000 miles from home, the Celtics got a couple of Boston Garden bounces. First, LA's Keith Erikson slapped the ball out of Havlicek's hand from behind. But instead of a turnover, it turned into a perfect pass to Don Nelson at the foul line. Nelson caught the loose ball and put up a jumper in the same motion. He back-rimmed the shot. The ball bounced straight up, higher than the top of the backboard. It dropped straight down through the net to force some air back into Boston's lungs with

1:15 left. A couple of stops and a handful of free throws over the next minute put it out of reach at 108–102.

The game summarized the NBA in the 1960s. Throughout the decade, from Elgin Baylor to Jerry West, LA always had the best individual player. (In 1969, in fact, West became the only player from the losing team named NBA Finals MVP.) But Boston always had the better team. The Lakers chased the Celtics for ten years and couldn't catch them—just as they couldn't catch them in Game 7 of the 1969 NBA Finals.

Afterward, Auerbach gloated in an ABC interview. "What're they gonna do with all those balloons up there?" he asked.

There were no balloons in the Celtics locker room. Nor was there any champagne. ("It's not superstition—we just don't have it," Havlicek said.) The team returned to Boston and a different sort of celebration. "I understand each player is going to get a rocking chair with a city seal on it," said the team's PR man, Howie McHugh. "I wonder if somebody is trying to tell them something."

That was indeed the end of the greatest sustained run in professional sports history. The official word came abruptly at midsummer. Russell announced his retirement in a first-person Sports Illustrated *article with the cover line I'M THROUGH WITH BASKETBALL. "I've lost my competitive urges," Russell wrote with typical candor. "If I went out to play now, the other guys would know I didn't really care. That's no way to play—it's no way to do anything."*

13

Patriots 32, Panthers 29
February 1, 2004

The Patriots' second Super Bowl win couldn't possibly match
the first for drama—but it came close

The 2003 Patriots were the NFL's stingiest team. New England had three shutouts over the last seven weeks, including a pair of 12–0 grinders. Then, in two playoff games at frigid Gillette Stadium, the Patriots limited a pair of top-five scoring offenses, Tennessee and Indianapolis, to fourteen points each (see games 67 and 40). So when the Patriots and their defense-minded opponent, the Carolina Panthers, were locked in a scoreless tie more than 26 minutes into Super Bowl XXXVIII, it wasn't a shock.

The shock was what happened after that. Each team scored twice in the last 3:10 of the first half. In between a pair of five-yard Tom Brady touchdown passes, Carolina quarterback Jake Delhomme—who had been 1-of-9 for one yard to that point—led the Panthers on a 95-yard touchdown drive. Carolina kicker John Kasay ended the half with a 50-yard field goal that made it 14–10, New England.

Then, after each had seemingly exposed the other's weaknesses (and after Janet Jackson had exposed something else at halftime), the teams went back to trading punts for most of the third quarter. Finally, Tom Brady put together an eight-play, 71-yard drive that concluded when Antowain Smith scored from two yards out ten seconds into the fourth quarter. New England had a 21–10 lead and the NFL's best defense to protect it.

But the Super Bowl's unique atmosphere, with its many delays and distractions and overarching sense of Great American Magnitude, can knock even the most disciplined team off stride. Up by eleven, the Patriots "played a little bit more conservative," defensive coordinator Romeo Crennel later admitted, "and [the Panthers] found some soft spots in our zone."

In fact, on the next drive the New England defense was as soft as flannel against Carolina's hurry-up offense. With the Patriots backpedaling after Delhomme completions of thirteen, eighteen, and 22 yards, Carolina running back DeShaun Foster leaked through for a 33-yard touchdown run. The Panthers went for two but failed. It was 21–16.

Brady gave the defense a chance to regroup with a drive that consumed almost five minutes. But it stalled at third-and-goal from the nine. A field goal would have put the Pats up eight—still a one-possession game. So Brady tried to force the ball to tight end Christian Fauria in the end zone. Panthers defensive back Reggie Howard intercepted it.

Playing with greater urgency now, the Patriots' defense harried Delhomme into a pair of incompletions that made it third-and-ten from the fifteen. It looked like New England might get the ball back with good field position and little harm from the turnover. But rather than try for a mere first down, Delhomme went for it all. He found Muhsin Muhammad behind safety Eugene Wilson, who injured his hip in a futile pursuit. Suddenly it was 22–21, Carolina (they missed another two-point attempt), with less than seven minutes left. The Patriots had lost their lead and their starting free safety on a single disastrous play.

Brady responded with a very Bradylike drive, using three different receivers and both running backs to move the ball to the Carolina one. At that point the Patriots showed another of their distinguishing characteristics—their malleable roster. On the previous touchdown, defensive tackle Richard Seymour had served as Antowain Smith's lead blocker. This time linebacker Mike Vrabel reported as an eligible receiver, and he ended up catching the go-ahead touchdown pass. With the lead at five, New England went for a two-point conversion for the first time all season. They got it with another offensive wrinkle: a direct snap to Kevin Faulk, who slipped into the end zone to make it 29–22.

But this strange, exhilarating game, with points clustered at the end of each half, was far from over. On the last play before the two-minute warning, Delhomme hit Muhammad again, on a pass that not only put the ball into New England territory but also knocked Rodney Harrison out of the game. Harrison, the Pats leading tackler, broke his right arm when he landed awkwardly out of bounds.

A secondary that had looked suspect even with its starting safeties turned into a sieve without them. Delhomme ended up with 323 yards passing on just sixteen completions. The last one, for the tying touchdown, was good for fourteen yards to Ricky Proehl, the former Ram who had also tied Super Bowl XXXVI with a late touchdown.

The odd score, 29–29, reflected a subtle difference between the Pats and Panthers. Each team had scored four touchdowns—but Carolina also had a field goal and New England had none. The score was tied because the Patriots had executed their lone attempt at a two-point conversion while the Panthers had failed twice.

And then another difference emerged: the kicking game. Having just tied the score with the PAT, the Panthers' John Kasay began his team's unraveling by booting the ensuing kickoff out of bounds. That gave the Patriots the ball at their own 40 with 1:08 left, all three timeouts, and Tom Brady at quarterback. Brady advanced the ball to the Carolina 23, the last seventeen yards coming on Deion Branch's tenth catch of the day. That left it to Adam Vinatieri—again. Vinatieri had had an off night to that point. He had missed a 31-yarder in the first quarter and had a 36-yarder blocked in the second. What's more, he had missed just four kicks indoors in his career, and all four had come right there, at Houston's Reliant Stadium.

But Vinatieri was like a go-to guy in the NBA. It didn't matter how many times he'd missed. With the game on the line, you went right back to him. From 41 yards, Vinatieri split the uprights with the precision of a diamond cutter. And after a cubic zirconia of a start, Super Bowl XXXVIII ended up being a gem.

The Patriots returned to the Super Bowl the next year and beat the Eagles (see Game No. 16). No team has repeated since.

12

Red Sox 3, Giants 2, 10 innings
October 16, 1912

It took an eighth game to decide this best-of-seven series,
and the Red Sox rallied from a run down in extra innings to win it

Fenway's first season might have been its best. The Red Sox went
57–20 in their new home in 1912, bracketed by come-from-behind
wins over the Yankees on Opening Day and in the September
finale. (The latter gave Boston a 19–2 edge in the season series—the
most lopsided in the rivalry's history.) But the 1912 team, which had
the best overall record in Sox history, 105–47, could win on the road,
too. In fact, it was during an epic 25-game road trip in June—yes, *25
games*—that this team came together. When they left Boston at the end
of May, the Red Sox were two games out of first. When they finally returned, on June 28, they were five games up, thanks to a 17–8 road trip.
They went on to win the AL pennant by fourteen games.

And that created an opportunity to clear up some unfinished business.

In 1904 the Red Sox were defending champions of the World Series.
But there was no World Series to defend. Boston repeated as AL champs
(see Game No. 86), but the National League pennant winner, the New
York Giants, refused to play them to determine an overall champion.
(At that time postseason series were essentially exhibitions, scheduled
at the discretion of individual teams.)

But now, eight years later, the World Series was officially sanctioned.
And that meant the Red Sox finally got a crack at the New York Giants,
who won the National League pennant again in 1912. No ducking the
confrontation this time.

Not that New York wanted to. At 103–48, the 1912 Giants were just as strong as the 1912 Red Sox. The teams were so evenly matched that the best-of-seven series still wasn't settled after seven games. The Red Sox had won games 1, 4, and 5 (by a total of four runs). The Giants had won games 3, 6, and 7. As for Game 2, at Fenway: It was called because of darkness after eleven innings, with the score 6–6. Per the rules of the day, the game wasn't suspended; it simply went into the books as a tie.

The series had a strange rhythm, partly because of that tie, but also because of the pitching rotation that Giants manager John McGraw set up. For Game 1, Red Sox player/manager Jake Stahl, Boston's first baseman, made the obvious call to go with his ace, Smoky Joe Wood. (Wood's 34 wins that year still stand as the Sox' single-season record.) But McGraw decided to reserve his number-one starter, Christy Mathewson, for Game 2. When the Red Sox won Game 1 behind Wood and battled Mathewson to tie in Game 2, they took command of the series. But despite building a 3–1–1 advantage after five games, they couldn't put the Giants away. Boston lost Game 6 behind number-three starter Buck O'Brien, which wasn't surprising. But they also lost Game 7, behind Wood—which most certainly was surprising. The only bright spot was that Wood lasted just one inning in an 11–4 pounding. That meant he would be available out of the bullpen in the final game, against Mathewson, if Stahl needed him.

Stahl did. It took until Game 8, inning 8, but the 1912 World Series finally produced the pitching matchup that everyone had anticipated.

The game was tied, 1–1, when Wood entered. The Giants had scored first, with a run off Sox rookie Hugh Bedient in the third. Sox right fielder Harry Hooper kept the Giants from extending their lead in the fifth, when he robbed second baseman Larry Doyle of a home run. Boston center fielder Tris Speaker, a future Hall of Famer, called Hooper's catch "the greatest, I believe, that I ever saw."

An unlikely source delivered the tying run for the Red Sox in the seventh: Olaf Henricksen, a reserve outfielder from Denmark. Pinch-hitting for Bedient, Henricksen drove home Stahl with a two-out double. It was his only at-bat of the series.

The game remained tied after nine innings. With one out in the top of the tenth, Giants left fielder Red Murray doubled to left. That brought up Fred Merkle, the Giants' first baseman. In 1908, Merkle's infamous baserunning "boner" against the Cubs had cost New York the pennant. Now, four years later, Merkle had a chance to collect a little karmic payback, with interest. A hit could win the World Series—and Merkle delivered. He singled to center, scoring Murray. With two outs, Giants catcher Chief Meyers nearly added an insurance run with a shot up the middle. Wood, however, made "a remarkable one-handed stop," the *Globe*'s T.H. Murnane reported, and threw Meyers out at first.

The inning was over, but not Boston's troubles. Wood, a decent-hitting pitcher (he'd batted .290 that season with fifteen extra-base hits) was due to lead off. But he had injured his pitching hand on that run-saving stop. So not only was Stahl forced to lift him for a lesser hitter (utility man Clyde Engle), but the Red Sox would also have to try to win without their best pitcher—and that was only if they could scratch out the tying run.

Engle lofted a routine fly to center. And when it came down, the Giants had a notorious muff to go with their infamous boner. Center fielder Fred Snodgrass somehow dropped the ball, and Engle ended up on second. (The *New York Times* reported that Snodrass's mother, who was following the game on an electric scoreboard at a theater in Los Angeles, fainted when the error was displayed.) Engle advanced to third on a long fly. (Snodgrass redeemed himself somewhat by robbing Hooper of a hit on the play.) After Sox second baseman Steve Yerkes walked, Tris Speaker popped one up in foul ground down the first base line. This was how Hugh Fullerton, one of the top baseball writers of the day, described what happened next: "Anyone could have caught it. I could have jumped out of the press box and caught it behind my back, but Merkle quit. Yes, Merkle quit cold. He didn't start for the ball…. Perhaps he was calculating the difference between the winners' and losers' [shares]."

In any case, the ball landed harmlessly in foul ground, and Merkle's karma account reverted from credit to debit. Given a second life, Speaker drilled a single to right. Engle beat Murray's throw home to tie the game, with Yerkes and Speaker advancing. Mathewson walked left fielder Duffy Lewis intentionally to load the bases. Sox third baseman Larry Gardner then won the game, and the series, in true dead-ball era fashion: with a walk-off sacrifice fly.

In its earliest years the Red Sox' new home was homey indeed; the 1912 World Series victory was the first of four that Boston won in their first six seasons at Fenway (although they actually played their home World Series games at Braves Field in 1915 and 1916).

11

Celtics 110, Lakers 107, OT
April 18, 1962

It took the Celtics the full seven games (plus five minutes) to win their fourth title in five years, against one of the best scoring duos the NBA has ever seen

The Celtics had just come from eight down at the half to beat the Lakers 119–105 at Los Angeles Memorial Sports Arena in Game 6 of the 1962 NBA Finals. So they flew home from LA that Monday night knowing there would be a Game 7—they just didn't know when. It was supposed to be at Boston Garden on Wednesday. But Celtics owner Walter Brown had petitioned the NBA to play the game on Thursday instead. Wednesday was the first day of Passover, Brown explained.

Lakers owner Bob Short needed to approve the switch. He didn't. Because if Game 7 were played on Thursday, the Lakers could be without the services of Pfc Elgin Baylor, who was on leave from the United States Army Reserve. In theory, Baylor was supposed to return to Fort Lewis, Washington, on Thursday.

You couldn't blame Brown for trying. Baylor's military commitment had limited him to 48 games that season. He had played in just four of LA's nine regular season meetings with Boston. The Lakers went 3–1 with him and 0–5 without him. No wonder Brown had presented him with a watch when he left for his service.

But by saving up his leave, Baylor had made it to every game of the NBA Finals. And in a seesaw series, he had been a constant. He'd scored 35 points in Game 1, 36 in Game 2, 39 in Game 3, 38 in Game 4, and 34 in Game 6. The outlier was Game 5 at Boston Garden. In that one, Baylor had torched the Celtics for 61 points (still an NBA Finals record).

With his athleticism and slashing style, Baylor had reinvented the small forward position. And in second-year guard Jerry West, he'd found the ideal complement for his skills. Like Baylor, West was both a prolific scorer (he'd averaged 30 points a game in the Finals) and an adept passer. Double-team one, and the other would make you pay.

In contrast to the Lakers, who derived the bulk of their offense from just two scorers, the 1961–62 Celtics were as finely balanced a team as the NBA has ever seen. Five players averaged between fifteen and 22 points a game. And unlike the Lakers, who lacked a dominant big man, the Celtics had defensive specialist Bill Russell as their anchor. And yet these two teams from opposite coasts, with opposite styles, were dead even after six games. (Heading to LA for Game 6, the teams had even shared the same commercial flight, which had to make an unscheduled stop at O'Hare when the landing gear failed to retract.) Not even home court had provided an edge; each had lost twice on their own floor.

Game 7 was more of the same—a predictable pattern leading to an unpredictable outcome. Again Baylor (41 points, 22 rebounds) and West (35 points) carried the load for the Lakers while the Celtics looked for the hot hand. Both Tom Heinsohn, their leading scorer, and Bob Cousy struggled, netting just eight points each. (Hampered by a sore right hand, Cousy was just 2-of-10 from the free-throw line.) Sam Jones, whose 35 points in Game 6 had saved the season, started slowly in Game 7, with just two first-half points. Fortunately for Boston, sixth man extraordinaire Frank Ramsey had seventeen first-half points. Jones finally got it going after halftime, with 25 points the rest of the way. And then there was Russell, who was a monster at both ends of the floor throughout the game: 30 points and 40 rebounds—twenty in each half. And although never known for his foul shooting—he'd made less than 60% during the season—he was 14-of-17 from the line.

Even so, the game was a virtual standoff. It was 22–22 after one quarter. It was 75-75 after three. And it was 100–100 with fifteen seconds left in regulation.

The Celtics had possession. The last time they'd had the ball with a chance to win on the last shot had ended in disaster. In Game 3, West had swiped a throw-in intended for Cousy and won the game at the buzzer on a breakaway layup.

This time the Celtics ran a play for Ramsey. But once again the result was a turnover, although Ramsey later claimed that LA's Rudy LaRusso mugged him as he drove the lane. In any case, the Lakers now had a chance to win the game and the title on the final shot.

After a timeout, LA's Frank Selvy inbounded the ball to guard Hot Rod Hundley at the top of the key. Hundley's top two options were obvious. But the Celtics had locked down Baylor and West so tightly that Hundley had to look elsewhere. He found Selvy, who had streaked toward the basket after inbounding the ball. Having not hit from the floor for almost the entire game, Selvy had scored twice in the last 90 seconds to tie it. Now he was wide open for a twelve-footer to win it all. But the shot bounced high off the rim and Russell grabbed the rebound. The game went to overtime.

OT started dismally for Boston. Ramsey committed his sixth foul, and Baylor hit two freebies to put LA ahead. The Lakers had a chance to extend the lead, but West was called for a key offensive foul. Russell countered with a dunk to tie the game, triggering a 7–0 run that put Boston ahead to stay. LA's last hope evaporated when Baylor fouled out with 2:20 remaining.

The Celtics had their fifth title in six years. Said Red Auerbach, who'd had to survive a double-overtime Game 7 to get his first one (see Game No. 8), "This is the toughest series we've had."

Such good times prompted inevitable speculation in the press that the end was nigh. A Globe *headline earlier that month had read: '62 LAST CHANCE FOR AGING C's? Russell wasn't so sure. "We may have a few more winning years ahead," he said.*

10

Bruins 2, Rangers 1, 3 OT
April 2, 1939

The Bruins won the first Game 7 in NHL history as the
"Sudden Death Kid," Mel Hill, scored his third overtime goal
of the series

The Boston Bruins and New York Rangers made history just by
showing up for the 1939 Stanley Cup Playoffs. That season the
NHL had devised what *Globe* hockey writer Victor O. Jones aptly
called a "cockeyed" playoff format. With just seven teams (an eighth,
the Montreal Maroons, had folded), NHL owners had decided on a single division for the regular season. Six of the seven teams qualified for
the playoffs. (The last-place Chicago Black Hawks, defending Stanley
Cup champs, were the only team to miss out.)

Here's where the cockeyed part came in. Detroit and the Montreal
Canadiens, the fifth and sixth seeds, played a best-of-three series in the
opening round. So did Toronto and the New York Americans, the third
and fourth seeds. The survivors, Detroit and Toronto, met in another
best-of-three series. The Maple Leafs won, to reach the Stanley Cup Final.

Meanwhile, the two top seeds, the Bruins and Rangers—the only
teams with winning records—faced off to determine the other finalist.
But rather than best-of-three, or even best-of-five, the Bruins–Rangers
semifinal was best-of-seven—an NHL first. Even the schedule was cockeyed. The series opened with one game at New York, followed by two
games at Boston (the top seed). The site then alternated game to game.

Although Boston had finished sixteen points ahead of New York,
the teams were evenly matched. Game 1 required 59 minutes, 25 seconds of overtime—almost the equivalent of a second full game—for the
Bruins to pull out a 2–1 win. Right winger Mel Hill scored on a feed

from NHL assists leader Bill Cowley just 35 seconds before the end of the third overtime, sending the subdued Madison Square Garden crowd home at 1:05 on an early spring morning.

Apparently, home-ice advantage helped the Bruins in Game 2; it took just 8:24 of overtime for Boston to pull out the 3–2 victory. Hill again scored the winner on an assist from Cowley. In the next game, the Bruins cruised to a 4–1 win and a 3–0 series lead.

With the score tied 1–1 late in the first period of Game 4, New York tried a new strategy. Basically, it was *Slap Shot* before *Slap Shot* existed. The Rangers couldn't win playing "Eddie Shore/old-time hockey," so they went full-on Hanson Brothers instead. Actually, they went full-on Patrick Brothers. Lynn Patrick and Murray Patrick (aka "Muzz"), the strapping sons of Rangers coach and GM Lester Patrick, were the primary instigators. And their primary target was … Eddie Shore, the Bruins captain.

The rough stuff started when Rangers center Phil Watson hit Bruins defenseman Jack Portland over the head. That triggered a melee that lasted thirteen minutes. The main event was Muzz Patrick vs. Eddie Shore. Shore got the worst of it—no surprise; Patrick was a former Canadian amateur light-heavyweight boxing champion. Shore's right eye was swollen nearly shut, and his nose was gushing blood as he left the ice. Victor O. Jones, in the *Globe*: "Eddie isn't sure whether this was the 12th, 13th, or 14th time that his nose has been broken."

To add insult to Shore's injuries, the Bruins then gave up a short-handed goal while Shore was in the dressing room. It turned out to be the final margin, as the Rangers avoided a sweep.

The ugliness got uglier in Game 5, back in Boston. Each team scored within the first eight minutes on power plays. After that, referee Norman Lamport decided to put the whistle away. By the third period, the game was out of hand. When Shore and Bruins left winger Roy Conacher were simultaneously staggered on hits that drew no calls, the Garden crowd showered the ice with debris, causing a ten-minute delay. During the stoppage a fan managed to grab at Lamport, and another fan hit Muzz Patrick in the jaw with an orange. The rowdiness continued when play resumed, prompting Lamport to finally call a penalty—on the Bruins' Dit Clapper, for boarding Lynn Patrick. The crowd responded by littering the ice with "beer cans, broken seats, papers, fruit and everything that wasn't nailed down," Jones reported. Remarkably, Lamport allowed play to continue throughout the disturbance. Skating on the trash-strewn surface, the Bruins killed the Clapper penalty. The game was still 1–1 at the end of regulation, and the intermission settled things down. When Rangers center Clint Smith scored the winner at 17:19 of over-time, the Garden crowd filed out in silence.

The Bruins, who hadn't lost more than two straight games all season, picked a bad time to suffer their first three-game losing streak. The Rangers won Game 6 at Madison Square Garden, 3–1, to force Game 7 at Boston the next night. In the NHL's first-ever best-of-seven series, the Bruins were in danger of becoming the first team to blow a 3–0 lead.

Boston fans still seemed to think that the officiating was to blame for this reversal of fortune. In the first period of Game 7, the crowd of some 17,000—Jones called it the largest in Boston's hockey history—again interrupted play by throwing things on the ice whenever a whistle went against the Bruins. The rowdiness abated somewhat after a girl in the first row was struck in the head by an unidentified thrown object and knocked unconscious. (Another fan was hospitalized after collaps-ing due to "malnutrition and overexertion induced by the excitement," according to a *Globe* brief.)

Despite the egregious injustices perpetrated upon them, the Bruins managed to battle to a scoreless tie through the first period. Finally, at 15:52 of the second, Boston took a 1–0 lead, thanks to a happy accident. George Allen, a rookie Rangers wing, fell down and lost possession in his own zone. The puck rolled right to the Bruins' Gord Pettinger, who immediately rifled the puck to Ray Getliffe, a center who had been demoted to third-line left winger after getting in coach Art Ross's dog-house. Getliffe slammed the puck past Rangers goalie Bert Gardiner from just outside the crease.

But again, the Bruins couldn't hold the lead. Just three minutes later, arch villain Muzz Patrick tied the game on a slapper from the blue line. From then until the end of regulation, Jones wrote, "the teams settled down to a grim but reasonably open game." The Bruins outshot the Rangers 10–1 in the first overtime period but couldn't score. The Rangers nearly made them pay for those missed opportunities with a flurry to start the second OT, but the Bruins survived. The game remained tied after 100 minutes.

Finally, after an epic seven-game struggle, the series ended as it began: in the third overtime, with Mel Hill, the "Sudden Death Kid," scoring on a pass from Bill Cowley to give Boston a 2–1 victory. When the Garden crowd showered the ice this time, it was with what Jones described as "sheer relief from the agony of putting their hearts through the ringer for four solid hours."

The relief didn't last long. Next up: The second best-of-seven series in NHL history, against the Toronto Maple Leafs. But the Bruins made things much easier on their fans this time, beating the Leafs in five games to win the Stanley Cup for the second time (the first was in 1929; see Game No. 60). Afterward the lingering Garden crowd offered a salute to that good ol' time hockey, chanting, "We want Shore!"

9

Patriots 16, Raiders 13, OT
January 19, 2002

Without the Tuck Rule (which was correctly applied, no matter what the Raiders say) and Adam Vinatieri's ability to kick in the snow, the Patriots' first Super Bowl win never would have happened

J ust 1:50 remained in the fourth quarter of Tom Brady's first playoff start, which was also the last game ever played at Foxboro Stadium. The Patriots trailed the Raiders 13–10 on a snowy Saturday night. New England had a first-and-ten at the Oakland 42.

In its play-by-play log, Pro-football-reference.com describes the next play, which consumed just three seconds of game time, like this:

Tom Brady pass incomplete

That's the abridged version.

What unspooled in real time was considerably more complex, not to mention controversial. Brady took the snap and dropped back. He started to throw, but stopped and drew his arm back. Oakland's Charles Woodson, Brady's former Michigan teammate, had an unblocked path on a corner blitz. Woodson nailed Brady and knocked the ball loose before Brady could secure it. Oakland linebacker Greg Biekert fell on the ball.

Nearly every person watching the game reached the same conclusion: Brady had fumbled. Oakland had recovered. And with the Patriots out of timeouts, the game was effectively over.

This was so obvious, in fact, that when referee Walt Coleman went under the hood to look at a replay, Oakland's radio announcers, Greg Papa and Tom Flores, wondered what aspect of the play could possibly be under review. "Whether it was a fumble or not, I guess," said Flores.

Could their eyes have deceived them? Moments later, the two harmonized on their interpretation of the replay: "That's a fumble."

Or not. "After reviewing the play, the quarterback's arm was going forward," said Coleman. "It is an incomplete pass."

"A bullshit call," Woodson said afterward.

Actually it wasn't. It was merely a by-the-book interpretation of the so-called Tuck Rule.

Coleman's initial explanation, like Brady's pass, was incomplete. Yes, Brady's arm had gone forward. But then it went back, which was where the confusion came in. Coleman understood what few others did: The backward motion was irrelevant. The Tuck Rule decreed that an aborted pass attempt still counted as a pass attempt until the quarterback had secured the ball—which Brady had not. In other words, the quarterback was granted immunity from fumbling on a pass attempt, even past the point where he has clearly decided not to attempt the pass.

A bullshit rule? Yes. A bullshit call? No.

And anyway, it's not as if the Patriots were awarded points on the play. They still trailed by a field goal in a snowstorm. The Tuck Rule gave them a huge break—but only if they took advantage of it.

They did. The drive continued to the Oakland 28. On fourth-and-nine, with half a minute remaining and the clock running, Vinatieri came on to attempt the tying field goal on a slippery field from 45 yards out. Long placekicks were such a dicey proposition that the Patriots had passed up a pair of opportunities in the first half and ended up scoreless. Oakland's mule-legged kicker, Sebastian Janikowski, had converted from 45 yards in the third quarter—but that field goal, which had extended Oakland's lead to 13–3, had come under far less pressure. Vinatieri's kick was New England's last chance.

He made it. Considering the circumstances and the degree of difficulty, that 45-yard field goal was the greatest clutch play in franchise history.

Here's an indication of what a long shot that kick was: The Patriots had a chance to go for another 45-yard field goal five minutes into sudden-death overtime—and they chose not to risk it. (One reason was that they were now headed into the wind—but still.) This time, on fourth-and-four from the Oakland 28, they went for it. Brady hit David Patten for six yards and a new set of downs. Five plays later, on third-and-goal from the Oakland five, Vinatieri returned to the field. Raiders coach Jon Gruden called a timeout to try to ice the kicker. But that ploy actually helped *de*-ice the kicker. Vinatieri & Co. used the extra time to clear a spot on the freezer-burned tundra of Foxboro Stadium—or Sullivan Stadium, Schaefer Stadium, [Something Unprintable] Stadium, or whatever name Pats fans chose to remember the place by. Regardless, a singular playoff game amid a January snowfall could white-out three decades of mostly bad memories at the old dump on Route One. Before the 2001 season, perhaps the best tenant the stadium ever had was the 1976 Patriots. That team, which finished 11–3, led the Raiders 21–17 in the waning moments of a divisional playoff game at Oakland Coliseum. But Raiders quarterback Ken Stabler scored from a yard out with ten seconds left, capping a drive sustained by five New England penalties, including a borderline roughing-the passer call on Sugar Bear Hamilton.

Now, thanks to the Tuck Rule, the Patriots were poised to settle an old score with the Raiders. And New England's homely old home could go out in style.

At 8½ minutes into overtime, Vinatieri nailed the winning kick from 23 yards. Instantly, Foxboro Stadium, that moribund aluminum monstrosity, transformed into an enormous commemorative snow globe, swirling in celebration.

Having dispatched one longtime member of the AFC aristocracy, the upstart '01 Patriots set their sights on another: the Pittsburgh Steelers (see Game No. 24). As for the Tuck Rule: It survived eleven more years before NFL owners voted it out. The Patriots abstained on the vote. The Raiders not only voted to abolish the rule, but they also sent a celebratory tweet when the results were announced: "Adios, Tuck Rule."

8

Celtics 125, Hawks 123, 2 OT
April 13, 1957

This was the most dramatic Game 7 in NBA Finals history—and it gave the Celtics the first of their seventeen championships

Rochester, New York celebrated an NBA championship before Boston did. So did Syracuse. Minneapolis, original home of the Lakers, celebrated *five*. During the league's first decade, when a road trip was a grim itinerary of backwater auditoriums, Boston was outclassed. As they began their eleventh season in the fall of 1956, the Celtics had never even won a division title, much less a league title. Even so, there was hope that things were about to change. Confidence, even.

The Celtics already had a solid foundation. They had a crafty, driven coach, Red Auerbach, and two future Hall of Famers, Bob Cousy and Bill Sharman, in the backcourt. And six months earlier, they had scored the richest draft-day haul not just in the history of the NBA but of any pro sport: Tom Heinsohn, a "territorial pick" from Holy Cross, and two members of the two-time NCAA champion San Francisco Dons: guard K.C. Jones and center Bill Russell. Three more future Hall-of-Famers. (Jones wouldn't join the team until 1958, after serving in the military.)

From the start Auerbach recognized that Russell, with his potential as a stopper, was the key component. "He's the greatest defensive center I've ever seen," Auerbach said on draft day. "He gives me a big man for the future."

To land Russell, Auerbach had to strike a deal with his former employer, St. Louis Hawks owner Ben Kerner. The two had a contentious history. Auerbach was the Hawks' coach in the 1949–50 season, when the team was based in Moline, Illinois. He abruptly resigned after the season—reportedly because Kerner had meddled in personnel moves—and joined the Celtics shortly after. Now, because St. Louis held the second pick in the 1956 NBA draft, Auerbach had to negotiate with Kerner to pull off the most significant personnel move of his long and legendary career.

The Hawks already had the game's preeminent big man, Bob Pettit, who had averaged 25.7 points and 16.2 rebounds per game that season. Kerner decided that Celtics center Ed Macauley, a St. Louis native and another future Hall of Famer, would be a better complement to Pettit than Russell would. But Kerner also insisted that the Celtics include rookie forward Cliff Hagan—yet *another* future Hall of Famer—in the deal. So it wasn't as if Auerbach had fleeced his old boss. In the short term, at least, the deal had made each team an instant contender.

Because of his commitment to the U.S. Olympic Team, which won the gold medal in Australia that autumn, Russell didn't join the Celtics until December 22. He made his debut at Boston Garden—against the Hawks, fittingly. In his first game he scored just six points in 21 minutes—but he also had sixteen rebounds. And he blocked three of Pettit's shots during crunch time. He was such a conspicuous defensive presence that the *Globe* ran a story two days later with the headline: WILL RUSSELL REVOLUTIONIZE PRO GAME?

The Celtics needed a last-minute rally to beat the Hawks in Russell's debut, 95–93, in a game that foreshadowed the 1957 NBA Finals. The two teams took different roads to get there. The Celtics breezed to an NBA best record of 44–28 to claim their first Eastern Division title and the first-round bye that went with it. They swept the Syracuse Nationals in a relatively low-stress best-of-five series to reach the finals.

Chronic underachievers, the Hawks (who went through three coaches that year) slogged to a pitiful 34–38 mark. Still, that put them in a three-way tie with Minneapolis and the Fort Wayne Pistons for the top spot in the West. Since there were only four teams in each division and the top three made the playoffs, this presented a problem. Which of those three losers deserved the first-round bye? In an improvised rock-paper-scissors tournament, St. Louis dispatched Fort Wayne and then Minneapolis in a pair of single-elimination tiebreakers to win the division. The Lakers then swept the Pistons in a best-of-three semifinal for the right to play the Hawks again in the best-of-five Western Division

Finals. Finally elevating their play to their level of talent, St. Louis swept. That set up a Hawks–Celtics finale.

With a better record, home-court advantage, and both the league's MVP (Cousy, with 20.6 points per game and 7.5 assists) and Rookie of the Year (Heinsohn, with 16.2 points per game and 9.8 rebounds) the Celtics seemed to hold a significant edge. Not for long; St. Louis won the opener at Boston Garden 125–123 in double overtime, as Pettit scored 37 points and Macauley, the former Celtic, added 23. The Celtics regrouped to win Game 2 by twenty, and the series shifted to St. Louis. That's when the underlying animosity between the two franchises went public. Just before Game 3, Auerbach demanded that the baskets at St. Louis's Kiel Auditorium be measured to ensure that they were regulation height. Kerner called him a "bush-leaguer." Auerbach responded by punching Kerner in the mouth. Some accounts suggest that Auerbach's bravado swung the series in the Celtics' favor. This makes little sense when you consider that St. Louis won Game 3, 100–98.

If anybody gave the Celtics inspiration in that tough road environment, it was Cousy, the seven-year veteran. Despite having a tooth knocked out in Game 4, Cousy led the Celtics with 31 points in a 123–118 victory. Cousy then set an NBA playoff record with nineteen assists as the Celtics won Game 5 in Boston, 124–109, for a 3–2 series lead. But the Celtics couldn't close the deal in Game 6 at St. Louis because they couldn't box out Cliff Hagan, the player considered a throw-in in the Russell trade. Hagan's put-back with two seconds left in Game 6 gave St. Louis a 96–94 win. The series was even at 3–3, and the question of whether Auerbach or Kerner had made the better deal a year earlier remained unresolved.

The Finals ended two weeks after they had begun, in the same place, Boston Garden, with a game decided by the same score: 125–123 in double overtime. But this time the Celtics won. And the tension was much, much higher. There was no more breathing room in the series, nor was there any in this game, which featured twenty ties and 38 lead changes. And it was the Celtics' veterans, succumbing to fatigue and to the pressure of having a championship within their grasp for the first time, who suffered most. Sharman was just 3-of-20 from the floor. Cousy was even worse—2-of-20. He even airballed a free throw that would have iced the game with thirteen seconds left in regulation.

Fortunately, Boston's rookies didn't know enough to be nervous.

Heinsohn was immense: 37 points on 17-of-33 shooting, with 23 rebounds.

Russell also came up big, with series highs for both points (nineteen) and rebounds (32), to go along with a slew of defensive plays that never made it into the box score. His end-to-end hustle was relentless. In what Heinsohn later called "the greatest play I ever saw in basketball," Russell made a full-court sprint to block a Jack Coleman breakaway layup that would have put the Hawks up by one with 39 seconds left in regulation.

But not even Russell had the instincts to anticipate the Hawks' last play. It was drawn up during a timeout by St. Louis player/coach Alex Hannum, who also pulled the trigger. Hannum, a forward who hadn't played at all in the first six games, chose a critical time to make his first appearance of the Finals: with just 1:37 left in the second overtime of Game 7. And he left himself open to second-guessing when he was called for traveling with just seventeen seconds left and the Hawks down by one. Hannum fouled Celtics forward Jim Loscutoff with one second remaining to keep the Hawks' faint hopes alive. Loscutoff hit a free throw to make it a two-point game. But the Hawks were 94 feet away from the basket, with just a count of one-Mississippi to execute a play. There wasn't time for a catch-turn-and-shoot maneuver, so Hannum instead directed his full-court heave at the Celtics' backboard—and nailed it.

When Pettit grabbed the carom, he was already squared up to the basket, with a great look from about ten feet. But his shot rolled out. The Celtics were NBA champions for the first time.

A lot of tradition can be traced to that afternoon—including the first shaving of a playoff beard. When Russell had arrived in December, he was wearing a goatee. He told a teammate that he intended to wear it until the Celtics won the Eastern Division title. "Then I decided to wear it through the playoffs," he said. "If we'd lost I was going to keep it on until we won the championship—no matter how many years it took."

Instead, the goatee survived exactly sixteen weeks. That's how little time had elapsed from the moment Russell had stepped onto the Boston Garden parquet for the first time and the moment he danced across it as the Celtics celebrated their first NBA championship. As he reflected on the greatest year any basketball player has ever experienced, Russell used a tone that indicated he still felt like the new kid in town. "Let's see," he said. "That's three championships in a year for me—NCAA, Olympics, and now with these fellows."

Russell had to wait an eternity (by his standards) for his next championship. In 1958 he severely sprained an ankle during Game 3 of a Finals rematch with the Hawks. He missed the next two games, and his mobility was limited when he returned in Game 6, with the Celtics down 3–2. Pettit took full advantage, scoring 50 points as the Hawks won 110–109 to take their first championship. That provided temporary validation for Ben Kerner. "I haven't seen the sun since the [Russell] trade," Kerner said. But Russell and the Celtics rebounded to win eight straight NBA titles, leaving no doubt who made the better deal in the 1956 NBA draft.

7

Bruins 4, Canadiens 3, OT
April 27, 2011

Yes, it was only the first round. But under the circumstances—overtime of Game 7 against the archrival Canadiens, a year after blowing a 3–0 series lead against the Flyers—there was no bigger victory for the Bruins on their march to the 2011 Stanley Cup

There's no more suspenseful scenario in sports. Game 7. Stanley Cup Playoffs. Sudden-death overtime. Next goal ends somebody's season. Could take five seconds or five hours. No clear advantage for either side. Each team battling exhaustion, desperate to hold traction on gouged ice, one funky puck hop from elimination. You don't need an angst-laden backstory on top of all that.

The 2011 Boston Bruins provided one anyway. A 39-year championship drought. An 8–24 record against their Game 7 opponent in 32 playoff series. Seventeen years since their last Game 7 victory—a stretch that saw the two worst collapses in franchise history. In 2004 they had become the first Bruins team ever to cough up a 3–1 series lead, in the opening round against Montreal. Then in the 2010 Eastern Conference Semifinal against the Flyers, the Bruins had joined the 1942 Red Wings and 1975 Penguins as the only NHL teams ever to blow a 3–0 series lead. And the Bruins took that infamy to a new level by blowing a 3–0 lead in Game 7. At home.

So how could the crowd of 17,565 at TD Garden possibly get comfortable in a game like this, with a *team* like this? So hard to gauge.

The Bruins had shown plenty of fight against the Canadiens during the regular season, whipping Montreal 8–6 in a February slugfest and whitewashing them 7–0 in March. But in between those two statement games at the TD Garden was a question-mark performance at Montreal's Bell Centre, a 4–1 loss most notable for Zdeno Chara's concussive hit on Montreal left winger Max Pacioretty. Those results magnified the significance of the Bruins' first-place finish in the Eastern Conference's Northeast Division. Boston held home-ice advantage for the 3–6 match-up with Montreal in the first round. Based on recent history, it appeared that they would need it.

The Bruins flushed that advantage while barely putting up a fight. They scored just one goal in the first two games at TD Garden, losing both. In the franchise's long and sporadically glorious history, 26 Bruins teams had fallen behind 0–2 in a Stanley Cup series. Not one had recovered.

The problem, said Bruins coach Claude Julien, was that "our team has not played at all close to the way we know we can." But they were playing exactly the way Bruins fans had come to expect.

And that's why the next two games, at the Bell Centre, were such a pleasant surprise. Boston jumped to a 3–0 lead in Game 3 and gutted out five Montreal power plays to survive for a 4–2 win. The Bruins showed even more mettle in Game 4, overcoming a 3–1 second-period deficit to win 5–4 in overtime and square the series at two games each.

After that, who knew what to expect? A double overtime win back at the TD Garden (see Game No. 43) to take a 3–2 series lead? Well, why not? A 2–1 loss back in Montreal with a chance to close it out? Well, of course. These were the Bruins, after all. And the opponent was the Canadiens.

And now Game 7, which was a distillation of all the ups and downs that this series—and the Bruins franchise—had to offer. Up: The Bruins had a 2–0 lead less than six minutes into the game. Down: They couldn't hold it. The tying goal, at 5:50 of the second period, was particularly hideous. With a man advantage, the Bruins were tentatively assembling in the neutral zone. Mark Recchi lost the puck just as he skated over the spoked-B logo at center ice. Canadiens center Thomas Plekanec swiped it for a shockingly easy breakaway. Tim Thomas had no chance on Plekanec's shot from point-blank range.

Among other things, the shorthanded goal meant that the Bruins' impotent power play (0-for-21 and counting) had generated more offense for Montreal than for Boston. Meanwhile, the Canadiens hadn't scored an even-strength goal since Game 5. Which meant that every penalty was now a psychological burden for Boston, regardless of which side drew the whistle. So it's understandable that Montreal occasionally took diving to new depths.

It caught up with them halfway through the third period. After some incidental contact from Chris Kelly's stick near center ice, Canadiens defenseman Roman Hamrlik flopped to the ice as if he'd been assassinated. Hamrlik lay there, awaiting a call that never came, while Kelly pressed ahead with the play and poked home the go-ahead goal on a rebound at 9:44. Now the Bruins had merely to stanch the Canadiens' attack for ten minutes to win the series.

They couldn't do it, of course—thanks to yet another penalty, with just 2:37 remaining. This one was especially frustrating, because it happened at the Montreal end, with the Canadiens posing no imminent threat. Patrice Bergeron was merely pursuing Montreal defenseman James Wisniewski behind the Montreal net when he brushed Wisniewski's face with his stick. It wasn't much, but it was obvious enough that it earned Bergeron two minutes in the box. He'd served just 40 seconds of his sentence before Canadiens defenseman P.K. Subban one-timed a rocket past Thomas from just above the left faceoff circle. Game 7 appeared destined for the worst possible outcome: a 39-year buildup that ends in sudden death.

But sudden-death overtime actually suited the 2011 Bruins. Give them an edge—whether it was a two-goal lead or a one-man advantage—and they didn't seem to know what to do with it. But at even strength they were the stronger team. And overtime is the ultimate test of even strength. No coming from behind, no protecting the lead. (And usually no penalties, unless the offense borders on a criminal act.) Just score once and be done with it. Already, the Bruins had done it twice in this series.

Make it three times.

Montreal carried the momentum into overtime and spent most of the first five minutes pressing the attack, forcing Thomas to make three high-stress saves. The Bruins' decisive counterattack, by contrast, was notable for its efficiency. Kelly started the sequence by flicking a soft wrist shot at Montreal goalie Carey Price, who caught it. That set up a faceoff in the Montreal end. Bruins center David Krejci won the faceoff at the left circle. It took twenty seconds for the puck to cycle behind the net, along the right boards and back across the ice, from Adam McQuaid to Milan Lucic to Nathan Horton, who had created just enough space to wind up and deliver the game-winner.

After all the disasters and disappointments, all the handwringing and hard times, the Bruins had delivered the ultimate shock. They had made a series-winning goal in sudden-death overtime against the Montreal Canadiens look simple.

Avenging the previous season's collapse against Philadelphia also looked simple, as the Bruins blew away the Flyers in a sweep. After that, Boston reverted to doing things the hard way, with Game 7 wins against Tampa Bay (see Game No. 17) and Vancouver (see Game no. 55) en route to the Stanley Cup.

6

Celtics 128, Suns 126, 3OT
June 4, 1976

No NBA Finals game was longer—or stranger

It *still* wasn't over. Not by a long shot. And there had already been several highlight packages' worth of those during Game 5 of the 1976 NBA Finals—including the low-percentage leaner that John Havlicek had just banked in from seventeen feet. That prayer, in the frantic last moments of the second overtime, had transformed what had looked like a one-point loss to the Phoenix Suns into what now looked like a one-point Celtics win. Fans flooded the parquet floor at Boston Garden in a premature celebration—not to mention an ugly one. (More on that later.)

This was an unlikely classic. The Celtics, top seed in the Eastern Conference, had run the table at the Garden during the playoffs: 8–0, including a couple of relatively easy wins over Phoenix in games 1 and 2 of the Finals. Phoenix, just 42–40 on the year and seeded fourth in the West, had evened the series on their home floor in games 3 and 4. But the Celtics immediately regained control back at the Garden in Game 5. Boston led 42–20 early in the second quarter and was still comfortably ahead at halftime, 61–45.

Eight minutes into the third quarter the game was tied at 68. And from that point on, the Celtics and Suns put on an extended demonstration of how to play basketball at a high level under extreme pressure. It wasn't just the stars; in this game *everybody* delivered, starters and subs alike.

It was the collective clutch play, rather than a collection of individual clutch plays, that made the game transcendent.

The Suns could have folded after the Celtics' opening blitz. They didn't. The Celtics could have choked when the Suns came all the way back. They didn't. The Suns could have let their attention drift to Game 6 once the Celtics pushed the lead back to nine with 3:49 left. Instead they chipped away, cutting the deficit to five with 1:03 remaining. Then Paul Westphal, an ex-Celtic, tied the game all by himself, with five points in thirteen seconds. After an offensive foul on Celtics center Dave Cowens, Phoenix forward Curtis Perry hit one of two from the line to give the Suns their first lead of the game, with just 22 seconds left. But Havlicek countered with one of two from the line at the other end, and it was 95–95 at the end of regulation.

The first overtime, in which each team scored just six points, was a relative lull. Then came the second overtime. It began with a flurry as Celtics point guard Jo Jo White (who led all scorers with 33 points on 15-of-29 shooting) and the Suns' rookie guard, Ricky Sobers, exchanged two hoops each. It ended with the most dramatic twenty seconds of play in NBA history.

The sequence started when White converted on a terrific drive along the right baseline, lofting a floater just over the fingertips of Phoenix forward Gar Heard and banking it in from high off the glass. With nineteen seconds left the score was 109–106, Boston. And in those pre-three-pointer days, that meant it was a two-possession game.

Phoenix called its final timeout, advancing the ball to half court. With several good scoring options available—Sobers, Westphal, and Perry all topped twenty points on the night—the Suns went to … Dick Van Arsdale, an aging backup guard whose left wrist was wrapped because he had broken it during the season. Van Arsdale dropped in a fifteen-footer, his only field goal of the night, to make it a one-point game.

Then came a Bizarro World interpretation of Celtics history. On a hurried throw-in to Havlicek from backup center Jim Ard, Westphal, of all people, made the steal. One reason the Celtics had dealt him to Phoenix a year earlier (for guard Charlie Scott) was that Westphal supposedly was slow afoot and a poor defender. Now he was back at the Garden, haunting the Celtics and turning an iconic Boston sports moment on its head: *Westphal stole the ball—from Havlicek!* While falling out of bounds, Westphal got the ball to Van Arsdale, who fed Perry. Perry missed his first attempt but grabbed the rebound and hit a jumper from sixteen feet to put Phoenix up 110–109 with just five seconds left.

And all of *that* merely set the stage for Havlicek's off-balance seventeen-footer that put the Celtics back on top—which was merely the prelude to the most stunning sequence of the night.

First, the ugly moment. Maybe it was the zeitgeist; the bicentennial was just a month away and Boston, crucible of the American Revolution, was in a revolting mood. Earlier that week, fans at Fenway had disrupted a Red Sox–Yankees game several times by throwing firecrackers on the field. Gene Kirby, head of Sox security, offered a response that is startlingly glib in hindsight. "Heck," Kirby told the *Globe*'s Will McDonough, "the police tell us that compared to what goes on at Boston Garden, going to our place is like going to choir practice."

Even more startling: Kirby was right. Said Suns general manager Jerry Colangelo, "The lack of security [at Boston Garden] is deplorable." Just thirteen Boston police officers were on duty for Game 5—not nearly enough to contain the crowd that spilled onto the floor after Havlicek put the Celtics ahead late in the second overtime. But the game wasn't over. One second remained. As officials tried to clear the floor, referee Richie Powers was assaulted by a fan—or a "boor," as CBS play-by-play man Brent Musburger called him.

It would have been a shame for such a terrific game to end on such a sour note. But the Suns were out of timeouts. They would have to inbound the ball from beneath their own basket, with just one second to advance the ball the length of the floor for a shot. There seemed to be little hope.

In Game 7 of the 1957 NBA Finals, facing an almost identical situation, the St. Louis Hawks came up with a creative play that at least gave them a shot (see Game No. 8). Mendy Rudolph had worked that 1957 game as an official. In 1976, Rudolph was at the Garden again, as a CBS analyst. And he predicted that the Suns would give themselves a shot with another bit of inspired creativity. "I would not be surprised now if they will call an extra timeout to gain the distance [to half court] and have a technical foul assessed," Rudolph said. "They could never score from 94 feet. They may from half court."

Right all around.

Just as Rudolph predicted, Phoenix called an illegal timeout and was assessed a technical. Jo Jo White sank the free throw to make it a two-point game. But the rulebook had a loophole. Other than the technical foul shot, the Suns' illegal timeout was treated the same as a legitimate timeout—including the right to inbound the ball from half court. (That's no longer the case; besides getting hit with a technical, a team now loses possession for calling an illegal timeout.)

The extra distance was crucial. With fans still ringing the floor, ready to reprise their celebration, Curtis Perry lobbed the ball to Heard at the top of the key. Heard caught the pass, turned, and released the ball just before the buzzer. "Honestly," Heard said later, "the moment I shot it, I knew it was going in."

On this night, of *course* Heard's shot went in. The game was tied at 112.

Attrition took its toll in the third overtime. With 3:23 left and the game tied at 114, Celtics forward Paul Silas joined Cowens and starting guard Charlie Scott on the bench with six fouls. Between them Cowens and Silas had grabbed 33 rebounds—more than half of Boston's total. But the departure of Boston's top board men simply evened the score; Phoenix was playing without a center. (Rookie of the Year Alvan Adams had fouled out late in regulation with twenty points and his backup, Dennis Awtrey, had fouled out in the second overtime.)

And thus the most critical 3½ minutes of the 1976 NBA Finals had the freewheeling feel of a pickup game, as each team went with a smaller, improvised lineup. Ard made back-to-back defensive plays to swing the game in Boston's favor. Phoenix had a two-point lead and the ball near the two-minute mark when Ard made a steal that led to the tying bucket on yet another Jo Jo White jumper in traffic. On the Suns' next trip, Ard tied up Perry for a jump ball. Ard tipped the toss-up to White, who tipped to Don Nelson, who threw an outlet pass to Havlicek, who fed a bounce pass to White, who drew the defense before dishing off to backup forward Glenn McDonald for the layup that put Boston ahead to stay with 1:38 remaining. Which isn't to say that the Suns went quietly. Even after two Ard free throws made it 128–122 with just 31 seconds left, Phoenix still wasn't done. A pair of Westphal layups, including one on a 360 spin, made it a two-point game with twelve seconds left. Westphal then got his fingertips on the ball during Boston's shaky advance to the frontcourt before Ard hot-potatoed a pass to White. While the spent Suns tried to get close enough to someone in a Boston uniform to commit a foul, White ended the game, fittingly, by staying a step ahead.

Game 5 ended early Saturday morning, and the teams then had to fly across the country for Game 6 in Phoenix Sunday afternoon. The outcome was predictably brutal; the Celtics led 39–33 at halftime, en route to an 87–80 victory that clinched their thirteenth NBA title. Jo Jo White, who scored fifteen points in the finale and averaged 21.7 points per game in the Finals, was named MVP.

2-5

Red Sox 6, Yankees 4, 12 innings
October 17, 2004

Red Sox 5, Yankees 4, 14 innings
October 18, 2004

Red Sox 4, Yankees 2
October 19, 2004

Red Sox 10, Yankees 3
October 20, 2004

This was the grandest achievement in Boston sports history. It consisted not of a single great game, but of four games stitched together

> *"Because the outcome of great events becomes so well established in our minds, there is a tendency to think things had to go as they did. But there is nothing inevitable about history."*
> —David McCullough

> *"For the 86th consecutive autumn, the Red Sox are not going to win the World Series."*
> —Dan Shaughnessy, the Boston *Globe*, October 17, 2004

So, no: Boston's first World Series championship in 86 years was not a foregone conclusion. At 30 minutes past midnight on Sunday, October 17, 2004, it was not even a foreseeable one. Having just been bludgeoned 19–8 in a game that felt more like rec-league softball than playoff baseball, the Red Sox had dropped into a 3–0 hole in the

American League Championship Series against the New York You-Know-Whos. "And, in this sport," Dan Shaughnessy's *Globe* colleague, Bob Ryan, noted in the Sunday edition, "that is an official death sentence."

So while Red Sox Nation awaited the coroner, Yankee fans awaited the coronation. Again.

But a peculiar thing happened at Fenway in Game 4 on that Sunday night. The Red Sox refused to tap out of the chokehold. They didn't submit when Alex Rodriguez, the most hated of the hated Yankees, put New York ahead with a two-run homer off Derek Lowe in the third. Nor did they submit when New York countered three Red Sox runs in the bottom of the fifth with two more in the top of the sixth to immediately retake the lead, 4–3.

Reliever Mike Timlin took the first tiny step. While his effort was hardly a masterpiece—three singles, two walks, and a wild pitch in two-thirds of an inning—Timlin retired Derek Jeter with the bases loaded to keep it a one-run game. And that's the way it stayed as the slow-footed Yankees squandered opportunities for an insurance run in the seventh (leadoff walk), eighth (leadoff walk), and ninth (leadoff walk).

So when Kevin Millar worked a walk against Mariano Rivera to start the bottom of the ninth, and Dave Roberts came on to pinch run, and Roberts, going on Rivera's first pitch to Bill Mueller, just beat Derek Jeter's tag at second on the throw from Jorge Posada, it felt like the start of a rally. And not just a rally to prevent the indignity of a sweep. But a rally with historic possibilities. With Pedro Martinez up next in the rotation, and Curt Schilling potentially available after that....

A rainout had absorbed the remaining travel day, so there would be no more breaks in the series. As long as the Red Sox won, there would be a game the next day, right through Game 7. And as the rally gathered strength, this continuity condensed it. It was like watching a well-edited thriller whose quick pace keeps you from dwelling on the implausible plot. This historic unfolding (from Boston's perspective) or folding (from New York's perspective) felt less like four discrete games than a single continuous thread. And that thread led to an outlandish outcome that, long before it arrived, seemed not just possible but, yes, inevitable.

But first Roberts had to score.

He did, of course, when Bill Mueller bounded a 1–1 cutter through the box and up the middle. The game was tied, headed to extra innings.

The thread began to unspool a little faster now. Curt Leskanic, with his 20.25 ALCS ERA, retired Bernie Williams (who was then the all-time postseason home run leader) with the bases loaded to end the top of the eleventh. Meanwhile, the Red Sox continued to burn through the New York bullpen. In the last of the twelfth, Yankees manager Joe Torre turned to aging, overworked righty Paul Quantrill to face Manny Ramirez and David Ortiz. Quantrill retired neither. Ortiz launched his two-run walk-off at 1:22 on Monday morning. That led to Pedro Martinez taking the ball at 5:11 Monday evening and breezing through the Yankees in the top of the first. The Sox offense then ground two runs and 34 pitches out of Mike Mussina in the bottom of the first, creating the odd dynamic of a team with a three-games-to-one lead approaching desperation mode. (All of this played out against a compelling subplot regarding Curt Schilling's potential availability for Game 6—a story that involved a ruptured tendon sheath in Schilling's ankle, an experimental surgery, Sox team physician Bill Morgan, and a cadaver to be named later.)

The Sox' early lead gave New York a sense of urgency. Bernie Williams homered in the second, and Mussina settled down and shut the Sox out over the next five innings.

And then the great rally's long thread snagged and threatened to snap. Trailing 2–1, the Yankees loaded the bases against Martinez in the sixth. Derek Jeter unloaded them with a double to make it 4–2, New York. Then the Yankees loaded the bases again, with two outs. Due up: lefty slugger Hideki Matsui, a.k.a. Godzilla, who was hitting .522 in the series with five doubles, a triple, two home runs, and ten RBI.

Matsui and Martinez had some postseason history. A year earlier, in the infamous eighth inning of ALCS Game 7, Matsui had doubled off of a laboring Martinez and scored the tying run. And yet now, with Martinez at 107 pitches and having walked one batter and hit two others in the inning already, and with the Red Sox one good swing away from having their Destiny Express irrevocably derailed, and with the Yankees' hottest hitter at the plate—in a favorable righty-lefty matchup, no less—manager Terry Francona stuck with Pedro. (*What, the guy never heard of Grady Little?*) Pedro responded by surrendering a rope to right field … that Trot Nixon caught while sliding on his knees.

Having failed to break the game open, the Yankees faced a growing backpressure. This was most apparent in the bottom of the eighth, when setup man Tom Gordon allowed a leadoff homer to David Ortiz that shrank the margin to one run. Gordon, a former Sox reliever who was once name-dropped in the title of a Stephen King horror story, now found himself trapped in a real-life horror show as King watched from the Fenway grandstand. "For whatever reason," Joe Torre later told writer Tom Verducci, "Tom Gordon was a mess out there." Gordon walked Millar after getting ahead 0–2 and then allowed a single to Nixon that put the tying run on third with no outs. For the second straight night Torre was compelled to summon Rivera in the eighth inning. The first hitter that Rivera faced, Jason Varitek, tied the game with a sacrifice fly.

From that point on every critical bounce in the series went Boston's way. In the ninth, Tony Clark's liner down the right-field line off of Sox closer Keith Foulke would have scored Ruben Sierra from first—if the ball hadn't hopped into the stands for a ground-rule double that kept Sierra at third, where he remained stranded. In the thirteenth, Tim Wakefield threw 34 pitches, three of which eluded Varitek behind the plate. In order, these three passed balls resulted in leadoff man Gary Sheffield reaching first after a strikeout; Hideki Matsui (who forced Sheffield) advancing to second; and then Matsui advancing to third while Jorge Posada (who had been intentionally walked) advanced to second. But despite putting the lead runner on against a knuckleballer whose catcher was reduced to playing goalie, the Yankees never used a pinch runner, never tried to steal, never attempted to put any pressure on Varitek. And like Sierra and Clark in the ninth, Matsui and Posada were marooned in scoring position.

Finally, in the last of the fourteenth, as the game approached the six-hour mark, with Torre again down to the dregs of his staff, Johnny Damon and Manny Ramirez drew walks off of Esteban Loaiza and Ortiz delivered his second straight walk-off hit, a single to center on the tenth pitch of an at-bat that was as taut as a guitar string.

From there, the undead Red Sox returned to New York to haunt Yankee Stadium. On the mound was Dr. Morgan's monster, Curt Schilling, oozing blood from his sutured right ankle as he limited the Yankees to one run through seven innings. His teammates gave him four runs to work with, all in the fourth inning, three on a homer by second baseman Mark Bellhorn, who had entered the game hitting .129. Umpire Jim Joyce originally ruled the hit a ground-rule double, believing that a fan had leaned over the fence to try to catch it, but the umpiring crew changed the call after a conference.

It was the first of two overturned interference-related calls, made without benefit of replay, that went Boston's way. In the bottom of the eighth, with one out, one in, and one on, Alex Rodriguez hit a tapper to Sox pitcher Bronson Arroyo, and the two had a footrace to first. They collided just up the line from the bag. The ball came out of Arroyo's glove as Rodriguez reached first and Derek Jeter raced home to make it 4–3. Now the dangerous Gary Sheffield would bat with one out and the tying run on.

Or not. After another discussion, the umpiring crew determined that Rodriguez had slapped the ball out of Arroyo's glove (which everyone back in Boston had already seen in repeated replays). The call: interference. A-Rod was out, Jeter was sent back to first, and Sheffield popped to the catcher. Inning over. Once Foulke tight-roped through the ninth (two walks, 28 pitches), the undead were dead even.

After the sustained stress of the previous three nights, the tension broke early in Game 7. Ortiz launched a two-run bomb in the first off Kevin Brown, who then loaded the bases in the second before giving way to Javier Vazquez, who served up a grand slam on his first pitch to Johnny Damon to make it 6–0. Damon added a two-run homer off of Vazquez in the fourth to make it 8–1.

There would be no Bucky or Buckner or Boone moment this time. Pitch by pitch, at-bat by at-bat, inning by inning, hour by hour, as one day blended into the next, the Red Sox had climbed from a three-games-to-none deficit at Fenway Park, one inning from elimination, to a seven-run lead in Game 7 at Yankee Stadium. And there was nothing anybody in New York could do but watch. The outcome was inevitable—history in the making.

The Sox completed their improbable run to the World Series by sweeping St. Louis—a nice bonus for Boomers who remembered the Cardinals shattering the Impossible Dream in 1967 and aging Sox nationals who recalled Enos Slaughter beating Johnny Pesky's relay throw with the winning run in 1946.

1

Patriots 20, Rams 17
February 3, 2002

The game that changed everything in Boston sports

The line for Super Bowl XXXVI, fourteen points, was less an indictment of the underdog Patriots than an endorsement of the favored Rams. As the millennium turned, St. Louis seemed about two touchdowns ahead of the rest of the NFL. Head coach Mike Martz had taken an Arena League refugee, Kurt Warner, and transformed him into a two-time NFL MVP. Warner's 4,830 yards passing in 2001 was the second-highest total in NFL history to that point, and almost 700 more than 2001 runner-up Peyton Manning. The Rams' offense, dubbed "The Greatest Show on Turf," seemed focus-grouped for mass appeal. Warner's weapons included two black guys with Hollywood-ready names, Torry and Isaac, a white guy named Ricky, and—as though a gesture of inclusion for troubled times—a Muslim, Az-Zahir Hakim. This was the offense of the future: Kurt Warner, the former Iowa Barnstormer, and a multicultural receiving corps performing dazzling feats in a place called the Trans World Dome.

But the Rams weren't simply a pumped-up Arena League team humming along in climate-controlled comfort. In fact, Warner had hit his high-water mark for the season playing outdoors on a cold night—in New England. He'd gone 30-of-42 for 401 yards in a 24–17 St. Louis win at Foxboro in November.

Patriots coach Bill Belichick had devised an array of blitzes for that game plan, which proved futile. Now, heading into Super Bowl XXXVI—indoors, at the Louisiana Superdome, where he wouldn't even have the elements on his side—Belichick had concluded that New England's best chance was to try to contain … Marshall Faulk. A running back.

And he was right.

St. Louis's flash was misleading. The Greatest Show on Turf was rooted in a traditional ground game. During Faulk's first three years with the Rams, St. Louis had a 37–11 regular-season record and two Super Bowl appearances—thanks in large part to Faulk's rock-steady dependability in the backfield. These were his rushing numbers:

YEAR	CARRIES	YARDS	AVG.	TD
1999	253	1,381	5.5	7
2000	253	1,359	5.4	18
2001	260	1,382	5.3	12

In addition, Faulk averaged 84 receptions over those three years. In 2001, his 83 catches and nine receiving touchdowns led the team. Whether through designed plays or dump-offs, he was a big part of the St. Louis air attack.

Limit Faulk, Belichick decided, and you could limit the Rams' effectiveness. That meant hitting Faulk hard all game long, whether he had the ball or not. According to David Halberstam's book *The Education of a Coach*, Belichick came up with a simple way to emphasize the importance of keying on Faulk. Before every play during practice before the Super Bowl, Belichick yelled "Where is he?" at his defense.

Message received. Faulk, who came into the Super Bowl riding a streak of eight games with a least one touchdown, didn't reach the end zone against the Patriots. And after shredding the Philadelphia Eagles for 159 yards rushing in the NFC Championship Game, he had just 76 against New England. On more than half his caries—nine of seventeen— the Patriots held him to two yards or fewer. Stifling Faulk, and jamming the speedy St. Louis receivers at the line, disrupted Warner's game.

The critical moment came early in the second quarter, with St. Louis leading 3–0. Faulk had just put together consecutive gains of five and fifteen yards. He appeared to be hitting his stride after a sluggish start. But on the next play Warner hurried a pass for Isaac Bruce on the right sideline at the St. Louis 47. Pats cornerback Ty Law stepped in front and took the pass back the other way for a touchdown. New England had the lead and a surge of confidence.

Once the Rams fell behind, Faulk played only a minor role in the offense. His biggest contribution, in fact, occurred on a play when he didn't even have the ball. Defensive end Willie McGinest was flagged for holding Faulk with 10½ minutes left in the game. On that play Warner had fumbled and Tebucky Jones had run the ball back 97 yards for an apparent touchdown. With the point after, that score would have put the Patriots up 24–3. The holding call not only brought the ball back, but it also gave the Rams a first-and-goal at the one. Warner cashed in, and that fourteen-point swing set up one of the most suspenseful finishes in Super Bowl history.

If the Patriots' defensive game plan had been bold in both design and execution, the offensive game plan was conservative almost to a fault. Newer Pats fans circa 2013 would hardly have recognized Tom Brady 1.0, the 24-year-old quarterback who managed the game for most of the night. Over the first 58 minutes, New England's longest drive in terms of both plays (seven) and time of possession (4:18) had netted just seventeen yards. No drive had gained more than 45 yards, and only one had produced as many as three first downs. During one stretch of the first half Brady went almost twenty minutes of *game* time—not real time—between completions. And before the game's final drive Brady was 11-of-19 for just 92 yards.

The objective was to avoid mistakes and win the turnover battle— which the Patriots did, 3–0. Those three turnovers had led to all of New England's points to that point.

But seventeen points hadn't been enough to beat the high-powered Rams in November, and it wasn't enough in February, either. After sputtering for most of the night, the Greatest Show on Turf finally clicked just past the two-minute warning, with St. Louis trailing 17–10. The tying touchdown came with dizzying suddenness: Warner to Hakim for eighteen yards; Warner to Yo Murphy for eleven yards; Warner to Ricky Proehl for 26 yards. Three plays, 55 yards. Elapsed time: 21 seconds.

The Patriots had out-hit and out-coached the Rams for almost the entire game. But they hadn't outscored them.

◆

Just as surely as the NFL's future in February 2002 looked like the St. Louis Rams, its past sounded like Pat Summerall and John Madden. The announcing duo had worked together since 1981, first at CBS and later at Fox. Theirs were the voices of import. If you heard Summerall and Madden, you knew it was a big game—the kind the Patriots had rarely been a part of.

Super Bowl XXXVI was Summerall and Madden's last game together. In hindsight their call was a fitting valedictory for an era—both in New England and in the NFL—starting with Summerall's player introductions. Because St. Louis was considered the visiting team, they were introduced first. The NFL gave each team the choice of introducing either its offense or its defense. St. Louis chose the offense. Summerall, whose intros were carried on the Superdome's public address system as well as on air, enunciated the names of each member of The Greatest Show on Turf as they sprinted out of the tunnel one by one. After a commercial break, it was the Patriots' turn. The NFL had allotted one minute, 40 seconds for player introductions. The Pats needed just ten seconds. "And now, ladies and gentlemen," said Summerall, "choosing to be introduced as a team, here are the American Football Conference champions, the New England Patriots." The team exited the tunnel en masse.

That was the moment when many fans across New England felt the change. It had been more than fifteen years since a Boston team had won a pro sports championship—and almost 30 since any team but the Celtics had. The two biggest draws, the Red Sox and Patriots, were riding a combined 0-for-124 streak. Few living Boston fans had ever celebrated a World Series title; none had ever celebrated a Super Bowl win. Both the Red Sox and Patriots had had some good runs in recent years, but those teams were often undermined by acts of selfishness, poor judgment, or both. The Pats' first run to the Super Bowl, after the 1985 season, was marred by Irving Fryar's "kitchen knife" domestic dispute (not to mention the unseemly spectacle of GM Patrick Sullivan detracting from what should have been a signature playoff win over the Raiders by taunting Howie Long from the sideline throughout the game). Months later manager John McNamara made several questionable moves in the '86 World Series, which led to years of backbiting (including Roger Clemens's disputing McNamara's claim that Clemens had asked out of Game 6, and pitching coach Bill Fischer's assertion that Oil Can Boyd was too drunk to pitch in Game 7). Then there was Clemens and his Ninja Turtle meltdown in the 1990 ALCS. And the Patriots' most recent trip to the Super Bowl, five years earlier, had ended with a sour taste not just because New England had lost, but also because of allegations that coach Bill Parcells had been planning his next career move (jumping to the Jets) when he should have been game-planning for Green Bay.

This edition of the Patriots was different. By all appearances it was a true team, and the coach set the tone. When the players had come up with the idea to be introduced collectively, Belichick supported them—even though NFL officials initially pushed back. In an ESPN interview years later, Belichick recalled telling NFL officials that supplying the names of either the offensive or defensive starters would be pointless because the players intended to come out as a group regardless of what the league said. "We're coming out as one," Belichick recalled saying, "because that's what they want to do." So the NFL relented.

The 2001 Patriots team had less in common with any previous iteration of the franchise than it had with the '67 Red Sox. Both were overachievers who had gone from distant also-rans to unlikely contenders. And with a minute and a half left in Super Bowl XXXVI, the 2001 Patriots seemed headed for the same fate as the '67 Sox. It appeared that they would come up just short of a championship. Against a team from St. Louis.

After tying the game, the Rams had momentum. And their momentum gained further momentum when they pinned the Patriots inside the twenty on the ensuing kickoff. New England had no timeouts. They had a young quarterback directing an offense that had played as if it had a governor on the throttle all night.

Madden, the voice of conventional wisdom, said on the Fox broadcast that the smart thing to do, the *obvious* thing to do, was for the Patriots to run the clock out and take their chances in overtime.

This was when Belichick again distinguished himself, and his team, from any who had come before. Belichick seemingly coached without fear. He had shown his spine already that season by sticking with Brady even after Drew Bledsoe, the erstwhile face of the franchise, had returned from an injury. Belichick had more faith in Brady to run the offense effectively, without giving up sacks or interceptions or committing other costly mistakes.

Never was Belichick's faith more apparent than it was at this moment.

First-and-ten at the seventeen. Brady in the shotgun. The pocket quickly collapsed. As Brady cradled the ball at the eight-yard line, defensive end Leonard Little got a hand on Brady's left arm. If the two had been a half step closer, the result could have been a sack—possibly even a fumble. Instead, Brady stepped up—something Bledsoe was loath to do—and, as he was being pulled down, dumped the ball off to running back J.R. Redmond for a five-yard gain.

If anything, that play reinforced the conventional wisdom. It had been a fairly high-risk play with minimal reward. Madden reiterated his opinion that the Patriots should run out the clock and play for overtime.

Brady hit Redmond again, for eight yards and a first down, then spiked the ball to stop the clock. Another completion to Redmond netted eleven yards. Moreover, Redmond got out of bounds. The Patriots had a first down at their 41 with 33 seconds left.

Madden: "Now I kinda like what the Patriots are doing."

After throwing the ball away to avoid a sack on a blitz, Brady hit Troy Brown for his longest completion of the game: 23 yards, to the Rams' 36, where Brown got out of bounds to stop the clock again. A final completion, to Jermaine Wiggins, moved the ball to the 30, well within kicker Adam Vinatieri's range. Brady, looking as calm as if he were conducting a training camp walk-through, called the team to the line and spiked the ball. It bounced straight up. He caught the ball in his outstretched left hand, tossed it to an official, and casually trotted off the field. Seven seconds remained—just enough time for Vinatieri to nail the game-winning kick.

Many Pats fans still deride Madden for second-guessing the Patriots when the final drive started. Not many remember what he said at the end. And that's too bad, because at that moment John Madden verbalized not only what he felt, but what all of New England did: "I'll tell you, what Tom Brady just did gives me goose bumps."

The pass-happy Rams were indeed the prototype for the new-millennium NFL, and no team did a better job of adapting to that model than the Patriots. Tom Brady led New England to two more Super Bowl titles, along with a 16–0 regular season in 2007 in which he threw a league-record 50 touchdown passes. And while it's impossible to prove that the Pats' winning ways had a positive effect on Boston's other teams, it's also hard to argue with that notion. Since the Patriots' landmark Super Bowl victory, the Red Sox, Celtics, and Bruins have all added titles. In fact, when the Bruins won the Stanley Cup in 2011, that left the Patriots—yes, the Tom Brady/Bill Belichick Patriots—with the longest current championship drought among Boston's four major professional franchises.

Notes on Sources

W riting this book was a two-step process. First I had to compile a list of 100 worthy games. I came up a good portion of the list right off the top of my head. I've lived in New England since 1982, and 60 of the games listed in this book took place since then—38 just since 2000, including seven of the top ten.

Evaluating games from the distant past was a matter of extrapolation—which Sports-Reference.com made relatively easy. I started by checking every postseason result of each major Boston pro sports franchise since its inception. Then I made some basic deductions. For example, any playoff series that went seven games warranted further research, as did any postseason game that the Boston team won in overtime or extra innings. Next I checked the box score of each prospective top-100 game to get a feel for its flow. Take Game 3 of the 1914 World Series. When I saw that the Boston Braves had scored two runs in the bottom of the tenth to tie the game before winning in twelve, I knew that that game belonged on the list. From there I just had to flesh out the details and put each game in the context of its time. (In the case of the 1914 World Series, I learned that, although Boston has been a solidly American League town since Day One, the city enthusiastically embraced its "Miracle Braves.")

My main sources for the second part of this process—writing individual game accounts—were the online archives of the Boston *Globe*, the *New York Times*, and various other dailies and wire services from around the country accessible through NewspaperARCHIVE.com. (The Syracuse *Post–Standard*, to cite one example, had a richly detailed account of the 1953 quadruple-overtime seventh game between the Celtics and the Syracuse Nationals in the NBA's Eastern Division Finals.) I relied heavily on the trove of highlight packages, newsreel footage, and entire game films archived on YouTube. I also searched dozens of other websites of varying veracity and assembled a small library of Boston sports books.

My written accounts of each game are my own interpretation of events based on facts culled from this diverse collection of sources, along with the words of the participants as quoted in news stories. When my sense of an event was colored by a specific writer, I cited the source (as when the *Globe*'s Victor O. Jones noted that the Boston Garden crowd, incensed over a call that went against the Bruins during an epic 1939 Stanley Cup Playoff battle with the Rangers, littered the ice with "beer cans, broken seats, papers, fruit and everything that wasn't nailed down").

I am both indebted to and jealous of all those who have documented Boston sports history on deadline since May 5, 1871, when the Red Stockings took on the Olympics in Washington, D.C., in Boston's first-ever game of professional sports.

Incidentally, that game set quite a tone. The Red Stockings overcame a 10–1 deficit to win 20–18. Future Hall of Famer Al Spalding was the winning pitcher. He also scored the go-ahead run on Ross Barnes's single in the ninth inning, when, in the words of *The Daily Milwaukee News*, "the excitement was now at a high pitch."

It still is.

**Number of
Games by Team**

Red Sox: 32
Celtics: 30
Patriots: 16
Bruins: 14
Boston College football: 3
Beaneaters/Braves: 2
Harvard football: 2
Boston University hockey: 1

**Number of
Games by Decade**

1890–1899: 2
1900–1909: 3
1910–1919: 5
1920–1929: 1
1930–1939: 1
1940–1949: 2
1950–1959: 3
1960–1969: 14
1970–1979: 5
1980–1989: 18
1990–1999: 8
2000–2009: 29
2010–present: 9

Made in the USA
San Bernardino, CA
13 December 2013